second edition

edited by **Sue Grafton**
with **Jan Burke** and **Barry Zeman**

Writing Mysteries

A Handbook by the
Mystery Writers of America

Lawrence Block

Michael Connelly

Tess Gerritsen

Tony Hillerman

Faye Kellerman

Jonathan Kellerman

Sara Paretsky

Ann Rule

WRITER'S DIGEST BOOKS
Cincinnati, Ohio
www.writersdigest.com

Writing Mysteries: A Handbook by the Mystery Writers of America. Copyright
© 2002 by the Mystery Writers of America. Manufactured in the United States
of America. All rights reserved. No part of this book may be reproduced in any
form or by any electronic or mechanical means including information storage
and retrieval systems without permission in writing from the publisher, except by
a reviewer, who may quote brief passages in a review. Published by Writer's
Digest Books, an imprint of F&W Publications, Inc., 4700 East Galbraith Road,
Cincinnati, OH 45236. (800) 289-0963.

Visit our Web site at www.writersdigest.com for information on more resources
for writers.

To receive a free weekly e-mail newsletter delivering tips and updates about writing
and about Writer's Digest products, register directly at our Web site at http://
newsletters.fwpublications.com.

05 04 03 02 01   5 4 3 2 1

Library of Congress Cataloging-in-Publication Data

Writing mysteries: a handbook by the Mystery Writers of America / edited by
Sue Grafton; with assistance from Jan Burke and Barry Zeman—2nd ed.
    p.   cm.
Includes bibliographical references and index.
ISBN 1-58297-102-1 (pbk.: alk. paper)—ISBN 1-58297-145-5 (hc.: alk. paper)
    1. Detective and mystery stories—Authorship. I. Grafton, Sue. II. Burke, Jan.
III. Zeman, Barry. IV. Mystery Writers of America.

PN3377.5.D4 W66   2001
808.3′872—dc21   2001056791
                                                         CIP

Edited by Jack Heffron and Meg Leder
Designed by Mary Barnes Clark
Cover designed by Matthew Gaynor
Cover photography by © 2001 Getty Images/JFB and
© 2001 Getty Images/Dave Krieger
Production coordinated by John Peavler

■ Permissions

Introduction by Sue Grafton. Used by permission.

"The Rules and How to Bend Them" Copyright © by Jeremiah Healy. Used by permission.

"Sparks, Triggers, and Flashes" Copyright © Marilyn Wallace. Used by permission.

"On Work Schedules" Copyright © 2001, Dick Lochte. Used by permission.

"Writing With a Partner, or . . . What Part of 'No' Don't You Understand?" Copyright © Warren Murphy. Used by permission.

"Expertise and Research" Copyright © Faye Kellerman and Jonathan Kellerman. Used by permission.

"Where Do I Find a Jewish Indian? or How I Stopped Worrying and Learned to Love Research" Copyright © Stuart M. Kaminsky. Used by permission.

"Background, Location, and Setting" Copyright © by Julie Smith. Used by permission.

"Characterization" Copyright © Michael Connelly. Used by permission.

"Rounding Up Your Characters" Copyright © 2001 by Margaret Maron. Used by permission.

"Writing a Series Character" Copyright © Sara Paretsky. Used by permission.

"The Amateur Sleuth" Copyright © Nancy Pickard. Used by permission.

"Vivid Villains" Copyright © 1990 by Sandra Scoppettone. Used by permission.

"In Search of a Novel" Copyright © George C. Chesbro. Reprinted by permission of the author.

"Building Without Blueprints" Copyright © Tony Hillerman. Used by permission of the author and *The Writer*.

"Outlining" Copyright © Robert Campbell. Used by permission.

"Perspectives on Point of View" Copyright © 2001 by Loren D. Estleman. Published by permission of the author.

"Dress for Success: Developing Your Personal Style" Copyright © 2001 by Carolyn Wheat. Used by permission.

■ About the Editor

Sue Grafton entered the mystery field in 1982 with the publication of *"A" Is for Alibi*, which introduced female hard-boiled private investigator Kinsey Millhone. *"B" Is for Burglar* appeared in 1985, and since then she has published fourteen additional mysteries, her latest being *"P" Is for Peril*. She's received numerous awards, including the Shamus, the Anthony, the Macavity, the Doubleday Mystery Guild Award, the American Mystery Award, and the Ridley Award. She is currently at work on *"Q" Is for Quarry*. The estimated completion date for the series has been revised upward from 2008 to 2015.

INTRODUCTION BY SUE GRAFTON 1

Part I: Preparation

1. The Rules and How to Bend Them ▪ by Jeremiah Healy 6
2. Sparks, Triggers, and Flashes ▪ by Marilyn Wallace 13
3. On Work Schedules ▪ by Dick Lochte 20
4. Writing With a Partner, or . . . What Part of "No" Don't You
   Understand? ▪ by Warren Murphy 26
5. Expertise and Research ▪ by Faye Kellerman and Jonathan Kellerman . .33
6. Where Do I Find a Jewish Indian? or How I Stopped Worrying and
   Learned to Love Research ▪ by Stuart M. Kaminsky 41
7. Background, Location, and Setting ▪ by Julie Smith 48

Part II: The Process

THE BEGINNING

8. Characterization ▪ by Michael Connelly 57
9. Rounding Up Your Characters ▪ by Margaret Maron 65
10. Writing a Series Character ▪ by Sara Paretsky 72
11. The Amateur Sleuth ▪ by Nancy Pickard 79
12. Vivid Villains ▪ by Sandra Scoppettone 86
13. In Search of a Novel ▪ by George C. Chesbro 91
14. Building Without Blueprints ▪ by Tony Hillerman 98
15. Outlining ▪ by Robert Campbell 105
16. Perspectives on Point of View ▪ by Loren D. Estleman 112
17. Dress for Success: Developing Your Personal Style ▪
    by Carolyn Wheat 121

THE MIDDLE

18. How to Write Convincing Dialogue ▪ by Aaron Elkins 129
19. Pacing and Suspense ▪ by Phyllis A. Whitney 139
20. Depiction of Violence ▪ by Bill Granger .148
21. Clues, Red Herrings, and Other Plot Devices ▪ by P.M. Carlson 160
22. The Book Stops Here ▪ by Lawrence Block 166

THE END

23. In the Beginning Is the End ▪ by John Lutz 173

24. Revision ▪ by Jan Burke 180

25. How to Find and Work With an Agent ▪ by John F. Baker 190

26. Dial M for Market ▪ by Russell Galen 197

27. The Mystery Novel From an Editor's Point of View ▪ by Ruth Cavin .205

Part III: Specialties

28. Writing Mysteries for Young Readers ▪ by Joan Lowery Nixon. 217

29. The Joys and Challenges of the Short Story ▪ by Edward D. Hoch . . .224

30. The Medical Thriller ▪ by Tess Gerritsen .233

31. Legal Thrillers ▪ by Linda Fairstein. 240

32. Historical Mysteries: The Past Is a Foreign
    Country ▪ by Laurie R. King. 246

33. From the Cradle to the Pen: The Evolution of a
    True Crime Writer ▪ by Ann Rule 253

34. E-Media—Crime Fiction E-Volves ▪ by G. Miki Hayden. 262

35. The Best of the Genre and a Reference List of Books on Writing
    and Technical Information ▪ by Angela Zeman and Barry Zeman 271

ABOUT THE CONTRIBUTORS 293

INDEX. 305

▪ Introduction

When I first learned that Writer's Digest Books had proposed a
second edition of *Writing Mysteries*, I was startled to realize that
nearly ten years had passed since the original was published in
1992. The Mystery Writers of America has sponsored a handbook since 1976 with much the same purpose in mind: to encourage
and support beginning mystery writers, offering counsel, direction, and practical advice about how to succeed in this form we so
love. In each of these guidebooks, well-known writers in the field
have contributed essays on every facet of the mystery, presenting a
wide range of viewpoints and suggestions developed after years
of hard-earned experience.

In this edition, we retain the wisdom of the masters while making
room for new talent whose "take" on various aspects of the craft
may be different. Writers whose chapters are reprinted have had an
opportunity to update, modify, and revise where needed. On reflection, many have concluded they got it right the first time around.
Others have taken advantage of the occasion to amend and refine.
While basic attitudes seem to prevail from one generation to the
next, trends do emerge. The past ten years have seen the flourish-
ing of the medical thriller, the legal thriller, and in nonfiction, the
in-depth coverage of true crime. The historical mystery has also
emerged as a strong presence in the marketplace, along with regional and ethnic variations on both the so-called cozy mystery
and the hard-boiled private eye. E-publishing has materialized, providing a new format, a new market, and easier access to writers
of every kind.

Regardless of the subject matter, I've been delighted with the
response, amazed as always at the generosity of mystery writers
addressing those who hope to join the ranks. Whether you're reading this how-to manual for the first time or returning to sample
its insights again, you'll find much to consider, ponder, and absorb.

If you're approaching the mystery for the first time, you may not
yet appreciate the profound mastery of the form required to succeed. If you've already written your first mystery (even your second
or third), you'll know just how exasperating, exhilarating, re-

warding, frustrating, and satisfying the genre can be. What we've done here is assemble some of the finest writers working in the field, describing with humor and candor the means and methods each has devised in tackling the mystery-writing process.

The creation of complex and believable characters is essential to the writing of a successful mystery. Whether it's a short story or a full-length novel, the narrative line needs to be strong, the prose style crisp, the pace relentless. But there are many other elements to conquer beyond the basics of character and plot. A mystery is more than a novel, more than a compelling account of people whose fate engages us. The mystery is a way of examining the dark side of human nature, a means by which we can explore, vicariously, the perplexing questions of crime, guilt and innocence, violence and justice. The mystery not only re-creates the original conditions from which violence springs, tracking the chaos that murder unleashes, but then attempts to divine the truth through the process of rational investigation and eventually restores an order to the universe.

That's a bit much, you may complain. How can you, as a mystery writer, accomplish such an impossible feat? You must become, first and foremost, a student of human nature, a self-appointed armchair psychologist, willing not only to analyze and understand your fellow creatures, but to inquire into your own soul and chart its contradictions. Translating your insights into fiction isn't easy, but the mystery is the perfect vehicle for the observations you have made. The term *mystery* is an umbrella that shelters a variety of subgenres: the traditional whodunit, the private eye, the classic puzzle, the police procedural, action/adventure, thriller, espionage, the novels of psychological and romantic suspense. You would do well to consider the assets and the drawbacks of each before you decide which is best suited for the particular story you wish to tell.

In addition to pace and suspense, there are questions of tone and atmosphere, the use of description, the balance of action, exposition, and dialogue. There are also requirements peculiar to the genre: clues, red herrings, the tying up of loose ends. As a mystery writer, you will need to acquire at least a nodding acquaintance with technical matters such as forensics, ballistics, and police procedure. We are, after all, writing about murder, which involves a number of specialists whose job it is to address the scientific and legal aspects of the subject. While you may not have to be a licensed expert yourself, you may be writing *about* the experts, and you'll need to know enough about a given subject to convey both data and attitudes convincingly. A mystery writer needs to have an understanding of how the judicial system works, a knowledge of investigative procedures, and access to specialized information, both mundane and exotic.

Aside from their technical proficiency, mystery writers are the magicians of fiction. We're the illusionists, working with sleight of hand in the performance of our art. With this book, we'll be taking you behind the scenes so you can see how the riddles are created and the illusions sustained. Keep in mind that the mystery is the one form in which the reader and the writer are pitted against each other. Your job, as a practicing mystery writer, is to lay out a believable tale of intrigue and ingenuity . . . always with the proviso that you play fair with the reader, who in turn will be doing his or her best to catch you at your tricks. You would do well, incidentally, to assume your reader is at least as smart as you.

We've designed this book as a walk-through, taking you from the first flash of inspiration to the point at which you'll search for an agent or an editor, finished manuscript in hand. Every work of fiction you write begins with an idea, sometimes quite fleeting, which you must work to develop, fleshing out the bare bones of theme and plot, layering in characters, making a hundred decisions about setting, tone, point of view, the style appropriate to the story you want to tell. As you progress through the book, you'll find suggestions about ways to research, approaches to character and plotting, techniques for outlining the story as it takes shape. You'll find advice about dialogue, about planting clues and building suspense. From beginning, to middle, to the rousing climax of your book, we're here, like an army of experts, to offer guidance and assistance. We'll even counsel you about stumbling blocks, what most writers think of as the three-quarter-mark sag, advising you what to do when you lose steam momentarily and the book sags under its own weight.

You'll hear many distinct points of view expressed here, but you'll also find many areas where our attitudes merge. It's been said that to learn something new, you need to hear it three times. You'll note the dictum at work here. Some points about the mystery are made over and over again from the perspective of writers whose work may appear very different on the surface. We've allowed the repetitions to remain, hoping you'll take comfort from the fact that so many of us agree on the basics.

The truth of the matter is that you must teach yourself how to write. We can offer guidance, the painful wisdom of our own hard-won experience, but in the end, you must hone your own skills, conquering the countless devils that will plague you as you learn. As a mystery writer, you will have to serve a long and some-times arduous apprenticeship. We offer encouragement, our own excitement at the prospect.

This, then, is our gift to you.

While the journey is yours, we offer you this road map. We warn you of the pitfalls. We point you toward the high ground.

As working members of the Mystery Writers of America, we wish you Godspeed.

—Sue Grafton

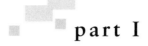

part I

Preparation

THE RULES AND HOW TO BEND THEM

▪ *Jeremiah Healy*

When Sue Grafton asked me to write this article, she suggested as a title "The Rules and How to *Break* Them." Now, having been both an attorney and a law professor, I naturally never break a rule. I have learned, however, that there are times when an old rule should be abandoned or a current rule should not be applied. In other words, the rule should be *bent*, usually because the reason behind the rule—the reason the rule was originally imposed—wouldn't be promoted by adhering to the rule.

For example, most states say that confidential communications between spouses are privileged from disclosure. What's the reason behind such a rule? Probably, the jurisdiction wants to encourage the exchange of intimacies that promotes a marriage relationship. However, if the wife has sued the husband for divorce, then at least communications thereafter should not be privileged, even though the couple is still technically "married." Why? Because the reason behind the rule just no longer applies. One spouse's filing for divorce shows that there is no longer a marriage relationship to promote.

Let me take a similar approach to the "rules" of mystery writing.

I will focus on the rules that supposedly govern the private investigator novel, suggesting the reason(s) behind each and where you can do some bending. Since most of us are aware of the Ten Commandments, let me follow that pattern in identifying the rules.

I. The Plot Is Everything

The first rule of mystery writing can be stated simply: The plot is everything. All other aspects of the book must be slaves to the story line. A solid reason behind this rule is that most readers come to a mystery because the genre promises an actual story, a characteristic that many find lacking in so-called mainstream fiction. Also, many readers truly want a tale in which the problem is resolved and the guilty party is punished, a disposition that is sadly lacking in many real-life bad acts. Given the reasons behind this rule, I would not try to bend it.

II. The Hero Must Be Male

The typical hero in a private investigator novel (as opposed to other types of mysteries) was a man. Why? Presumably, there was a perception that the public would accept as a private investigator only a male with certain physical strengths and acquired capabilities, like being a good shot or a tough street fighter. At first blush, this reason behind the rule wasn't completely crazy: Many real-life private investigators were former law enforcement or military service personnel, professions that were almost exclusively male until relatively recently.

However, society has changed dramatically. I served with female military police officers in the 1970s, and there are now plenty of women in civilian law enforcement as street cops or investigators. Accordingly, the perception has changed, and with it, the reason behind the rule as well. Thanks to Sue Grafton, Linda Barnes, and Sara Paretsky, we now have Kinsey Millhone, Carlotta Carlyle, and V.I. Warshawski, respectively. This "rule" can be abandoned so long as the character, male or female, is credible.

A common aspect of the *stereotypical* private eye was that of heterosexual rogue, presumably to attract and satisfy an audience thought to aspire to that questionable status. Happily, the reason behind the rule no longer supports this aspect either. My own investigator, John Francis Cuddy, is heterosexual but not a rogue: He remains faithful to the memory of his dead wife until he meets a woman to whom he can commit. Joseph Hansen's Dave Brandstetter is neither heterosexual nor a rogue: He chooses his gay lovers carefully and stays with one for many of the books in the series. So long as the character is carefully drawn, he or she is no longer subject to expectations of orientation or promiscuity.

III. The Setting Will Be Los Angeles

The classic setting for a private investigator was L.A. Historically, Raymond Chandler chose that city for Philip Marlowe. Current authors have followed that tradition (e.g., Arthur Lyons for Jacob Asch and Robert Crais for Elvis Cole). I don't believe this choice was ever a rule, especially given Dashiell Hammett's setting of San Francisco for Sam Spade. The reason behind this presumed rule was that the "city of angels" provided a variety of social classes, ethnicities, and corrupt officials. With all respect, a lot of cities (and many large towns) have these advantages. Witness Marcia Muller's selection of San Francisco for Sharon McCone, Jonathan Valin's Cincinnati for Harry Stoner, Loren Estleman's Detroit for Amos Walker, Lawrence Block's New York for Matt Scudder, and Benjamin Schutz's Washington, DC, for Leo Haggerty. The reason behind the rule of setting should be to have a place that provides a suitable backdrop for your story line and a pool of different characters for your cast. Therefore, choose your setting based on a combination of your needs and your familiarity.

IV. Some Violence Is Required

There must be some violence in a private investigator book. The reason behind this rule is that without violence our knight-errant is neither tested nor confirmed in his or her physical courage. However, the trick is to make the violence rational and advance the story line. In real life, a private investigator who discharged his or her weapon (outside a firing range) three times in a year, even without hitting anybody, would surely lose the permit to carry that weapon. Accordingly, be sure your violence, particularly if committed by the hero, is proportionate to the provocation involved. Also, have your violence occur at different points of the book to pace the plot and revive the reader. If you are philosophically troubled by blood onstage, have some of your violence occur offstage.

The one mandate that the rule of violence still carries, at least for a private investigator novel, is that there must be at least one death-by-criminal-act in the book. There are some current practitioners who do not observe this rule, and frankly I come away from their work feeling unsatisfied as a reader.

V. Certain Violence Is Prohibited

The mirror image of the previous rule is that there are some types of violence that are not acceptable, even in fiction. The virtually taboo areas include graphic scenes of child abuse, rape, and cruelty to animals. The reason behind this rule is common decency. I once skated close to this prohibition, having my private investigator protagonist discover a kitten flayed alive by a bad guy. I quickly received "I had to stop reading the book" from fans and "I wish you hadn't done that" from booksellers. Even though the act occurred offstage and the scene advanced the plot, the rule-as-taboo was deemed broken.

VI. Write in the First-Person Narrative

Returning briefly to the gods, there is a sense that the private investigator novel must be written in the first-person narrative style rather than the third-person narrative because that's the way both Hammett and Chandler did it. By way of comeback, both Hammett and Chandler wrote detective stories in both the first- and third-person styles, so this "rule" never really was a rule. However, the reason behind it is instructive: When the narrator speaks to the reader as "I," the reader comes to identify with the narrator and accepts the limitations of information that the typically chronological progression of first-person imposes on the structure of the book.

Only a few practitioners in the private eye field use the third-person narrative. The most successful examples are the Whistler series by the late Robert Campbell and the Alo Nudger series by John Lutz. Both these masters manage to engage the reader's interest and loyalty. Unless you are an accomplished writer, however, I believe that the rule of first-person narrator is a good one to follow. Just remember that what the first person giveth the first person also taketh away: All your story line development has to occur through the eyes (and therefore the restricted field of vision) of your narrator, and many great "words" would sound false coming from his or her lips (and therefore your vocabulary options become restricted as well).

VII. The Hero Cannot Be the Culprit

The rule also has a mirror image: The culprit cannot be the hero. It is particularly difficult to develop a plot in which the first-person narrator turns out to be the culprit. Also, the reader, having come to identify with the hero, feels betrayed when the person the reader trusted turns out to be the criminal. Finally, the hero as criminal is presumably someone the reader (or the potential editor) feels he or she cannot adopt as a series character. Accordingly, at least in private investigator fiction, the first-person narrator being the culprit should be avoided, unless the traitorous hero is virtually crucified at the end of the book as retribution for the betrayal of the reader.

VIII. The Culprit Must Appear Early

A rule that makes a lot of sense is that the author must introduce the culprit early. I believe that the name or label of the character who is to be the culprit should be introduced in the first few chapters, with the actual face-to-face meeting of the investigator and the culprit occurring before a third of the novel is gone. The reason behind this rule is ultimate fairness to the reader: At least part of the reason he or she is plowing through your book is a sense of solving the puzzle before the investigator, and crucial information as to each suspect—and especially the culprit—is necessary to play fair with your investigating companion.

IX. Use Only Two-Character Scenes

A rule many of us observe without stating it is that each scene should involve only the protagonist detective and one other character. The reason for this is basic: The writer can alert the reader to a change of speaker simply by a change in paragraphs without annoying the reader by a lot of express signals. My favorite example of this is Robert B. Parker's Spenser books, in which the dialogue simply flows with only occasional cues of "I said" or "Susan said" for the reader who has lost his or her place.

If you need to have more than two characters populating a scene, then be sure each has a distinctive "voice" so that you don't confuse the reader by not providing express signals. Though not a "private investigator" novelist, I think Elmore Leonard is the best example of a writer who can capture a different voice without offensively caricaturing the social class or ethnicity of the character speaking.

X. Authenticity Is Required

Most writers believe in the need to be authentic. The reason behind this rule is that you do not wish to offend a "ringer" reader who knows more about the subject than you do. To expand a hypothetical I've used before, Robert Randisi and Parnell Hall have to be sure they are using the right subway lines in their books about Manhattan and Brooklyn. On the other hand, Nancy Pickard and Bill Pronzini can create credible, but fictional, towns outside Boston and San Francisco in which Main Street can run either north-south or east-west. However, none of us can afford to have a character fire seven bullets from a Smith & Wesson Combat Masterpiece without reloading. The interpretation of this rule is simple:

You must be authentic when you are trying to be authentic. Accordingly, research and perhaps the help of an "expert" as proofreader is vitally important when you are dealing with real-life facts.

Conclusion

There are rules that can be bent and others that should be observed strictly. With a little thought, you can be your own lawyer in determining when the reason behind the rule permits bending or dictates adherence.

chapter two

Sparks, Triggers, and Flashes

■ *Marilyn Wallace*

A t book signings, conferences, and conventions, a mystery writer can be sure that, eventually, three things will be asked: Someone will wonder whether you use a word processor to compose, someone will inquire about your work habits, and an eager questioner will surely ask, "Where do you get your ideas?"

The replies to the first two are fairly predictable.

"I always/never/after first draft work on a computer."

"I work every morning/afternoon/evening for four/six/eight hours."

It's in response to "Where do you get your ideas?" that writers take the opportunity to be really creative. "From Cleveland/Macy's/the cosmic pipeline," the writer explains. The questioner goes away entertained but unsatisfied. The respondent worries whether glibness is the proper refuge from such a familiar query, decides brevity was the required virtue, and goes home to work on her book.

The work consists of pushing, prodding, pulling, and otherwise trying to wrest a book or story from a glimmer of a notion. And while she's so engaged, she realizes that it would have been helpful to provide the answers to several more specific questions: What sparks you to write a mystery? What triggers the decision to turn an idea into a novel or a short story? If you can't start working right away, how do you keep the flash of an idea from fading away completely?

Of course, what works for one writer won't necessarily be effective for another. And what's useful today may not have the same result a month later for the same writer. Still, the questions are worth exploring.

What Sparks You to Write a Mystery?

Since mysteries deal with people in the throes of powerful emotions—greed, fury, revenge, love, lust—it helps to be attuned to those emotions in yourself and in others. What makes your blood boil? What are you desperate to protect? To gain? What makes you angry, afraid, confused? What issues or incidents most often bring you closest to hostile confrontation with other people? In what circumstances do you find yourself evading or embellishing the truth? What self-deceptions, manipulations, obsessions are part of your personal repertoire? Paying honest attention to your own feelings is one starting point of crime fiction. Since most of us will not directly experience the acts we write about, what we can do instead is be aware of our emotions and what incites them. This is a variation on the often repeated principle of writing what you know: Write what you *feel*, and you're on your way.

What musings take you on extended mental journeys? For me, questions that engage my curiosity are often the starting point of fiction. "The Sentence" followed after weeks of pondering the nature of obsession. *Primary Target* came out of discussions with friends about what life would be like for the first woman to run for president of the United States.

Pay attention to those things that interest you deeply. A story infused with the writer's passion to tell it is always more engrossing. Dick Francis cares about horses; Tony Hillerman cares about Navajos; Mary Higgins Clark cares about ordinary people caught in extraordinary circumstances. Enough said?

Every pearl of mystery fiction begins with a grain of an idea that serves as an irritant.

For many writers, the fascination and, indeed, the *mystery* of human behavior is the starting point for fiction. Because we're such a mobile, gregarious society, access to other people's lives is commonplace; potential stories abound. A snatch of conversation between a mother and her adult daughter, overheard in the airport, leads you to wonder about the lives of the people you're so shamelessly eavesdropping on. Why is the daughter hissing orders at the mother? What will happen after the mother boards her plane? The direct gaze of an unshaven man dressed in tatters pierces you with the knowledge that he was once someone's son. What sequence of events robbed him of his hope?

Personally, my tolerance for lack of closure must be very low— I feel compelled to explain these things to myself, and that practice lends itself to creating fiction.

Your storytelling may be stimulated by a newspaper article that reports something unusual or intriguing. I was electrified by an article about a woman who, under hypnosis, recalled the details of a murder that she claims she saw twenty-five years earlier. What happened to bring the memory to the surface now? How will law enforcement officials react to a chain of evidence a quarter-century old? The questions and images generated by reading about this case may take years to work their way toward fictional life, but I can tell by my visceral response that I'll eventually use it in some way.

Susan Dunlap says that when she's writing her Jill Smith series, all she has to do is sit back and read the local papers about Berkeley, California. The town, she admits, provides her with endless material. Of course, if you've chosen a city less colorful than Berkeley, you may have to work a little harder to identify its fiction-provoking qualities. Look for the conflicts inherent in the social, political, and economic life of a region, and you may find a starting point for a mystery.

When Mickey Friedman was interviewed by Carolyn Wheat at a writers' breakfast, she revealed that hot climates intrigue her. Her face became transformed as she spoke of the decadence, the decay, the *slime* of Venice, Florida, India, the south of France—

all places she's captured wonderfully in her mysteries. Some places are so thoroughly imbued with menace, either blatantly (mean streets, moody moors) or in contrast to an idyllic patina (cozy villages, relaxed resorts) that a writer's imagination is stirred into action. Novels of suspense, particularly those with ties to the gothic tradition, rely heavily on such laden settings. Watch for places that excite strong responses in you.

Most writers are also incurable readers. Intriguing facts, gleaned from eclectic reading, can push buttons. Did you know that a suicide who wears glasses almost always takes them off before jumping to his death? What if a jumper is found splattered on the sidewalk . . . still wearing his glasses? Scientific oddities, historical trivia, or even unusual psychological or spiritual systems can spark the beginning of an idea.

Wherever you find that initial inspiration, learn not to censor yourself too early in the writing process. Something that at first glance seems to be a cliché can be given a spin that will take it out of the realm of the ordinary, while an idea or an image that seems too strange even for fiction can often be tamed into usefulness. Sticking too close to the origins of an idea can keep you from seeing its dramatic possibilities. Allow your mind to play awhile; see what catches fire, what continues to simmer, and what turns to cold gray ash.

What Triggers the Decision to Turn an Idea Into a Novel or a Short Story?

The answer to this is very nearly straightforward.

If a trick ending, a gimmick, or a title presents itself first, or if you've imagined a moment in which a character says, "Aha!" it's likely that the idea is best suited to be a short story. A gimmick hardly has the heft to carry the burdens of character and plot development required in a novel. On the other hand, the impact of a punch ending, along with Poe's "unity of effect," are hallmarks of the mystery or suspense short story.

"A Tale of Two Pretties" began its fictional life as a title that popped into my head when I wasn't looking. It tickled me, and

I got to thinking about Dickens and the noble melodrama of Sidney Carton and Charles Darnay. And suddenly, from a title that appeared unbidden, I was working on a short story in which two women decide that the way out of their personal problems is to trade places.

If, on the other hand, you're intrigued by a relationship or a moral dilemma or a social situation, it's clear that you need the larger canvas of a novel on which to explore. A vague idea, unformed but seductive, has potential for development as a novel. In the next stages of work, the themes will emerge and the plot and characters take shape, but sometimes that can't happen until your initial idea has a companion.

You may be one of those people for whom it takes at least two major ideas to make a novel. When something gnaws at you and refuses to go away, even though you can't figure out how to use it, don't discard it. It might just be waiting for a complementary piece to make it workable. It's not always predictable when and how those lone notions will match up. But at some point, the two parts become interwoven and take on a shape that's not one or the other but a third, new configuration.

My first novel, *A Case of Loyalties*, provided me with the inkling that mystery fiction might work this way. A painter-friend who lives in a small town about three hours north of New York City called one day and told me that her sixteen-year-old daughter had just been arrested for stealing a car. I listened to her concerns, her frustration, her anger, her desire to do the right parental thing, and it struck deep emotional chords in me.

That was the first thread.

Four days later, a painter-friend who lives in Oakland, California, called to talk about the drive-by shooting she'd seen from her apartment window.

The two threads began to intertwine. Perhaps the proximity in time and the fact that they both involved painters and cars led to this merging. But then the story developed a life of its own. The painter-mother in the book is neither of my friends, and yet she's both of them. The fictional events don't resemble their sources except in the most superficial terms. But it still took both threads for that novel to happen; it grew from my emotional connection to both situations.

Deciding the most appropriate form is only one of the decisions you face after you have that first idea. In fact, growing a novel is much like doing an acrostic puzzle. You start with a character or a place or a fact or a situation, and eventually, by a back-and-forth process, you fit in all the pieces that weren't part of your generating spark. You ask: What if? What next? Why this? Sooner or later, you know what really happened and you know what appears to have happened. You make decisions about how the truth will be revealed. From one step to the next, especially when you're writing a novel, the original idea may become so transformed that you're surprised to see where it's all led.

For me, that's part of the excitement of writing.

If You Can't Start Working Right Away, How Do You Keep the Flash of an Idea From Fading Away Completely?

Suppose you're one of those writers constantly assaulted by glimmers of ideas. "So many ideas, so little time" is your lament. Perhaps you're already writing a mystery and you're so afraid of losing a hot new concept that you're tempted to start writing another book before you've finished the one you're already working on. (All you can learn from this process is how to *start* a book. Besides, I haven't seen any half-books in my local bookstores lately.) Maybe you're inundated by the work that's paying your bills until you can "quit your day job." How do you hold onto ideas that seem exciting until you're ready to work on them?

Some writers say that the measure of a good idea is its ability to survive without being written down. A bad idea, they contend, will slip into the murky depths of memory unretrieved and die a well-deserved death. But if you've accumulated so many tidbits of data (the telephone numbers of your three best sixth-grade friends, all the words to the Grateful Dead's "Ripple," the names of all the bones in your foot) that things are getting crowded in your brain, you may not feel very secure about being able to recall an unformed idea a year later.

Write down those elusive wisps of ideas. Write down a key phrase or a twenty-page outline, but commit the thought to paper. It may lie in the bottom of a drawer and, mercifully, never rise above the underlayers. One of these long-forgotten notes may become the key to a scene, or a story, or even a novel. The physical act of writing something down will reinforce it in your mind, and the idea will gain legitimacy so that you'll be better able to remember its existence. Even if you never find the piece of paper, having written it down will fix it more firmly in your mind. Something to do with a writer's wiring, I suppose, but I'm not especially concerned with explaining it. I just know it works!

Gillian Roberts goes a step further when she suggests storing characters who interest you in an imaginary apartment house. Diabolically efficient—the characters will bring their individual conflicts to this new community and will begin to interact and perhaps may even develop stories on their own.

Two Final Caveats

First, don't talk your ideas to death. This is a hard lesson to learn, but you soon discover how quickly the need to create fiction fizzles after you've told the plot of your new novel to the fourth or fifth friend who has the patience to listen. If you don't altogether kill it, the desire to write it may become so diluted that it's hard to get your storytelling juices going again.

And, especially, don't ever be afraid of running out of ideas. I promise you, more will come.

Mysteries have an enduring appeal because they tell stories of people and passions, conflicts and consequences; they chronicle the moral dilemmas and interpersonal collisions of our times. And since change is one of the constants of our world, you can be sure that new collisions and fresh dilemmas will continue to arise to spark your imagination, trigger your desire to tell a story, and ignite your flash of inspiration.

chapter three

ON WORK SCHEDULES

■ *Dick Lochte*

E very writer has to have some sort of work schedule, even the
writers who don't actually do any writing. These nonwriting
writers busy themselves with their real occupations, usually something that keeps them firmly in the public eye—such as repeating
a working writer's lines every night on stage, or appearing on television in a three-story tic-tac-toe construction. They have definite
schedules that they shift imperceptibly to include infrequent meetings with the ghosts who are putting their thoughts on paper, or
with the publicists who are arranging for their media appearances
to promote the books that they haven't written. We can learn
nothing from the work habits of those nonpractitioners of the art.

And, to tell the truth, I'm not sure that there's much more to be
gleaned from the specific habits of genuine practitioners, since the
systems one uses to create a work of fiction are as individual as
one's taste in clothes.

Take the great Raymond Chandler, for example. In one of his
collected letters, he described a rather Spartan technique for forg-
ing ahead on his novels. He would set a number of hours aside each
day in which, while he did not force himself to write, he refused

to allow himself the pleasure of doing anything else. He just sat there in his room. Since he completed only six novels in twenty years, it follows that he spent a ghastly amount of time staring at blank walls and even blanker sheets of paper. No wonder he wound up hitting the sauce.

Dick Francis takes a few months to complete his research, a few months at the keyboard to write his novel, and the rest of the year traveling or promoting his books, which appear annually like clockwork. It's a schedule to be revered.

John D. MacDonald wrote from four to eight hours a day, six days a week. Mickey Spillane, on the other hand, at least during his early years, would sit down at the typewriter, slip the end of a roll of butcher paper under the platen, and keep typing for as long as it took to complete a novel. Then he'd cut the pages, send them to his publisher, and ignore the literary process for a while, until his accountant called to tell him his pile of money needed topping.

The first thing to realize is that your specific lifestyle or livelihood will always dictate your work habits, and it would be a mistake to try to adopt the schedule of a novelist just because you like his or her books.

Due to changing employment circumstances, I myself have shifted into several different work patterns during my three decades at the keyboard. My first, which lasted six years, was built around a nine-to-five job at a magazine in Chicago. I was left with few options. At least three nights a week, as soon as my cohorts would wander off to sample the happy-hour wares of nearby saloons, I'd clear my desk of the day's toil and shift into gear on my own work, which then consisted of interviews, articles, and critiques for local newspapers. I'd stay with it until the need for food or sleep forced me to call a halt.

That sort of moonlighting may sound grueling, but it was a walk in the park compared to my next schedule, which I adopted when I became a 100 percent freelance writer in southern California. What I had not realized was the importance of having an official end to the workday, after which I would be ethically free to pursue my private muse. Once I made the commitment to a freelance career, I never again felt that freedom. If I wasn't trying to meet a deadline, I was hustling new work. That narrowed down the time for creative writing to odd, very late nights and occasional weekends.

Under that system, it took me nearly three years to write my first novel, *Sleeping Dog*. And at least a third of that was completed during a period of two months when I steadfastly refused to do any major journalism projects. Fortunately, the success of that book allowed me to alter the emphasis of my schedule. Since 1986, I have been fitting my nonfiction work around my book writing, being much, much choosier about accepting magazine and newspaper assignments.

But I'm still forced to push my current manuscript aside from time to time. I write a column of mystery reviews that appears every other week in the *Los Angeles Times,* and review books and audios for other publications; this eats up about two days a week. Then there are the odd movie and TV jobs that are hard to turn down because they're so lucrative. Unfortunately, they're always we-need-it-right-away situations that force me to put the book on hold.

So, while I long ago established a system of at least six hours a day at the word processor, I still haven't quite worked out which of those hours will be spent on behalf of a book or any number of other writing projects. How, then, can I help you with your scheduling problems? Well, unless your work history is identical to mine—and I wouldn't wish that on you—you probably won't have a scheduling problem. You'll have a pretty good idea of the hours you can carve out of each week for your project. The important thing is to make those hours count. And there's where I can help you by describing some of the techniques I use.

1. I welcome the occasional insomnia. Usually, I can nod off without much effort, sometimes at a party in a roomful of nattering people. But on those nights when sleep won't come, I'm not unhappy. I never try to force it. Nor do I get out of bed to read or watch TV. What I do is think about the book in progress, going over the construction of the chapter I'll be working on in the morning. Either of two things happens: The mental effort puts me to sleep, or I wind up with a totally thought-out chapter.

2. I try to use the novel (or short story) to push personal problems out of my mind. Easier said than done, of course, but unless this is accomplished, you might as well forget about your book and spend the day going to the movies.

3. I do my best to ignore the sluggish traffic and the ghastly sound of NSYNC coming from the car radio when I drive my kid to school in the morning. Here, the idea is to use every spare task—particularly those that require little or no thought—to pre-pare yourself for the magic moment when you'll be allowed to put words on paper. For example, don't turn on the radio while you're getting dressed. You don't need to watch the *Today* show while fueling up on your morning coffee. Katie Couric may help you sell your book, but she won't help you write it. And, by all means, do not carry a cellular phone. Even if it doesn't give you brain tumors, it's a distraction and an annoyance to others. Think about the novel, instead.

4. I try to schedule errands—from posting mail to banking to visiting the doctor—in a bunch, or singly, as early in the day as possible. You can noodle with creative ideas while running around the city, but when it comes to actually putting words together, I think you have to clear the decks. I have a friend who carries a laptop, jotting down bits and pieces of his novel in between haircuts and business meetings. He actually writes sections of his books in short sprints, and I don't know how he does it. It takes me an hour just to warm up.

5. Research—on the Internet or at libraries or other locations—should be completed before you start to write. When I'm writing fiction, I keep research to a minimum. It's too easy to get so over-whelmed by information, particularly in hopping from one Web site to the next, that, even if you don't forget the purpose of your search, your sorting and editing brain cells short out. You get smothered by your notes or printouts. The late Thomas Thompson (author of the best-selling true crime novels *Blood and Money* and *Serpentine*) used to refer to this destructive postpone-the-novel process as "the tar baby syndrome."

6. I try not to interrupt writing to deal with correspondence or phone calls. Before starting work, I download my e-mail, but I ignore most of it, zapping all spam and saving the newsgroup items for later perusal. Snail mail gets handled during the lunch break. The bills get put aside, unopened, until I'm ready to pay them. The flyers and promotional material get dumped unopened. Magazines get thrown onto a pile that eventually tumbles over when it reaches knee height. I do read personal mail right away. (It goes without saying that checks get very special attention.)

7. Though the temptation is great, I don't screw around with my computer when I should be working. I use it to process words, period. No Buffy the Vampire Slayer pinball game. (At least not until work is done.) No goofing in chat rooms. During the workday, my computer is merely a sophisticated typewriter. I even force myself to put off fiddling with word counts and spell checkers until I've decided to call it a day.

8. I rely heavily on my phone answering machine, letting it take calls. If the writing is going particularly well, I'll even turn off the sound.

9. When I sit down at the word processor, I read whatever I've written the day before, making small changes. Then I segue into the new material. I rarely go back any farther in the book than the previous day's work. What you want to do is finish the first draft before going back to check those opening chapters. Otherwise, you rarely get past the opening chapters.

10. I do whatever I can, short of losing friends for life, to avoid meeting people for lunch. You may think you deserve a break, but you'll lose all the morning's momentum. Better to fix a quick

salad or nuke a frozen pizza (to use both ends of the calorie spectrum) and get back to that keyboard before it cools.

11. I'm flexible about my quitting hour. When I was single, I'd often work until two or three in the morning. Now, I usually click off the computer at about five P.M. I try not to quit at the end of a chapter. It's easier to start up again if you're in the middle of something.

12. Finally, there are times when, as a crime novelist, you'll be asked to participate in projects that aid and abet the mystery genre, such as this handbook. Such requests will invariably take their toll on your work schedule, and you should always turn them down. Just like I do.

chapter four

Writing With a Partner, or . . .
What Part of "No"
Don't You Understand?

■ *Warren Murphy*

(Author's note: The following piece is based on extensive interviews with other writers and not, *except where obvious, on personal experiences. Not even to me could God be so nasty.)*

So you want to write with a partner, huh?

I know how that goes. Get a partner and you have somebody to stand alongside you while you suffer the inevitable slings and arrows of a philistine world.

Get a partner and you have somebody to share the good times too, and they *will* come, because—as the old jazz musician said—if you hang around long enough, sooner or later they get to you.

Get a writing partner and you'll have someone whose strengths will fill in the gaps created by the weaknesses in your work. And vice versa.

And, of course, you'll have a kindred spirit who will understand just what it is you do. Because, don't we all know that only a writer understands a writer?

Sounds great, doesn't it? What could be better than writing with a partner?

Well, for a start, how about prostate surgery? Frontal lobotomy? Electroshock therapy has many adherents.

As the proverbial been-there-done-that, supported by my vast amounts of field research, here's my advice on partnering:

Don't. Don't. Don't.

If they were alive, you might ask Gilbert and Sullivan. Maybe they'd talk to you; they sure didn't talk to each other. And whatever happened to Art Garfunkel or Jim Messina or . . . well, you get the idea. And don't give me the writing team of Ellery Queen because, from what I could deduce, they argued like cats in a bag until they came up with the technique of one plotting and the other writing.

Writing in tandem? It almost always starts out like Damon and Pythias. It almost always winds up like the Worldwide Wrestling Federation.

Okay, you want specific? I don't know if you can handle specific. But here's the distillation of what I heard from some writing teams I talked to.

First up, there is the care and feeding of a partner. You think a puppy's trouble? Wait until you get somebody who goes angsting around, all aquiver with outraged indignation over the deletion of a comma. One of the real problems with partnering is all the time you waste trying not to hurt your partner's feelings, and in the end, it won't do you a bit of good because your partner knows you are a crass, unfeeling egomaniac interested only in yourself.

And wait until you are forced to spend time with someone who hates you because, walking into a room together, six people know your name and only five in the room know your partner's. Clearly you have been up to something criminous at his expense.

And the writing itself . . . the joint writing . . . oh, my God. Two months into the partnership and you will wonder how you ever managed to get yourself saddled with a logically challenged half-wit who is a functional illiterate to boot. Your partner, meanwhile, thinks exactly the same thing but blames it all on your Alzheimer's and sends you a box of Depends on your birthday . . . just in case.

And then there's the absolute senseless, random nature of the tensions involved in partnering. Here's a writer talking: "So lightning strikes and Hollywood calls me about a book we wrote. And I talked to them and it looked good, and I called my partner and instead of asking me about their offer, he said, 'Why did they call you? Why didn't they call me?'

" 'I didn't ask.'

" 'You should have.'

" 'Maybe it's because your phone is unlisted?'

" 'Well, they sure didn't try too hard, did they?' And he hung up on me."

Same writer later: "So my partner sends me to Hollywood to negotiate a deal and gives me specific minimums that he demands must be met. I come back with 125 percent of his demands and he turns down the contract because, he said, it was clear that if somebody as dumb as me could get 125 percent, anybody with sense could easily have gotten 150 percent. Go figure."

Not convinced? Still going to go ahead with it, despite all these warnings?

Okay, you can't say I didn't try.

Now listen carefully. If you're going to do it anyway, then follow this one piece of advice:

Get it in writing.

Let me clarify that thought.

Get it in writing!

Get what in writing?

Get everything in writing. Everything you can think of. Who negotiates for the partnership. Whose agent represents you. Who approves necessary expenses for researching a book. If the partnership breaks up, who owns what.

Who has to pay for the coffee. Who buys the gas. Whose travel agent books planes and hotels. (One writer I know looked around the hotel his partner's travel agent had booked and said, "Nice. Who was the last person she booked on vacation? General Wainwright at Corregidor?")

And most, most important of all: How are you going to work? Are you going to work together? Apart? Who plots? Who writes first? Who rewrites? Who edits? Who's in charge of preparing and delivering the finished manuscript?

Now all of this may sound like a quibble or a joke, but it's neither. Anything you can think of that two people can argue about, two writing partners will definitely argue about.

And the thing they'll argue about longest and loudest will be just how they are going to work together.

Few writers I know can actually write together at the same time, much less in the same place. Instead, one plots; the other writes. Occasionally they switch. But those work rules have to be decided in advance.

Same for rewriting. Your partner may have written a scene that just oozes royal purple on the page, something so ghastly that its publication will make you both laughingstocks. Naturally, he thinks it's his best work. How do you change it?

And that is the real heart of darkness, the biggest nagging problem of equal partnerships: who decides. You have to work all this out first, before it ever actually comes up, and then you have to live up to it. If one partner plots, he decides on the plot. If the other partner does the writing, he makes the writing decisions. And one of you has to be the final rewrite authority. Sure, you can discuss and you can negotiate at every stop of the way (although neither of you will ever change your mind about anything). But unless one of you has the power to say, "No, no, a thousand times no," there will most likely be no book.

Instead, the partnership will just deteriorate into a vicious kind of "who said, you said, I said, what said" chaos that leads always to bad partial manuscripts and sometimes to homicide.

So agree on how you're going to work, and then try to anticipate everything else that might have to do with the business of authoring and put it in writing and both of you sign and send copies to your lawyers. (Naturally, you will have separate lawyers since neither of you trusts the other's attorney not to steal the pennies off your dead eyes.)

Trust me on this: 90 percent of lawsuits are filed because someone says, "Oh, I thought you understood that." Nobody under-stands anything. Get it in writing because later, when your partner starts to rewrite the history of the terrible time he spent with you, you'll be amazed at all the things you're alleged to have said, all the deviltry you're accused of having committed.

Get it in writing. If you're unsuccessful and never make a nickel from writing, then neither of you will much care. But the moment the first dollar bill is slid under the door, all bets are off, so get it in writing.

That said, and all those caveats notwithstanding, then maybe—just maybe—a writing partnership can endure.

I speak from experience. I started in the business partnered up and spent my first quarter century as a writer working with the greatest partner anyone could have. We wrote and sold a lot of books, but partnership was different for us and, for the record, none of the things I just complained about had anything to do with me and Richard Ben Sapir.

Even before we ever wrote a book together or published any-thing, Dick Sapir and I were best friends. We stayed best friends. I tended his pet boa constrictor when he was out of town. He never knew it, but I once put a guy on a government payroll to body-guard Dick when he insisted upon going into ghetto-area gin mills late at night and hustling the locals at the pool tables. We played drunken football in the hallway of an Atlantic City hotel. We seized a radio station once and broadcast Radio Free Hoboken until they chased us out. We were driving on the Jersey Turnpike when we heard that JFK was dead, and we pulled off to the side to weep. Dick was the godfather of my children. I was at his wedding; he was at mine. When he missed one, he said, "Don't worry, I'll make the next one."

Workwise, we knew exactly what the other was doing. We'd think of some vague story, and Dick would write the first half of the book and send it to me. No outline, no suggestions, just wonder-ful characters doing strange things. He left it for me to figure out. I wrote the second half of the book, and then, without his knowl-edge, I rewrote the whole book so it was seamless. I always pre-tended I was just retyping it.

Dick never called me on it. He had a reading dysfunction and thus never read any of our books in print, so he didn't know what it was I did. Talk about a great partner: one who doesn't complain about your work because he doesn't read your work. It doesn't get better than that.

It got sticky only once. Dick called and said he feared he had destroyed our careers because in his last half-a-book, he had killed off one of our heroes who had now turned out to be wildly popular with readers. "It's okay," I said. "He's still alive. I changed it."

"Without asking me?" It wasn't exactly high dudgeon; maybe medium dudgeon, but I was apologizing for weeks.

Years later, as he was writing his first solo book, he called me and said, "You Irish bastard, why didn't you tell me?"

"Tell you what?"

"How hard it is to finish a book. I've been writing all these beginnings for us, and I never knew how tough it was to write an ending until I had to do it myself on this book of mine. Why didn't you tell me?"

"I didn't want to brag," I said.

"All these years, I thought I was carrying you."

"Same here."

Dick was in New Hampshire. I was in New Jersey. I finished work at 5 in the morning, just as Dick was starting his day. He could never quite figure out how that worked so he called me every day at 7 A.M., just to see if I was up yet. Sometimes these calls were real important. He once called me to ask me how to spell *that*.

I suggested t-h-a-t.

He said t-h-a-t had been his first guess but it didn't look right; was I sure? I suggested he call his therapist. T-h-e-r-a-p-i-s-t.

In our entire career together, we had one argument over money. Dick had done some extra work, and I said I owed him five thousand dollars. He said it was three thousand dollars. I sent him a check for five thousand dollars. A check for two thousand dollars came back.

The matter was never resolved because around that time I lent him my brand-new car and when I went to get it, I found it in front of his house, smashed, with a red ribbon neatly attached to the hood. He didn't remember how it happened but it cost two thousand dollars to fix, so that resolved the big money dilemma.

He was the writer I respected most in the world. He had only one speed: overdrive. He never saved anything for later; he gave you his best work every day. Drunk, sober, happy, sad—none of it mattered. The pages flew from his typewriter with the implacable regularity of an *I Love Lucy* assembly line, luminescent, pulsating with an intelligent hilarity. *The New York Times* called him "a brilliant professional."

So that's how a partnership can and should work, huh? Based on trust, friendship, and respect, right?

No.

Because then he went and died on me.

Partners do that, you know. One day you look up and the person you knew would always be there isn't there anymore.

That sucks eggs and . . . .

Well . . . anyway . . . partnerships. Dick Sapir and I had a survivor's agreement, forced on us by a publisher who wanted to give us a lot of money but wanted protection should one of us shuffle off this mortal coil. We thought it totally unnecessary, but today it allows the series we created to continue, through ghostwriters, even though Dick died fifteen years ago. As I was saying, we got it in writing.

Summing up about partnering:

Don't do it; it's harder than it looks and more trouble than it's worth.

If you must do it, pick a friend to partner with, but nevertheless, decide who does what, live up to your rules, and put it all in writing. You'll thank me later.

Then give it a shot. Hope for the best. But be prepared to say good-bye.

chapter five

EXPERTISE AND RESEARCH

▪ *Faye Kellerman*
▪ *Jonathan Kellerman*

How Much Is Necessary? How Much Is Too Much?

Is it necessary to be an expert to write from an expert's point of view?

Some contemporary crime and suspense novelists do just that:

• Robin Cook, a physician, writes about doctors, in peril, solving heinous crimes.

• Aaron Elkins, author of the Gideon Oliver series, shares a background in anthropology with his fictional protagonist.

• Andrew Greeley, a priest, creates mystery novels that center on the Catholic Church.

• John Katzenbach, a journalist, uses his professional background to create a reporter protagonist in his first novel, *In the Heat of the Summer*.

• Jonathan Kellerman, a child psychologist, pens the Dr. Alex Delaware series. The hero: a child therapist-cum-sleuth.

• Lia Matera and Scott Turow, attorneys, each produce novels that allow the reader entry into the clandestine corners of the legal system.

Varying styles, but each possesses an unquestionable sense of technical authenticity.

Such a tight match, however, is by no means necessary to produce a successful crime novel or any other work of fiction. Most crime writers have, in fact, assigned to their protagonists professions and roles with which they've had no direct experience. This *needs* to be so for the crime novel to survive, because, though cops and private eyes with a talent for fiction do exist—Joseph Wambaugh, Paul Bishop, William Caunitz, Dorothy Uhnak, Joe Gores, and Gerald Petievich come to mind—they comprise a very small club, indeed. The same need for flexibility applies to gender: If possession of female (male) genitals were necessary to write from a woman's (man's) perspective, a vast number of notable literary works would never have been created.

The operative word is *fiction*. We novelists make things up. Ours is a Walter Mitty world and that's the fun of it. We convince ourselves that we can write from any point of view we damn well please, because we have inherited the cloak of (or at least a shred of) authorial majesty. We can be American and pen English novels. Ninety-eight-pound weaklings with literary alter egos of Schwarzen-eggerian proportions. Our private eyes, mega-cops, and super-spies engage in stunts that, in the "real" world, might very well result in revocation of license, criminal prosecution, or ignominious death. Our characters may be immune from basic physiological needs if eating, drinking, healing, etc., get in the way of telling the story. And though their creators may be inept at putting together a jigsaw puzzle, our sleuths are able to solve crimes of Rubik's Cube complexity with elegance and panache.

It's all part of The Great Mystery Fiction Geneva Agreement: We provide the thrill. The reader suspends disbelief, allowing members of the clergy, barkeeps, dentists, cabdrivers, college professors, senior citizens with no discernible source of income, and even animals to get to the root of felonies and horrors that stump the law enforcement experts. In some cases, the insult to the gendarme is carried to the point of injury: The expert is written as a mere foil—a straw person set up to be mulishly stupid so *our* guys can walk right over them.

A grand seduction, this crime fiction business, not wholly unlike a quick-shuffled Three-Card Mental Monte. But to pull off the scam, the *illusion* of authenticity is necessary: enough sense of place and time to get the mark to grab at the lure, but not so much technical information that he loses interest.

How then can knowledge and expertise, obtained either through direct experience or research, be optimally exploited?

There are no commandments etched in stone, but a few suggestions come to mind:

Technical data should never interfere with the flow of the story, nor should it be so jargon-laden or esoteric that only another "expert" understands what you're trying to say. Spare the reader lengthy recitations of statistics or verbatim transcripts of lectures you've received from your sources. And don't talk down to the reader. A sure sign of weak or amateurish writing is over-inclusion—trying too hard to explain too much, too quickly.

Transfer of information should sound natural, never pedantic. Unless, of course you're trying to create a pedantic character (a risky business, at best). The reader should never be yanked out of reverie of the story and say to herself, "Aha, this guy is trying to *teach* me something."

The data should be *interesting*. Some fields of endeavor are just inherently more interesting than others. But all fields are composed of both the interesting and the dull—usually a soupçon of the former struggling to maintain integrity while swimming in a vatful of the latter. Concentrate on the fascinating. The part that would turn *you* on if you read it in someone else's book. Resist the pressure to include everything you've just learned about the mating habits of the aboriginal yellow-footed tree frog just because it's taken you a month to learn it.

The expertise should be *germane* to your story, both in terms of plot construction and the development of character. Rewriting is especially useful in this regard. You may find yourself larding your manuscript with nuggets of esoterica that seem fascinating upon first reading but lose luster in the cold light of an editorial morning-after. Like a sculpture, the novel often takes form gradually. Don't be afraid to chip away until what remains is really important.

Here are a few examples of expertise-based prose that we feel work very well.

An explanation of voir dire from Scott Turow's *Presumed Innocent*:

> Late in the morning, questioning about the juror's back-grounds begins—this process is called voir dire, truth telling, and it continues throughout the afternoon and into the second morning. Larren asks everything he can think of and the lawyers add more. Judge Lyttle will not allow questioning directed to the issues of the case, but the attorneys are permitted to roam freely into personal details, limited largely only by their own reluctance to give offense. What TV shows do you watch, what news-papers do you read? Do you belong to any organiza-tions? Do your children work outside the home? In your house, are you or your spouse in charge of the monthly bookkeeping? This is the subtle psychological game of figuring out who is predisposed to favor your side.

The definition of a borderline personality from Jonathan Keller-man's *Silent Partner*:

> At first glance, they look normal, sometimes even super-normal, holding down high-pressured jobs and excel-ling. But they walk a constant tightrope between madness and sanity, unable to form relationships, incapable of achieving insight, never free from a deep, corroding sense of worthlessness and rage that spills over, inevitably, into self-destruction. . . .
>
> Borderlines go from therapist to therapist, hoping to find a magic bullet for the crushing feelings of empti-ness. They turn to chemical bullets, gobble tranquilizers

and antidepressants, alcohol and cocaine. Embrace gu-
rus and heaven-hucksters, any charismatic creep promising a quick fix of the pain. And they end up taking
temporary vacations in psychiatric wards and prison
cells, emerge looking good, raising everyone's hopes.
Until the next letdown real or imagined, the next excur-
sion into self-damage.

What they don't do is change.

The printing of counterfeit money from Gerald Petievich's *To
Live and Die in L.A.*:

"Rick likes to do the whole printing all at once. He'll
start in the morning by burning the images on the alu-
minum plates. When he finishes the plates, he puts the
plate on the press and starts running off the fronts of
the bills. Then he starts right off on the backs . . ."

And Petievich on aging counterfeit bills . . .

"I buy me a plastic trash barrel and fill it with water. I
pour in a bottle of Creme de Menthe and about one
bottle of black India ink. I soak the bills in the shit and
then dry 'em with an electric fan. They come out perfect. The soaking and drying make the bills look dirty,
like they've been in circulation for a while; takes away
the crisp look that's a sure tipoff to the cashiers when
you pass 'em."

Widely varying voices, but the common thread is the *simplicity*
of the language. It may be useful to reread the above selections
to appreciate this. All three authors are dealing with material well
known to them because of personal expertise but generally unfamiliar to the reading public. Yet, in each case, not a single word
has been used that would cause the lay reader to run to the
dictionary.

Any time the reader has to sit back and analyze what you're

talking about, you blew it. Unless, once again, the aim is to portray a character as being deliberately snobbish and confusing (e.g., a pompous blowhole using jargon to intimidate the opposition). This is not to say that specialized lingo is unacceptable. Like dialect, technical language can be utilized for verisimilitude and richness of texture. Just make sure that the reader can read between the lines of argot and understand what the character is saying.

Expert novelists often grant their greatest endowment of smarts to the hero of the story—following the old saw to write what they know, and/or luxuriating in the Walter Mitty ego trip that makes writing a better job than most. But don't underestimate the value of an expert *secondary character*. A couple of examples:

• A forensic odontologist helps Detective Sergeant Peter Decker identify the charred remains of two teenagers in Faye Kellerman's *Sacred and Profane*.

• A pair of memorable entomologists at the Smithsonian Institute expose a vital clue by pinpointing the habitation of a rare moth—the trademark of a serial killer—in Thomas Harris's *Silence of the Lambs*.

So much for the use of expertise, once we've got it. But how do we get it?

The answer, of course, is research. And research is by no means limited to the uninitiated. Most fields of technical knowledge change rapidly and even the experts must work at keeping their knowledge current. What was standard procedure when a given sourcebook was written may be outdated by the time the book is published. This applies to works of fiction as well. Sometimes, as in the case of Jonathan Kellerman's *The Butcher's Theater*, set in a city, Jerusalem, where events occur at breakneck pace, a specific date is used to anchor the novel in time.

The first step in researching is obtaining the *flavor* of the field by immersing oneself in written material.

Articles in peer-review journals—technical periodicals whose contents are evaluated by experts prior to acceptance for publication—may be more current than books, but due to publication lag in academia, even they may be old news by the time they make it into print. Libraries—especially university facilities—are likely to include in their holdings newsletters and bulletins that offer maximal freshness. Scan a year or so of these to get a feel for what's been done. This may be less than a grand frolic: Professional journals often possess all the excitement of a tractor manual. The literary mind screams: Where's the editing! But it's good to read the boring stuff, too. You'll know what not to do.

After you have a general familiarity with terms and concepts, the next step is find someone in the field. If you want to write from the point of view of a gynecologist, call up a gynecologist. Not every OB/GYN is going to chat with you, but you may find a few who are more than willing to give you some time. Some may even be thrilled. Especially if you give them an acknowledgment in your opus.

Many of us who've written cop or private eye novels have benefited from listening to what cops and/or PIs have to say. We've visited police stations, ridden in police cars, read crime charts and weapons manuals down to the individual firearm specifications.

All the information is out there. Footwork, a forthright manner, and a nice smile help reel it in.

As you amass your information, try to organize it in a way that suits your novel. Index cards or their computerized counterparts work wonders. Multigenerational and historical mysteries, especially, may require heroic feats of organization.

Live with the data until your confidence level rises. Try to think and feel like an expert. But don't fake it. If you don't know what you're talking about, leave the information out or ask an expert for clarification. Even if your facts are completely correct, there are detail junkies lurking out there, just waiting to pounce. It's much more fun to read their letters when they're dead wrong.

And speaking of fun, have some. If you love what you're learning, you're a lot more likely to transmit a sense of adventure and vitality to your readers. Fun's also terrific for its own sake: One of the most enjoyable aspects of professional writing is the opportunity to learn things we never had the time, or desire, to study in school. To sit in the stacks of a university library—just you and a bunch of musty old volumes no one else has touched in decades, to come upon the ultimate technical clue that helps your novel take final shape—is sheer heaven. Enjoy the luxury of exploring new worlds. Give yourself straight As. There's no pop quiz tomorrow morning.

chapter six

WHERE DO I FIND A JEWISH INDIAN? OR HOW I STOPPED WORRYING AND LEARNED TO LOVE RESEARCH

Stuart M. Kaminsky

I was deeply into doing research long before I learned to give it a name and all the excess baggage that went with the word and its implication of academia and long hours under dim lights in libraries that smell of reassuring slow decay.

When I was working on my master's degree in Literature at the University of Illinois, I took a course in research. It consisted of a series of questions, a long series, handed out in the first session of the class by the professor. We were, in those days before the Internet, supposed to live in the library and return on specific dates with specific answers.

We searched through books, asked librarians, went through volumes of periodic reviews of literature and the indexes of obscure literary journals with Greek or Latin names.

After hours spent in vain and neglecting my other classes, my job as a waiter, and my sleep, I came up with a solution, a solution from my education as an undergraduate journalism student. It is one that has served me well ever since.

I asked an expert. Not an expert at the University of Illinois, since they all knew the assignment and wouldn't contribute to undermining it by doing my work for me, but one at Notre Dame University. I got his name by asking directory assistance at Notre Dame. I was connected to a professor in the English Literature Department. I told him I had some questions and knew he was the one person in the United States who could answer them with ease. After three questions, he told me I had the wrong man. He transferred me to an associate professor who not only answered all my questions but told me far more than I wanted to know, even citing sources and telling me to call him again if I had more questions.

I imagined a lonely little man in a dungeonlike office poring over thick tomes that spewed dust while he waited for someone just like me to find him. I made two people happy. Him and me.

Point of this story? You have a question? Find the expert. You can still call your local university, but it is a lot easier to find experts now than it was when I started writing. Now we have the Internet, which means we have too many experts. If you don't have access to the Internet or don't know how to use it, you should probably stop reading right now, in midsentence, and go out and get the necessary equipment. You don't even have to purchase it if you are willing to make frequent trips to your nearest library.

Let me give you a few examples. I write about Russia and wrote about the Soviet Union while there still was one. I read and collect books about life, education, medical care, even heating and air-conditioning. I still read such books. I like reading books. The problem with books is that I get absorbed in the text. For example, when doing research about the Russian Orthodox Church for a novel I was working on, I became fascinated with the church and moved on to the Greek Orthodox Church. I spent more time reading about religion than writing about it. My goal was information to form a believable background for my story. I hope that was one result. The other was that I learned a great deal. I gave myself a course in a specific religion and then applied it.

I suggest to all who wish to do research on a general subject to read books about that subject, to do so with some vague general questions but with an open mind. Read with the understanding that your research may take you in a direction you hadn't considered, a direction much better than the one you would have followed had you focused solely on the answer to your specific question.

And, by the way, when I say "books," I don't necessarily mean those usually identified as nonfiction or textbooks. I've learned far more about daily life in St. Petersburg, Russia, in the 1860s from Dostoevsky than I have from any textbook. In Dostoevsky's journals and novels, I have walked the streets of St. Petersburg and seen the details of life in that milieu.

Now, I could have gone to the Internet and found answers to specific questions, but I would have missed the details, the things that brought the place to life.

The Internet, however, is invaluable. I am slightly ashamed at how little time I now spend in the library and how much better my time is spent in front of my computer screen.

Again, for my Russian novels I have located and now correspond with a young filmmaker in Moscow who answers any questions about daily life that I might have. I am in direct contact with an officer at the Moscow Criminal Investigation Division. I found him simply by searching under "Police, Moscow." Of course I got listings for Moscow, Idaho (which has a very nice site), first, but I found him and get answers quickly. When I wanted to learn about Mir and the Russian space program, I found myself in direct contact with Star City, which is just outside of Moscow where the cosmonauts are trained. Within five minutes of searching, I was getting answers to my questions from a Russian colonel who sent me photographs, diagrams, history, geography, and more.

There are several million experts out there waiting for you. The trick is to find them and then ask the right questions. The Internet doesn't think. If doing a search for "Fingerprints" doesn't give you the connection you want, think of other ways to refine the search. Check Web sites and Web pages. Discard the fakes and lunatics.

Many universities have Web sites that will connect you to sources. I have found criminal investigation agencies—from the CIA and FBI down to my local Sarasota police chief—willing and happy to answer any questions I might have.

A couple of tricks of the trade:

- Don't lock yourself into a question so specific that after two or three tries you find that you can't get an answer. If the door doesn't open, go through a different one. Don't get hung up on research. Don't use it as a crutch or an excuse. If, within a few minutes, you can't find out who discovered the paper clip, forget it. On the other hand, if, without looking for it, you stumble on the name of the person who invented the paper clip, hold onto the information. It may fit into something you are doing.

- If you can't find the answer to your question, create an answer that makes sense and attribute it to a character. It becomes his or her information, not yours. Humans can be wrong. Characters can be wrong.

- Keep a notebook in your pocket or purse. Carry two working pens or pencils. When some fact strikes you in the newspaper, a magazine, a book, a store window, wherever, write it in your notebook. I have notebooks full of information. I use about half of it at most, but it is there for me somewhat unneatly arranged in my desk.

- While you wait for the physician, dentist, barber, or hairdresser to get to you and you find something in one of the waiting room magazines that interests you, simply ask if you can take the magazine home. I've got a pile. On the cover of each of the magazines, I put a Post-it giving the page number and subject of the article that interested me.

- Frequent used bookstores. Look for the things people normally have no use for. You may have no immediate use for a certain book, but something tells you it might contain information you can use. For example, I have purchased many an out-of-date gun magazine, ratty brown paper–covered books issued by the government in the 1960s about protecting oneself from communicable diseases, 1940s histories of Los Angeles, collections of money-saving recipes from 1937, a bound volume of issues of *Harper's* (sans cover) from 1942 to 1943. I love this stuff. Research is not a chore for me. It is sometimes my favorite part of the job.

• Ask a librarian. I mentioned this earlier. I emphasize it now. At lunch with some friends less than a month ago, an argument arose about the practice of scalping. One friend said the British and French had introduced it to the American Indians. Another said the native peoples had been taking scalps long before white men came. A member of our group called the library. A few days later, at no cost, the library found and provided an article on the history of scalping. At another lunch with the same group, the question came up about whether the Spanish introduced syphilis to America or the Indians of Central America gave it to the Spanish. Again, the librarian happily came up with another article. By the way, the Native Americans were scalping long before the British, French, and Spanish came to America, and Central American Indians gave syphilis to the Spanish conquistadores. Research librarians live for such questions.

• If you are writing and find that you need the answer to a question, don't use it as an excuse to stop writing. Make one quick effort to get the answer. If you can't find it in ten minutes, keep writing and go back for the answer when you finish your manuscript.

• If you can get it, watch *Court TV*. Not the movies but the trials. See what they're really like. Even better, watch some trials in your town. Good seats are almost always available.

• Use your own experience as potential research material. About a year ago my eighty-five-year-old mother got suddenly sick and dizzy when I was with her shopping. I took her to the emergency room. We were put in a small room near the nursing station. While my mother rested, I eavesdropped on staff conversations, wrote a description of the equipment, and asked each person who came in to deal with my mother what that day had been like. Each one, from the lady who cleaned the rooms to the doctor in charge, was more than willing to tell me. No one had ever asked them. Instead of sitting bored for five hours, I filled a small notebook with material I could use for a scene I knew I would have in an emergency room.

I had an accident five years ago in a Kmart store. I had a concussion and was unconscious. I woke up in the hospital, my head throbbing and bandaged. My very first thought was, *This is damned interesting. I've got to remember how it feels and get it in my notebook.*

• Do research as a great no-guilt excuse for having fun. I love reading old newspapers and magazines. Whenever I do one of my Toby Peters mysteries, I spend two days in the local library looking at issues of the *Los Angeles Times* and *The New York Times* for the period I'll be dealing with in my book. I read the radio listings, the comics, the ads, the society news, the war news, and the human or inhuman interest stories that are often no more than a paragraph or two long. If I were to stop writing Toby Peters novels, I'd still find an excuse for reading the *Times* from the 1940s and going through *Life* magazines reading everything including the Goodyear and Cresta Blanca ads.

• Search lists of magazines. For years I had a subscription to *Prison Life*, a magazine put out by prisoners in state and federal institutions. The magazine was a treasure trove. There are magazines on just about everything. For years I collected circus magazines. I love the circus. I've written two novels with circus backgrounds. Eventually, however, I ran out of space for my circus magazines and gave them to a collector. There's a magazine called *Casket and Sunnyside* for undertakers and morticians. Ah, what a source.

In short, while I've given you some ideas, I'm sure you could give me some too. If you are creative enough to write a publishable story, true crime or novel, you should be creative enough to find the information you need.

I have heard people who conduct writing seminars and have read articles by these same people saying, "Write about what you know about." I've known many writing students and aspiring writers who heard this and decided they had essentially dull lives or could only write about being homemakers, pharmacists, or insurance adjustors.

Research gives you the opportunity to know about anything. Research and imagination.

Use both.

I close by saying that if there is one book a person who writes about crime should have within arm's reach it is *The Writer's Complete Crime Reference Book* by Martin Roth. I just flipped it open at random and found myself in the middle of a section on the details and requirements of parole. As it turns out, I don't need this section. I know two ex-convicts currently on parole. One, who served time for conspiracy to commit murder, is an accomplished painter; the other is a former armored car robber who is now an author. Both men are quite willing to talk about their experiences in prison and on parole. It helps to have the right friends, a computer, and a good book or two within easy reach.

chapter seven

BACKGROUND, LOCATION, AND SETTING

■ *Julie Smith*

The backdrop of a mystery, the world in which the action takes place—the scenery, so to speak—has the potential to be as important as character or plot. Indeed, if painted vividly enough it can become a character in itself, or it can determine plot. It can set a mood, create an atmosphere. It can express an opinion. It needn't do any of that; it can simply add richness and color.

But it should do at least some of the above.

You could leave it out; you could set your mystery indoors and never give the reader any sense of the city in which the action occurs. But if you do, your work may lose a dimension. There are exceptions, of course—Stephen King did it in *Misery*, but we're talking here about the master of creating atmosphere; he aims for the claustrophobic terror of confinement and succeeds.

Failing such special effects, your setting must be rich and vivid and colorful if your mystery is to be first-rate. The reader should get a strong sense of it, a blast of grit and conflict if the story is set in Chicago, a cacophony of construction noise and yelling; the gentle feel and sound of lapping waves if the setting is Port Frederick, Massachusetts.

Describing the landscape will go a long way, but there are wicked, lovely ways of drawing out the power of a setting, making it release its essence, that go far beyond that. They are ancient ways in our genre, going clear back to Chandler's thirties. Consider the first paragraph of "Red Wind":

> There was a desert wind blowing that night. It was one of those hot dry Santa Anas that come down through the mountain passes and curl your hair and make your nerves jump and your skin itch. On nights like that every booze party ends in a fight. Meek little wives feel the edge of the carving knife and study their husbands' necks. Anything can happen. You can even get a full glass of beer at a cocktail lounge.

I'll never forget hearing Joseph Hansen, author of the Dave Brandstetter mysteries, lecture one cool summer night at a rustic lodge in the redwoods. "Put weather in!" he told his audience. And then, warming to his subject, he stamped his foot: "Put *weather* in!"

Yes, put weather in. But don't just say it's raining. Make us feel the sodden weight of a wall of water driven by winds gusting at sixty miles an hour. If a Santa Ana's blowing, make our hair curl and our nerves jump and our skin itch.

If the weather, the land, the milieu are to play an important part in your book, you may want to say so up front. Mickey Friedman's *Hurricane Season* begins with an artful prologue in which Friedman establishes her locale as an important character in her book, maybe *the* most important, but she is working two sides of the street here—her story takes place in 1952:

> Hurricane season comes when the year is exhausted. In the damp, choking heat of August and September, the days go on forever to no purpose. Hurricanes linger in the back of the mind as a threat and a promise. The threat is the threat of destruction. The promise is that something could happen, that the air could stir and

become clammy, the heat could lift, the bay start to wallow like a huge humpbacked animal.

If a hurricane came, there would be something to do besides drink iced tea on the front porch and take long, sweat-soaked naps in the afternoon; there would be something to talk about besides how hot it is.

Palmetto is in northwest Florida on a corner of land that juts into the Gulf of Mexico. Tourists bound for Miami, or Palm Beach, or Fort Lauderdale do not see Palmetto or know about it. In their rush to the south, they do not pass near it. They want palm trees and hibiscus; Palmetto has scrub oak and miles of sawgrass through which salt streams meander, and acres of pine woods. It has broad, slow-moving brown rivers lined with cypress swamps.

Water is a presence, and people live in connection with it. They fish, or deal in oysters, scallops, and shrimp. On the beach road, there are fisheries built on pilings over the water, corrugated iron oyster shacks, shrimp boats, swathes of net. People travel by boat where the roads don't go—across the bay to St. Elmo's Island or down the sloughs deep into the river swamp.

Notice how Friedman first creates a mood—of stillness waiting to be broken. And then she uses geography to segue into rich description, along the way giving a painless, hidden lecture on the economy of the town. By the time we're on page two, we know what the place feels like, what it looks like, and how it makes its living. We're practically wiping away imaginary beads of sweat and we find ourselves on the way to the kitchen to make some iced tea. We now have a perfect picture of Palmetto, a veritable slide show.

In my own book *New Orleans Mourning*, I used Mardi Gras as a vehicle for understanding the town. In an early chapter we learn, from the point of view of Skip Langdon, the cop, what Mardi Gras looks like:

The huddled masses stood several hundred deep on both sides of the avenue, some with ladders for their kids or themselves, some with toddlers on their shoulders, risking the kids' lives, in her opinion—one bump and baby hit the pavement. . . . They really did holler and beg— just like the guidebooks said they did. It seemed to be proper Carnival etiquette for the hoi polloi. The aristocrats, (the male ones, anyway), grandly conveyed on floats, were supposed to demonstrate their largess by casting trinkets into the crowds. Little strings of beads, mostly, and Carnival doubloons.

It doesn't create much of a mood or even convey much information, but it does tell you what you'd see and hear on the street, a nuts-and-bolts item in even the shortest short story. This is the part of the tale where the fiction writer acts as reporter. She must be on the scene to record the sights and sounds of her setting, its tastes and smells too, if they're important. Then she reports; she takes you on a tour. I heard Joe Gores say once that he drives through the area he's going to write about, taking notes on a tape recorder, before he sits down to write.

But what if you have a scene in the Grand Canyon and you don't have a vacation coming up soon? Do the next best thing to going there—look at all the pictures you can find and interview everyone you know who's been there recently. But never cut corners by simply leaving out the description.

You can make it short; you can make it pithy; you can make it metaphorical and ambiguous. Just don't try to make the reader believe you're not mentioning what things look like because it doesn't matter—he'll see right through you.

Sometimes the feeling of a place is best conveyed by information other than description. In *Diamond in the Buff*, Susan Dunlap tells you more about Berkeley than talk of brown-shingled houses ever could:

As I drove downhill I thought about Leila Sandoval and Berkeley syndrome. . . .

Like the street artists on the Avenue, Berkeley syndrome was a phenomenon that flourished here. Many
Berkeleyans had come to town as students. Caught by
political awareness, social concern, or artistic aspira-
tion combined with disdain for material possessions, they
had stayed. After graduating, or dropping out, they had
worked for the good of their fellow man, or they'd followed their muse, sitting in the warm sunshine of commitment. They had stored good karma against the chill
of a middle age they were sure would never find them.
They worked twenty hours a week to pay the rent, but
they knew they were not insurance or real estate agents;
they were union organizers or metal sculptors. And, in
Berkeley, everyone else knew that too. They were not
ne'er-do-wells as they would have been back East, they
were people "who'd gotten their priorities straight."
    Berkeley syndrome had blossomed in the Sixties, and
bloomed well through the Seventies. By the mid-
Eighties, the syndromees were well into their forties. Eyes
that had peered into blocks of stone and seen visions
of beauty now needed bifocals; teeth that had chewed
over the Peace and Freedom platform required gold
crowns that part-time jobs would not pay for. And the
penniless life with one change of jeans and a sleeping
bag to unroll on some friend's floor was no longer viable.
The need of a steady income became undeniable. And
so they scraped together the money, took a course in
acupressure, herbalism, or massage, and prepared to
be responsible adults.

As it happens I live in Berkeley and can vouch for the fact that
no citizen thereof will be able to read that passage without saying
to herself, "That's my hometown."
Background determines plot when events are inextricably tied to
the place where they happen. In my own *New Orleans Mourning*,
I set the murder at Mardi Gras and have the motives and passions

grow out of politics and societal attitudes that exist only in New Orleans.

Reaching back in history, Hammett's *Red Harvest* could only happen in the milieu where it's set—never mind that the town is imaginary, we'll never forget it. Los Angeles has traditionally been the American symbol of corruption, new money, recklessness, ambition, peculiar ways for society to go awry. Mystery writers have been mining it since Chandler; lately, the Miami crime novel has sprung up along the same lines.

Chandler's novels, for instance, could take place only in Los Angeles—they are *about* L.A. and its corruption. Ross Macdonald's novels, also set in southern California, could probably be moved to some other locale without losing much more than a few canyon fires and oil spills—they are *about* family secrets and the past affecting the present.

Tony Hillerman's novels have to happen where Navajos live, but they are about the Navajo religion rather than the land; yet the Navajo religion is deeply bound to the land. So the setting, though not quite a character in the Hillerman books, plays an integral part in their structure. A new author who lives in a unique locale, where events can be determined by the place itself, would do well to exploit it.

Background can also be used to express opinions, political or otherwise. An intimate acquaintance with the seamy underside of New York is a big part of what gives Andrew Vachss's novels their bite and sting. Vachss uses the whole rotten social fabric as his scenery. When he zeros in on a street corner, you know just how his hero (and, one might imagine, the author himself) feels about it:

> Wall Street was expanding its way up from the tip of Manhattan, on a collision course with the loft-dwelling yuppies from SoHo. Every square inch of space was worth something to somebody and more to somebody else a few months later. The small factories were all being converted into co-ops. Even the river was disappearing as land-greed took builders farther and farther offshore;

Battery Park City was spreading its branches into the
void left when they tore down the overpass for the West
Side Highway. Riverfront joints surrendered to
nouvelle-cuisine bistros. The electronics stores that
would sell you what you needed to build your own
ham radio or tap your neighbor's phone gave way to
sushi bars. Antique shops and storefront-sized art gal-
leries shouldered in next to places that would sell you
some vitamins or rent you a videotape.

People have always lived down here. The neighborhood
used to be a goddamned art colony—it produces more
pottery than the whole Navajo nation. The hippies and the
artists thought the winos added just the right touch of
realism to their lives. But the new occupants are the kind
who get preorgasmic when you whisper "investment
banking" and they didn't much care for local color. Lock-
smiths were riding the crest of a growth industry.

Vachss gives us social history and social comment all wrapped
up in two neat paragraphs that also convey a pretty good idea of
the look and feel of the place.

Notice how different a feeling you get from these two paragraphs
and the description in *Hurricane Season*. Quite simply, you're
transported—in one case to New York, in the other to Florida in
the fifties.

And that, ultimately, whatever other functions it performs, is the
goal of location and background—to scoop up the reader on a
magic carpet and take him to the world of your book.

Seven Ways to Make Settings More Real

1. Don't treat background as secondary; use it to advantage. Set
your book in a place that lends itself to atmosphere and exploit
the locale to the fullest.

2. Use ordinary description, but go beyond it as well—give us
feelings, sounds, tastes, smells, metaphors, impressions, opinions.

As in all writing, show don't tell. Involve all five senses. Above all, give us strong images. Don't tell us it's a pretty day; show us the sun glinting through a violet canopy of jacarandas.

3. If it's appropriate, let the character of a place shine through and become a character in your book.

4. Don't cut corners. Visit the location of each scene, get the feel of it, take copious notes, then report. If you can't do that, research it well with books, pictures, and interviews—especially interviews. Pay attention to people's personal takes on a place.

5. Don't overlook the obvious. If you're setting a cozy in Miami—probably a poor idea, but let's just say you've found an idyllic pocket in the suburbs and you want to plant a body there—at least *mention* drug smuggling; orient the reader to the larger community.

6. Note from the examples herein just how far a couple of paragraphs can go. Slip in nuggets of information—economics, history, social history, geography—but don't get carried away. A little does a lot.

7. Put weather in.

part II

The Process

CHARACTERIZATION

▣ *Michael Connelly*

From somewhere in my memory, either amateur hour TV or the boardwalk in Venice, I remember a sideshow act called plate spinning. The object of this entertainment endeavor is to rotate plates balanced on thin wooden dowels. The practitioner gets several pieces of supposedly good china spinning at once and then must quickly move from dowel to dowel, keeping everything spinning and aloft. Paid particular attention is the plate in the middle of the formation. By virtue of its position, it is the most important of plates. If it goes down, it invariably takes several other plates with it and you have broken china all over the ground and an empty tip bucket.

In my mind I often liken writing a book to spinning plates. There are many, many different things you have to keep up and spinning at all times. Each listing within the table of contents of this book is a plate the writer must keep spinning from beginning to end. Plot structure, dialogue, prose style, research, rhythm and pacing, on and on. There are many, many plates to keep off the ground. The writer moves frantically from one to the other during the course of writing a book.

And without a doubt the plate at the center of the formation, the most important plate, is character. It is the plate that takes down everything with it if it falls. Everything. A book lacking in true and believable characterization is just so many pieces of broken china on the ground. A good plot is empty unless filled with the blood of character.

I don't profess to be an expert. I am no teacher. Nothing I write here is new. It's all been said before. But what I write here is an attempt to explain what has worked for me. I believe there are no rules to writing. You find what works and then you work it. What follows here is a scattershot listing of thoughts, theories, practices, and borrowed adages that have worked for me. There are a few examples and anecdotes to help illustrate them as well.

Character is defined by quality not quantity. It is a mistake to think that your characters will come to life if you pump multitudes of details into them. True character can be hidden in those details. Most of the time, less is more if the details you do use open a window into your character's interior. I call these the "telling" details of character. They are the nuances that create an empathic strike between your character and reader. They are details that show your reader your character's true world. And when you get one, you know it. The empathic strike is like hitting a steel plate with a ball peen hammer. When you hit it, your whole body knows it.

Here's an example of a telling detail. I once spent a week tagging along with a homicide squad. I was going to write a story for a magazine. I was also collecting the details of this difficult job so that I could later use them in my novels. During the week, three homicides occurred, and the squad responded accordingly. At each crime scene, I noticed that the squad sergeant would squat like a baseball catcher next to the victim, take his glasses off, hook the earpiece in his mouth, and study the body. At the end of the week, I was sitting in the sergeant's office conducting my last interview for the story. At one point the sergeant took off his glasses and put them down on his desk blotter. I looked at them and saw the plastic earpiece had been deeply grooved by his teeth. The sergeant obviously clenched his teeth on the earpiece when he squatted down and studied the victims of homicide. The ball peen hammer hit the steel plate. That was a telling detail. A character nuance that said so much about this man and his job and how the two related. I knew it was something I could use in fact or fiction and my reader would be drawn closer to the character I was trying to delineate. That one detail would say more about his world than a hundred details without resonance.

Whether you stumble upon it as I did in that story or it comes out of your own creative genius, your life as a writer must be the pursuit of the telling details of character. One telling detail will take you further than a page of description. Character is in the details that work toward showing the world and your protagonist's relationship to it. Telling details pierce the facade everyone builds around themselves.

Character is conflict. That is probably said in every writing classroom in the world. Your protagonist is defined by how he faces and overcomes the conflicts in the path ahead. You should endeavor when you write to put obstacles in the path of your characters at every turn and at every level of their lives.

In crime fiction there is always a built-in baseline conflict—the crime that must be explained and solved by the protagonist. But the writer cannot be satisfied with this alone. The writer must build in other conflicts. There must be personal stakes and turmoil for the protagonist. So that when he explains and solves the crime he is also explaining and solving something about himself. In so doing he is revealing himself. That is character.

I think Kurt Vonnegut summed this up best when he gave this advice to writers: Make sure on every page everybody wants something, even if it's just a glass of water. Or words to that effect. What he was again saying is that character is conflict. All persons are defined by their wants and needs. Their desires. Attaining the things we want creates conflict within ourselves and in our relation to the world. This natural human condition must be embedded in the people you write about. It helps define their characters. It makes them real. In my own writing, Vonnegut's adage is never far away. I consciously work to make sure the conflicts are there on every page, whether running above or below the surface. Often my protagonists are constructed so that in addition to the built-in conflict of the case at hand, they are in the midst of inner dilemmas or turmoils that carry toward how they view and investigate the cases. I add other conflicts, such as the obstacles of bureaucracy, and I am almost there. I was once told that the best crime novels are not about how a detective works on a case; they are about how a case works on a detective. I try never to forget that. I know that it is by putting my protagonist on a path littered with conflicts and obstacles that I can achieve that. And achieving that creates character. It's a circle—like a spinning plate.

These conflicts can be big and small. They can be as seemingly minor as wanting a glass of water or a cigarette. Because it is how a person goes about quenching his desires or living with them unrequited that the readers get a glimpse of his true character. It is one thing to say a character felt like having a cigarette. It is another to have the same character, in a moment of stress, reach his hand to the empty pocket where he used to keep his smokes. One is description; the other is characterization.

Here is another example. It was a small moment, but I think I used it to say a lot in terms of character. In a book I wrote called *The Last Coyote*, the protagonist, Detective Bosch, needed information from a bureaucrat. He visited her in her little cubicle at City Hall, where she was burrowed in like a fiddler crab, drinking fruit punch from a large cup with a straw. As is typical in such situations, she was reticent to help him. She more or less dismissed him and left the cubicle, using a well-practiced pirouette move to slide through the narrow channel between her desk and the wall of the cubicle. Left alone, Bosch simply got up and pushed the desk a couple inches closer to the wall. When the bureaucrat came back she went into her pirouette move to get behind her desk and— bang—her thigh hit the desk and her fruit punch went over, spilling across her blotter.

This moment had nothing to do with the story or the plot or even the solving of the crime Bosch was investigating. It was all about character. Though it could be taken as comical or mean-spirited on Bosch's behalf, his action was also an insight into his world and how he operates in it. It said this is a man who doesn't suffer fools well, who has little patience with the bureaucracy that stands between him and solving a case. These are important character elements. They are part of a personal code. The problem is you can't always tell your reader these things about your protagonist. You must show it. If I had simply written that Bosch was a man who did not suffer fools well, it would have been a detail. Showing Bosch not suffering a fool well became a telling detail, a piercing of the facade. That's what you want. That's characterization.

Raymond Chandler said there is a quality of redemption to anything that is art. I think it is true. I think there is a quality of redemption to anything that is true character. What I mean is that the protagonist of a crime novel should be on an arc that runs parallel but still may be wholly separate from the arc of the crime investigation. There must be something that fuels him. He can find the fuel in the crime he is investigating, but most often it is something else. Something inside, something from the past. He must turn the difficulties, even horrors, of his past into the fuel of the present. Most often that puts him on a redemptive arc. The detective is making up for something in the past. It can be in the distant or close past, but it is back there somewhere behind him and it is what drives him whether it is his conscious motive or not.

From the fires of the detective's past, a personal code is also forged. The protagonist must have a code that is adhered to no matter what the costs or consequences. He must protect this code like a mother protecting a child. In his code is his character.

The detective cannot state his code to the reader. It must become apparent through action. If part of his code is that he doesn't suffer fools well, then he must show this through action, not state it. If his code is that he will go to the ends of the earth to see justice win the day no matter the consequences to himself or others, then the story should be constructed so that the detective follows a path leading to a point where he faces the choices that illustrate this.

Everything should be in service of character. When I write, I consciously devote myself to thinking about how each chapter, setting, plot point, even page can be used to further illustrate the character of my protagonist. The plot is in service of character. To go the opposite way, to put character in service of plot, is to construct a book that might be highly entertaining but ultimately will be short of attaining a higher level of art and empathic connection to the reader.

Don't get me wrong. Plots evolve in and of themselves. An idea hits you and a plot forms, often independent of your protagonist. In my own experience, almost all of the books I have written began with a plot. But the writer's job is to harness that plot, mold it, and put it in service of the characterization of the protagonist. The task is to take the story and make it uniquely the protagonist's story.

The writer should never miss an opportunity to brush on a character stroke. From the selection of a name to the types of clothing worn to the car driven to whether bottled or tap water is preferred, each brushstroke is all-important because it bespeaks character.

But the writer must be careful. There is a fine line. Description is not necessarily character. The writer who layers his pages with the obvious surface details of a life is not communicating character to the reader. It's the telling details that do that.

There is a delicate relationship between story flow and characterization. One should never be sacrificed for the other. A story that speeds along without characterization is a hollow missile. A story with its flow choked off by too much or inappropriately located characterization is a dud. The art of delivering characterization requires finesse and balance. The story must always move forward and backward at the same time.

By that I mean that the writer's task is to deliver a set of full-blooded characters to the reader. In particular, the protagonist. As discussed above, you do that with actions, personal nuances, and the telling details of his world. The other component is the past. We are all products of our pasts. So, too, are our characters.

But the key is to not stem the flow of a story while taking a journey into the past. The art is to keep the story moving forward with force and momentum at the same time you are delivering—almost secretly—the past.

Here's another example we can look at. *The Black Ice* opens with Bosch on the back deck of his hillside home watching a brush fire burn up the side of the mountain across the pass. His eyes track the fire helicopters as they drop water on burning homes and brush. Here is the paragraph with the line I'm talking about highlighted:

> Bosch watched the squadron of helicopters, like dragon-flies from this distance, dodging in and out of the smoke, dropping their payloads of water and pink fire retardant on burning homes and trees. *It reminded him of the dustoffs in Vietnam*. The noise. The uncertain bob-bing and weaving of the overburdened craft. He saw the water crushing through flaming roofs and steam immedi-ately rising.

Within that paragraph the story kept moving forward while at the same time it moved back. In a short eight-word sentence, I was able to deliver characterization through the past without dis-turbing the forward progress of the story. What was said here? First of all, I said this man we are about to ride with through this story is of a certain age and experience. He obviously saw action in the Vietnam War. Not only that, but more than two decades later, the memories are never far from him. In fact, something right out of present-day life can suddenly bring him back to his war experience.

This to me is important stuff. To me it is characterization, a nice stroke of it on the very first page. But in getting it to the reader, the onward flow of the story was not disturbed in any way. If at that moment I had instead diverted from the narrative to a flash-back sequence, it could have been useful in more thoroughly deline-ating Bosch's war experience, but it would have impacted the forward movement of the story. It would have stopped it cold. Instead, as in most cases when seeding the story with the past, less was more. Less creates interest and intrigue in a character. It's a finesse game, and the writer must always be on top of it, must always be conscious of the balance between story flow and characterization.

I have preached here that everything should be in service of character. So let me discuss how the paragraph above came about. The fire described in the opening of the book has nothing to do with the plotline other than its metaphoric and mood qualities. I wanted to impress on the reader from the beginning that while Los Angeles is a place of great beauty it is also a place of natural cataclysms, such as fires and floods and earthquakes—a place where anything can go wrong. Once I chose the fire I had that. I then consciously pursued ways of turning this opening vignette into a passage that also said something about Bosch's character. I finally came up with the line about Vietnam and with those eight words was able to tie Bosch's past and present together and to infer that this is a man who carries some baggage.

This was one paragraph on one page. It is something I try to pursue on every page. Not coming close to that mark but hitting it enough times with enough telling details to build a full character in the minds of the reader. I hope, at least.

The discussion here has been focused primarily on the characterization of the protagonist. But to borrow a phrase from Detective Bosch's personal code, everybody counts or nobody counts. No character is a throwaway. The writer must labor over all characters in the story in the same way. Remember Vonnegut's rule: Make sure *everybody* on every page wants something. All characters are important. The writer cannot shirk his duties in constructing any of them, good, bad, or indifferent.

This after all is in service to your protagonist. There is an adage that your hero is only as good as your villain is bad. I think there is an element of truth to that. But it should be carried forward to the whole slate of characters who populate a novel. They all act in concert to support the protagonist. The fuller they are—the more real they are with desires and secrets and telling details—the better and fuller your protagonist will be in their reflection.

This of course underlines the writer's difficulty. So many plates to keep spinning, so little time. The writer must jump from character to character, making sure they remain balanced and turning. I have never tried it before, but I get the feeling that spinning real plates is a lot easier.

ROUNDING UP YOUR CHARACTERS

■ *Margaret Maron*

My favorite reading is a traditional fair-play mystery novel. For me, that means an ingenious plot peopled by engaging characters in a fully realized setting. Ideally, these three elements are seamlessly integrated into a satisfying whole. Yes, I have enjoyed books where the plot is totally outrageous or so complex that one needs a diagram and a timetable to follow all its twists and turns. I have also spent pleasant evenings immersed in settings so unusual that I was willing to overlook the predictable plot in exchange for this guided tour of an unfamiliar world. But I seldom finish a book if its characters are flat and two-dimensional.

Indeed, the mysteries that linger longest in my memory are not those with the never-would-have-guessed-it plot nor the behind-the-curtain look at places I'll never go in real life. I may muddle the plots of my favorite writers, but I'll remember forever the characters they made me love: Elizabeth Peters's Amelia Peabody Emerson, Jonathan Gash's Lovejoy, Virginia Lanier's Jo Beth Sidden, to list but a few, and, of course, any character even glancingly mentioned by Josephine Tey.

In the pantheon of writers from the first Golden Age of Mysteries, Josephine Tey (1896–1952) is usually ranked below Agatha Christie (1890–1976), whose elegant plots have never been bested, and Dorothy L. Sayers (1893–1957), whose plots were occasionally over the top but who compensated with better-rounded characters and more interesting backdrops. But while Sayers lovingly embellished her upper-class Lord Peter Wimsey and his true love, Harriet Vane, giving them intellectual passions even nonintellects could understand and sympathize with, her secondary characters seldom rise above their labels: village rector, spinster typist, aristocratic snob, obliging police inspector.

When I decided to get serious about teaching myself how to write, Christie and Sayers were the classic prototypes to which I first turned. It was only then, while prowling the mystery section of the Brooklyn Public Library, that I stumbled across Josephine Tey (the *T*s being shelved immediately beneath the *S*s). Her *Brat Farrar* was a revelation.

In *Busman's Honeymoon*, Sayers sends the newly married Wimseys to a village that Harriet had known as a child. The class-conscious villagers are pictured as so bedazzled to find a lord in their midst that it's hard to differentiate the personalities beneath all those virtual curtsies and pulled forelocks.

Contrast this with Brat Farrar's tour of the country farms he's supposed to have known as a child. Every farmer, every farmer's wife springs instantly to life, individuals caught in the middle of their daily chores and each as different as lettuce and potatoes. The way they express their pleasure at seeing him alive after years of thinking he'd died eight years earlier even lets Brat form a partisan picture of Patrick, the young man he's pretending to be.

Including Brat himself, there are seven major characters in *Brat Farrar*: Bee Ashby, who stepped in to run her brother's stud farm and act as guardian of his five children after he and his wife were killed in a plane crash; Simon, twin brother to Patrick; Eleanor, their younger sister; and the still-younger twins, Jane and Ruth, who are as different from each other as Simon and Patrick had been. At least a half-dozen secondary characters float in and out of the story, and another four or five appear in only one or two key scenes. Yet even the minor characters are given enough traits and lines to make them memorable.

There are also several horses, three of which play roles designed for their specific personalities. Fourposter is ten-year-old Jane's old pony, "more of a conveyance than a ride." Jane doesn't want to meet this newly returned brother, but "it was never possible to back away from anything that Fourposter might happen to be interested in; he had no mouth and an insatiable curiosity. So forward came the reluctant Jane on a highly interested pony." The scene is made amusingly vivid by this depiction of a nosy horse who, by staying in character, literally carries poor Jane into the homecoming.

Timber is Simon's purebred gelding, a magnificent animal but a conceited rogue, which only strengthens his similarity to his master and prepares us for Simon's roguery.

Chevron is well bred, sweet tempered, and dependable, a symbolic reflection of the Ashby family at its best: "She loved jumping and was taking her fences with an off-handed confidence. One could almost hear her humming."

As I let myself sink into the book, I realized that Tey had even made me anxious to meet Great-Uncle Charles, who has retired from foreign service in the Far East and who is slowly wending his way home by ship. He is a very minor character. His only function in the book is to delay Simon's coming-of-age party until "Patrick" can be proven the true heir or an imposter and later to offer a solution for Brat's real identity. Although he doesn't actually appear "in the flesh" until the very end, we catch glimpses of his nature through the eyes of the children as they remember the exotic gifts he sent them every birthday and Christmas, and we see him through Bee's loving memories: "Charles loathed horses . . . and if ever against his better judgment he was lured within smell of a stable, he made friends with the stable cat and retired with it to some quiet corner until the process of horse exhibition was finished. He was rather like a cat himself; a large soft man with a soft round face . . . [who] padded as lightly on his large feet as though he were partly filled with air."

One could do worse than to take this short book (approximately two hundred pages) and dissect each sentence as a text for building memorable characters.

For the first twelve years of my professional writing life, I wrote short stories. In those years, plot took first precedence for me. I would try to put myself in Agatha Christie's mind and think of a clever twist. After I'd worked out the mechanics for executing it logically, I would then create characters to do the work. Their sole purpose was to jump through the hoops I'd placed in their paths. Nevertheless, having created them, the least I could do was try to imbue them with life and breath by applying the techniques I was learning from Josephine Tey and Dorothy L. Sayers.

This worked quite well until I came to write my first full-length novel. That's when I discovered that while plot may be the engine that runs a short story, characterization is the fuel that carries a novel across that wide expanse of manuscript pages.

It is not enough, for example, to say that Mary is a beautiful girl with a kind heart. (Your reader thinks, "Oh, yeah?")

Nor is it enough to describe in excruciating detail her shining hair, olive skin, flashing brown eyes, and lush figure. (Your reader yawns.)

Furthermore, it definitely isn't enough to have her complacently acknowledge those features in a mirror or to have another character say, "Gosh, for a beautiful girl, Mary, you're so sweet!" (Your reader groans.)

But . . .

If you establish that Mary's mother had been a noted beauty and if you let us see the mother glance at Mary with proprietary pride while a third person sees the glance and thinks (snidely or charitably) how lucky Mary was to have inherited her mother's looks instead of her father's . . .

If you have young men stand a little straighter and older men suck in their stomachs as she holds the elevator door for that mother pushing a stroller across the lobby . . .

If she's hot and sweaty after mowing a sick neighbor's yard and a desirable guy still says, "I've been wanting to buy you a drink ever since I first saw you," as he hands her a bottle of cold water . . .

Then Mary's inner and outer beauty are both on their way to being firmly established in your reader's mind.

It's the old "show, don't tell," and this can work in a variety of narrative voices, too. Omniscient third person, for instance:

> Nobody liked Detective Jones. He hadn't been likable as a child and he wasn't likable now. No one at the station willingly partnered with him. Merely driving out to a crime scene was enough to make a colleague want to stick his head out the window. Jones sucked all the air and light out of a car.

Close third-person viewpoint:

> Chuck's heart sank when he saw that he was partnered with Jones. The guy was gloom and doom with a sour take on everything. Just the thought of getting into a car with him made Chuck's chest tighten. He found himself breathing deeply as if his body already sensed the need for extra oxygen, as if the car were a diving bell with only enough air for one.

First-person viewpoint:

> I gave a mental groan as I heard the lieutenant partner me with that asshole Jones. My chest tightened, and I knew I'd be gasping for breath by the time we got to the crime scene. Riding with Jones was like riding beside a black hole. No light or air for anyone else.

(In the above examples, you probably noticed that the last two told almost as much about Chuck as about Jones, a way of letting descriptions do double duty.)

While it's relatively easy to differentiate between characters when there are only two or three, how does one keep six to ten of them distinctive in the reader's mind without running through a repetitive description every time a character reappears after an absence of several pages?

Small mannerisms can give major help. If you establish that Tom is a pacer when things get tense while Jack becomes irritable and Susan just wants to feed people, those mannerisms will keep the reader reminded who they are. Does someone absentmindedly twist a lock of hair when pensive? Nibble at a hangnail incessantly? Automatically switch on the radio as soon as she turns the ignition key or walks into a room so that all the action takes place against a backdrop of news and weather?

Speech patterns also help. One character might speak only in the present tense; another ends all her declarative sentences in an upward lilt that suggests question marks. Still another throws in an "Okay?" after every other sentence or overuses phrases, such as ". . . like he goes, '*Duh!*' and like I'm even caring, y'know?"

In one of my books, I kept a character from using a single contraction. As omniscient narrator, I never said she didn't use contractions, nor did I let any of the other characters comment on it; but this small grammatical oddity reinforces the reader's subliminal awareness of her careful, deliberate nature and her habit of thinking before she spoke.

Upon beginning a new book, some writers will draw up a cast of characters and write a thumbnail sketch of each one. They'll list the obvious first: age, sex, physical appearance, profession or occupation, then move on to class, education, birthplace, birth order, hobbies, sports, favorite food and drink, preferred mode of transportation, and so on. The author may even decide which political party a character votes for and whether this one likes classical opera better than classic country, or if that one favors the missionary position over others more exotic. This works very well if you are having trouble keeping the characters straight yourself.

Other novelists will take several random objects, such as a lawn chair, a pair of Nike sneakers, a chocolate bar, the Statue of Liberty, and a pink plastic flamingo, and then jot down each character's thoughts and feelings about those items, making sure that no two perceptions of the same object are the same. Deciding why

Sally thinks the flamingo amusing kitsch while Janice just doesn't get it should give you a good grasp of their basic natures.

Still other writers will give no thought to a character's stand on issues or items until actually confronted with the need to know in the third chapter, at which point the authors will go inside their character's head and simply ask.

An eye-opening exercise is to take two of your characters, imagine them in your mother-in-law's living room, and "ask" them to describe it. The wealthy art collector will be kind but patronizing about the prints your mother-in-law chose to match the couch, while the day laborer might decline to take a seat on that couch, afraid his dirty clothes might stain it. Both are looking at the exact same room, but their views are colored by their past experiences.

In the end, there is no right or wrong way to bring a character to life. Whatever works best for you is the method you should use, but there are two universal points worth keeping in mind:

1. In your desire to have your readers love your heroine and hate her enemies, remember that the wholly angelic is almost as rare as the wholly evil. If you want to keep your characters believable, think of Superman and sprinkle a little Kryptonite over them all. Good characters should have a few flaws, bad characters should have a few virtues, and all should be vulnerable in at least one area, just to keep them human.

2. Characters are not checkers to be pushed around the board that is your plot. If a character isn't alive to you, he will never live for your readers. (And even your corpses need life!)

chapter ten

Writing a Series Character

■ *Sara Paretsky*

Amy [graciously] criticised the artistic parts of the story, and offered hints for a sequel, which unfortunately couldn't be carried out, as the hero and the heroine were dead.

—*Little Women*

The death of the hero need not spell the demise of a series character, as Conan Doyle found to his dismay. In general, though, a story that brings decisive closure to the protagonist's life precludes a series about that character. Closure need not entail the death Jo March meted out for her heroes. Instead it means the decisive resolution of conflicts plaguing the protagonist in such a way that a sequel can destroy or intrude on the reader's relief in the resolution. In a story suited for a series, the resolution of plot conflicts becomes more important than that of character conflicts, however credible and intriguing the central character may be.

Peter Dickinson, one of the greatest of contemporary crime writers, has done both series and nonseries work. His Inspector Pibble books all deal to some extent with the problems of a man who is an outsider, by temperament and upbringing, both to the police force and to the world of financiers or landowners whose crimes he is supposed to solve. His intelligence and perceptions are such that he can figure out who committed the crimes without much difficulty. But to impose a solution on a society that regards him as alien remains a major hurdle for him.

Over the course of the series, Pibble nags at this problem from different angles. It is only in the final—or at least most recent—book, *One Foot in the Grave*, that he is truly triumphant. And to triumph he has to become extremely disconnected from normal life: Dickinson gives us an indigent, elderly, infirm Pibble stuck in a dreadful nursing home. He is not there undercover—he is there as one of society's discards. But he finally masters both his physical incapacity and his anomie. With *One Foot in the Grave* Dickinson has resolved the central problem of his character, and the series feels complete.

In contrast is Dickinson's *King and Joker*, one of the most brilliant crime novels of the last decade. The book tells the story of the coming-of-age of a royal princess in Buckingham Palace. The two main characters are a thirteen-year-old girl and her ninety-plus nurse, disabled by a stroke and dying. Dickinson's poignant, empathic presentation of these women—one just starting her life, the other ending it—is awe inspiring. The lesser characters are drawn just as credibly, and with equal care. At the end of the book, the major interest of the reader is not the solution to the crimes plaguing the palace. It is Princess Louise's acceptance of her heritage, and the final tying of the knot in Nurse Durdon's life that enables her to die at peace.

These characters are so vivid, so beguiling that Dickinson could not resist the temptation to bring them back in a sequel, *Skeleton-in-Waiting*. And in this book Princess Louise becomes flatter, less interesting. Her important problems were resolved in *King and Joker*. No one, even such a master as Dickinson, can write effectively about people whose major life issues have already found some kind of resolution.

If you have an idea for a story, or a character, or a group of characters, and you wonder whether you should be planning a series or a stand-alone book, you should think the matter through along the lines of the Dickinson stories. The first question you have to ask is what kind of story you want to tell. In particular, you need to think about what kind of problem you want to solve.

The last thing that should influence you is what you think publishers want, or what you think may sell. Writing to a hypothetical, unknowable marketplace instead of from your interests is the best way to produce flat, uninteresting work. A decade ago many publishers thought the private eye story was dead and didn't want to see such manuscripts. But people in love with the form continued to write in it. And because they wrote what interested them they created stories that have found a receptive readership.

Some publishers are now saying that the tough, independent woman investigator is passé, and that future books will hark back to softer women such as Mrs. North, working in tandem—perhaps even in subordination—to clever, strong men. Even if I believed such prophecy, for me to abandon my tough, independent investigator for that mythical market would mean I was writing something I didn't believe in. And if I can't believe in it it's a cinch no reader will.

Almost any form of the crime novel is suitable for a series: Amanda Cross and Emma Latham have created long-running, successful books with professional people turned amateur sleuth; George Smiley makes his weary way through Le Carré's spy stories; and police officers and private eyes almost demand a series. It's not the type of book you want to write that determines whether or not you have a character suited for many stories, but how you see the story itself.

All my own books so far have been first-person private eye novels with the same protagonist, V.I. Warshawski. Although I see her as a fully realized character, I also see her in relationship to a variety of stories. At this point I'm interested in such social questions as how large institutions affect the lives of ordinary people, and how the criminal justice system treats large-scale white-collar crime. These are issues for which I don't have a personal answer, and so I keep exploring them. They seem to be best addressed through the voice of my series character, rather than in stand-alone thrillers.

My detective has certain conflicts in her life for which I also don't have answers. These lie primarily in a tension between her need to be alone and her need for intimacy. The story that resolved that conflict for my hero would probably be the last in the series, just as *One Foot in the Grave* becomes the final Pibble story by resolving Pibble's personal issues.

In addition, solving my detective's personal emotional problems would mean telling a much different kind of story than the ones I've written so far. In series books, the emphasis is on solving the crime: finishing the plot. If the focus became the detective's conflicts, with the plot problems secondary, then I'd be better off with a stand-alone book such as *King and Joker*.

If you think your story idea, or your character idea, will work best with a series character, you should consider some of the special advantages and pitfalls of using a recurring hero.

The major problem with a series character is the need for continuity, but a continuity with enough change that the reader sees you are not going through rote motions in succeeding books. You have to show your hero—perhaps fat, a gourmet, an orchid fancier—in such a way that the reader who has read all your books learns something new, while the reader who's seeing your hero for the first time can understand him pretty completely.

This is a relatively small technical problem, and can be fixed by extending the hero's skills, as Sayers does with Lord Peter Wimsey, or presenting him from the viewpoint of a different character.

In *Strong Poison* we learn about Wimsey's virtuosity with music through the eyes of Miss Murgatroyd, for whom he plays a Bach sonata "with a curious impression of controlled power, which, in a man so slight and so fantastical in manner, was unexpected and even a little disquieting." In *Murder Must Advertise* she makes his grace and athletic prowess apparent in the scene where he dives from the top of a fountain into a shallow pool, and again when she presents his skill as a cricketer. These are all ways in which a highly skilled writer shows, rather than describes, her hero.

When you are writing your first book, and the first of many books about your hero, you want to avoid annoying characteristics that may come back to grate on you in future books. Harriet Vane, the crime-writer heroine of the Sayers series, wishes that she hadn't made her own detective, Robert Templeton, a man with a taste in violent checks and plaids.

People with whom the hero associates regularly—family, colleagues, police friends, or adversaries—have to be portrayed consistently from book to book. Arthur Maling has been heard to moan over his Potter series because in the first book he gave the man partners and gave all the partners families. These characters have to be moved consistently from book to book. It's considered cheating to kill them off.

You should keep some kind of file on the salient traits and facts of your recurring characters. One of my own people is a doctor with a storefront clinic. Because I thought I remembered important data I didn't find out until after my fourth book was published that I'd moved her clinic by more than a mile. It's too late to fix that blunder now.

One of the most serious issues to decide is how to let your character change. Will she or he age? At the rate of a year per decade, or not at all, or with the passage of time as it affects you, the writer? Christie let Poirot and Miss Marple age very slowly, but she felt she had made a mistake in starting two series with heroes whose ages were already well advanced.

Sayers supposedly thought that Wimsey was too much a buffoon in her earliest books and tried to invest him with seriousness and a love life in the later ones. Some readers find the last few books heavy and clumsy compared to the early ones. Sayers changed her hero but not necessarily for the better. Whether it was a good alteration or not, she worked it out quite carefully. In the passage cited earlier from *Strong Poison* we get one of several cues the book provides on the deeper aspects of Wimsey's personality—of the controlled power his mask of buffoonery hides. *Strong Poison* provides all the clues to the change in Wimsey's affect that becomes fully realized in *Gaudy Night*.

Other detectives change without so much conscious direction from their creators. Chandler once said he thought he was writing parodies of himself in his last work. Marlowe changes—he goes from scoffing at those who know Proust to spouting Shakespeare as he takes on a denser, more literary character—but he doesn't age.

Other series characters, like Nero Wolfe, remain relatively static. Wolfe and Archie don't age. There is an illusion of perpetual youth about Archie, but he does in fact lose his brashness in the later books. He develops a palate and becomes finicky about his eating. His speech becomes less idiosyncratic and more like Wolfe's.

These are changes of which Stout may have been unaware.

As you yourself change, the way you see your characters probably alters as well. You cannot force yourself into an unnatural stasis; nor can you expect to be able to do that with your character. It is of course better to direct alterations in your character consciously, as Sayers did. Unfortunately, as I have learned to my sorrow, that is much easier said than done.

A series character offers several advantages to the writer. The problem of change has as its obverse the pleasure in developing a set of people in detail, showing the progression of their lives, not abandoning them at one climax when we all know most lives have many pivot points.

The other advantage a series character offers is something I mentioned earlier in a different context: the opportunity to explore a set of issues from the same perspective.

In my own work, I didn't set out to create a series character. I was trying to prove to myself that I could write a novel. I wanted to write a crime novel with a woman protagonist. And because I live in the ultimate hard-boiled city, Chicago, it was impossible to think of my protagonist except as a hard-boiled detective.

As time has passed, though, the kinds of crimes that interest me, and the perspective that interests me, make the voice of my PI hero the most effective one to use. I find that she gives me the opportunity to look in depth, and over time, at issues of law, society, and justice. I wouldn't be able to explore these as effectively in a stand-alone thriller. This does not mean a different writer couldn't do so, just that I can't do so.

For example, Dorothy Salisbury Davis's amazing novel *A Town of Masks* is a profound exploration of society and justice. She shows, with heart-wrenching poignancy, how the difference in our self-perception and the way our neighbors view us can lead to tragedy. The characters in *A Town of Masks* speak with finality: There is no place for their lives to go at the conclusion of the novel.

Every crime novel can be written in a number of different ways. Every story I tell could be told as a police procedural, even as a spy novel, if you accepted corporate espionage as a form of spying.

And most of them could be written as stand-alone thrillers. I choose to tell them as PI novels because I like that particular voice. It comes naturally to me. And I have a continuing curiosity about my character's life and those of some of her recurring friends and associates.

THE AMATEUR
SLEUTH

Nancy Pickard

Advantages and Disadvantages

In its simplest definition, an amateur in any field is someone who does not get paid for what she does.

She may be a "wannabe," that is, an amateur who is working for nothing, but only until the day that she begins to earn some money. Unpublished writers are that kind of amateur—which only goes to show that you can be very, very good at what you do, but if you don't earn a living at it, the world will still insist on calling you an amateur. In that sense, Vincent van Gogh—who never received a sou for his paintings—was an amateur.

Or, she may be an amateur in the sense of being a true volunteer—that is, she's doing the work for nothing, and she's doing it either because she loves it or because it furthers her ambitions or answers her needs that have little or nothing to do with money. That kind of amateur will never be a pro, because no matter how *pro*ficient she becomes, she'll never request or receive payment for her work.

The amateur sleuth belongs to that second category of amateur.

With that designation come all of the pitfalls of being a volunteer, whether it's a volunteer candy striper at a hospital or a volunteer crime solver. Those disadvantages are: First, you don't get paid. To borrow from the comedian, you don't get no respect. You get stuck with the dirty work nobody else wants to do. You feel a lot smarter than everybody seems to think you are. Not only do you not get paid, but you also don't get much gratitude, except maybe once a year at an "Appreciation Awards Banquet." The place wouldn't easily run without you, but nobody acknowledges that. If management would hire enough pros, pay them well enough, and if those pros did their jobs well enough, they wouldn't need you. You have to do it in your spare time. You have to buy your own silly uniforms. And, people are always patting you on your head (or worse) and telling you how cute you are, and why don't you run along now while the real professionals take over?

On the other hand, as a volunteer, you get a few perks that the real pros don't, to wit: You don't have to do it. You don't have to do it by the rules. You don't have to take it. You can talk back. You can quit. You can be late, or fail to show up, and they don't dare reprimand you, because they know they need you a lot more than you need them. And all that stands between you and retirement is your own conscience, which, however, volunteers seem to possess out of proportion to the rest of the populace.

If you decide to create an amateur sleuth to solve your fictional mysteries, those are some of the advantages and disadvantages that she'll face as she goes about solving the murders to which the professionals haven't a clue.

But what about you, the writer?

What advantages/disadvantages will *you* face in the creation of that sleuth?

The most important apparent *disadvantage* you'll face has to do with that familiar fictional term, suspension of disbelief. Which is to say, why is this amateur sleuth attempting to solve this murder? Why not let the cops do it? Why does this amateur sleuth keep tripping over dead bodies? And why doesn't she mind her own business? A private eye or a cop never has to face those questions, because solving the murder is literally their business.

For those of us who are lucky enough to write about amateur

sleuths, it turns out, however, that suspension of disbelief is not actually much of a problem. Fans of amateur sleuth novels are *eager* to suspend their disbelief. They *want* to temporarily suspend their belief in the need for real police officers to investigate real crimes. They *want* to believe for a little while that a fairly ordinary, smart person (like themselves?), using common sense, sensitivity, good humor, and fair play, can bring a villain to justice. For the time that it takes for them to read your book, they *want* to believe in the, perhaps, more idealistic, innocent, and fair world that you have created; they *want* to suspend their belief in a real-life justice system that does not always work; and they *want* to suspend their belief in their real-life experience of witnessing unsatisfying endings to unsatisfying lives.

Your fans don't really want cops on the scene. If they wanted cops, they'd read a police procedural; if they wanted private investigators, they'd read novels starring those professionals. Your readers *like* amateur sleuths, so you don't have to fret very much about justifying the existence of yours.

Still, even though your readers love to watch an amateur solve the murder, and even though they may not want cops on the scene, in an amateur sleuth novel you will still need to make it appear at least marginally believable that the cops aren't any more than peripherally involved. There are many time-honored stratagems for getting around that obstacle. Sometimes the amateur takes over after the professionals give up on a case. Or maybe the amateur steps in because he or she has an intense personal interest in the case. Or it could be that the amateur is acting on the request of a friend or family member. Or maybe the amateur thinks the cops have botched the case—accidentally or purposely—and so she attempts to solve it herself. The amateur sleuth might even be romantically involved with a cop, and that brings him or her onto the scene. Or it might even be for the simple reason that the amateur sleuth happens onto the scene of the crime and follows the path of his or her natural curiosity about it.

I've used those stratagems—and combinations of them—in my Jenny Cain series. In *Generous Death*, Jenny gets involved in the case because her own life and livelihood, as well as the lives of some of her friends, are threatened. She has several excuses for getting involved in *Say No to Murder*: She is on the scene; she's romantically involved with the detective; and her own father is a suspect. *No Body* brings her onto the case at the specific request of her beloved former sixth-grade teacher Miss Lucille Grant. In *Marriage Is Murder*, she gets involved because she is so worried about the effect that the case is having on the detective she wants to marry. *Dead Crazy* sees her involved for three reasons: A "client" requests it; she happens onto the scenes of the murders; and she feels personally driven to solve the crime because of family reasons. In *Bum Steer*, Jenny is a suspect herself, always a compelling reason to find the real culprit!

A *second* apparent *disadvantage* that you'll encounter in writing an amateur sleuth novel is that most amateurs don't use weapons. Indeed, most of them aren't even trained in self-defense. By and large, they don't jog five miles a day, wear a black belt, or work out down at Gold's Gym three times a week. (Can you imagine Miss Marple lifting weights?) That means your sleuth will have to rely on her wits, and sometimes on whatever makeshift weapons she happens to have on hand, like knitting needles. Jenny Cain gets herself backed into a corner in her first adventure, *Generous Death*, and, in desperation, defends herself by attempting to strangle the villain with her (Jenny's) bra! In *No Body*, she uses her panty hose to tie up a murderer. Cops and private eyes rarely have to resort to such desperate maneuvers. Guns are quicker than underwear. And remember: If you do teach your amateur sleuth karate, or train her at the firing range, you'll be edging her into the realm of the pros and away from the pleasure that readers take in watching an ordinary person make the best of an extraordinary situation.

A *third* apparent *disadvantage* to the amateur sleuth is that she needs some way to support herself that won't interfere with the plot. That's difficult to do if you give her a nine-to-five job. It accounts for why so many amateur sleuths are independently wealthy, like Lord Peter Wimsey and Mrs. Eugenia Potter. Lately, amateur sleuths seem to be attempting to live off more modest means: Claire Malloy and Annie Laurance are booksellers; Jane Jeffrey supports her three children on the modest income of her late husband's life insurance and his family's pharmacy. Other famous amateur sleuths are academicians with holidays, sabbaticals, and summers off, like Professors James Owen Mega, Beth Austin, Harry Bishop, Kate Fansler, Peter Shandy, and Gervase Fen, and schoolteacher Amanda Pepper. Or they might be actors, artists, or writers—like Harriet Vane, Tessa Crichton, Jocelyn O'Roarke, and Patience McKenna—who are supposed to have at their disposal great chunks of free time. Or maybe they're medicos or clergy—like Sister Mary Helen, Rabbi David Small, Nurse Hilda Adams, and Brother Cadfael—whose very professions make it natural for them to snoop.

When I created Jenny Cain, I decided to make her the director of a charitable foundation because I knew that foundations derive most of their funds from bequests. I figured that where there is money and death there is the potential for foul play. John Putnam Thatcher, the famous fictional sleuth who is the head of the trust department of a bank, enjoys many of the same detecting opportunities. Their jobs are basically nine to five and they do get paid, but that only makes them professional businesspeople, not professional crime stoppers.

The jobs of investigative reporter and lawyer would appear to be ideal for an amateur sleuth. But they're not really amateurs, since their actual job is to investigate the crime for their editor or client, respectively. Lawyer sleuths are admitted to the bar of The Private Eye Writers of America, so I guess we can't count them into the ranks of amateurs. Rebecca Schwartz, Willa Jansson, and Howard Rickover are examples of fictional lawyers who have as much of the intimate, between-you-and-me charm of the amateur as they do the cool calculation of the pro. The same could be said of the fictional investigative reporter Samantha Adams. But since those sleuths all get paid for investigating their cases, I guess we have to reluctantly draw the line at those professions, even though we'd like to include those characters in our club of civilized sleuths.

A fourth apparent *disadvantage* to writing an amateur sleuth novel is that you generally can't use as much bad language, violence, sex, or gore as you could in some other types of mysteries.

And isn't *that* a relief? And isn't your mother grateful?

So it seems that even the apparent disadvantages of writing about an amateur sleuth can be turned into advantages.

There are other advantages to be had, as well:

For example, an amateur sleuth doesn't have to be an expert at anything, except perhaps at understanding people. As that archetype of the amateur sleuth, Miss Jane Marple, is often heard to comment, ". . . living all these years in St. Mary Mead does give one an insight into human nature."

The amateur sleuth also enjoys the advantage of great reader identification. We can all identify—assuming we want to—with an average Jane or Joe who just happens to stumble onto a crime and then just barely manages to solve it solely by dint of courage, wit, and common sense.

In addition, the amateur doesn't have to be as "tough" as a cop or private eye, which has the advantage of opening the way for a more normal sort of character who is allowed to show more emotion than might be acceptable in a professional. Readers often say they feel as if they could sit down and have a cup of coffee with their favorite amateur sleuth. They might not feel quite so comfortable sharing a beer with some of the tough guys and loners who inhabit the darker worlds of private eyes and cops.

Another advantage to writing about an amateur sleuth is that you don't have to know nearly as much about police procedure (or guns!) as do the authors of private eye and police procedural novels. Sometimes you'll be able to avoid the police altogether in your novels; other times, you'll need to insert a modicum about procedure or weaponry, which you will verify by research— which can be as easy as calling a police department and asking.

There is one more apparent *disadvantage* to writing amateur sleuth novels. I've saved it for last because it is the one that you will hear most frequently and most passionately advanced by those few poor, benighted souls who don't care for the genre.

"Amateur sleuths," they object, "aren't real."

To which you may reply, "Pshaw."

Amateur sleuth novels don't purport to be about "real" crime fighters. What they *are* about is real feelings, real motives, and the very real effect of murder upon people and relationships.

Like every other kind of mystery, including police procedurals and private eyes—in fact, like any kind of *fiction*—there is about the amateur sleuth novel a certain air of fantasy that its readers *really* enjoy. Maybe *real* life is not so civilized, maybe *real* murderers do not so frequently get their comeuppance, and maybe *real* justice is not so commonly done, but mystery readers appear to have a *real* need to believe all of that is possible in this world. The amateur sleuth, like her private eye and police counterparts, allows us to believe in that better, more logical, and reasonable world, at least for a little while.

It's a great advantage to you, the writer, to be able to provide that kind of pleasure for your readers.

VIVID VILLAINS

■ *Sandra Scoppettone*

I f the point of your story is "whodunit," the culprit needs to be
worth the finding. Often the nature of the villain, and how
absorbing a character he or she is, will affect the flavor of the whole
rest of the story—as is certainly true of "Buffalo Bill" and "Red
Dragon" in the novels of Thomas Harris (*The Silence of the Lambs*;
Red Dragon), to say nothing of Harris's riveting villain Dr. Han-
nibal Lecter.

Often I start working out a story in terms of its villain. Sometimes
he's more interesting than anyone else. I'm curious about what
makes a murderer who he is. Was he born missing some human
quality? Did his early environment shape him? Or was it a combination of both?

For a long time I was intrigued by "the nice quiet boy" who kills
his whole family. When I decided to do a book about one of these
kids, I first researched the subject. Had I made him a monster created by his family, there would have been no one to like, no one
to root for. So I decided to give him a brain tumor. That turned
into *Such Nice People*.

The villain in *Innocent Bystanders* was invented, but there had been a true crime case I knew of in which a patient murdered her psychiatrist's wife. Why? Was she in love with her doctor? Did she have delusions? What was her family like? Out of this came Hedy Sommerville and her family.

If you're going to go into the mind of a murderer, you should know something about his kind of pathology. All murderers are not alike. There are those who commit the so-called crime of passion, the professionals (hit men, gangsters), and the sociopaths or psychopaths.

The reason I say *so-called* crime of passion is because I believe that this kind of killer is a narcissist. It is often a man who cannot bear rejection by his lover/wife, and rather than let her go on to a new man, a new life, he kills her. I don't believe that this has anything to do with love. Nevertheless, you can make this villain interesting.

To me, the least engrossing killer is the professional, who may be a sociopath, but does it for money.

What's the difference between a sociopath and a psychopath? Simply put, according to *The Random House Dictionary*, the sociopath is hostile to society; the psychopath is mentally ill. The psychopath usually kills victims known to him or, in his mind, is provoked to kill. The sociopath murders indiscriminately and often without any specific reason.

Charles Willeford creates this kind of killer in *Miami Blues*. He's Freddy "Junior" Frenger, and he's so fascinating that he almost takes the book away from Hoke Moseley, Willeford's series character.

The sociopath walks among us almost always undetected. In *Donato and Daughter* I created the character of Russ Lawrence. He's an upper-middle-class married man with two children. He's learned how to behave like the rest of the world, and his family has no idea who he really is. I thought he was interesting in a horrifying way: Writing about him was like watching an accident. Yet one editor said he was boring and wanted me to lose his point of view. I refused, lost the contract instead, but went on to sell the book elsewhere. And then readers wrote and told me how mesmerizing and chilling they found him. Sometimes we know better than editors.

The practical question here is how are we going to know how to write about the villains? Surely they aren't among our good friends or even acquaintances. So if you wish to understand their thinking, what do you do?

I read. I've read a number of books about the psychopath/sociopath. *The Murdering Mind* by David Abrahamsen, M.D., is an excellent book, giving insights into the perspective of these people. Others are *The Murderers* by Emanuel Tanay, M.D., with Lucy Freeman, and *Murderers Sane and Mad* by Miriam Allen Ford. There are many others that are valuable and that can be found at your library. One of the best is Tim O'Brian's *Buried Dreams: Inside the Mind of a Serial Killer*, which is written from the point of view of John Wayne Gacy, the serial killer from Illinois. O'Brian really gets into the mind of this murderer, and the book helped me to understand the thinking process of a sociopath. Although Gacy wasn't an upper-middle-class member of society, he certainly was respected in his area and apparently fooled those who crossed his path, including Nancy Reagan.

Ted Bundy was a flawless example of the charming, good-looking sociopath who duped everyone. Almost any of the books about him are worth reading.

Another book that I used to research one of my villains is *Fatal Vision*, Joe McGinniss's account of Jeffrey MacDonald, who was convicted of killing his wife and two children. Again, MacDonald was the perfect portrait of a normal man: doctor, Green Beret, devoted husband, father. MacDonald denies his guilt. So what's new?

To my knowledge I've never had the opportunity to talk with a psychopath/sociopath, but I suppose one could arrange this through a prison warden if so desired. From my reading I've learned that these killers are more than willing to talk about themselves, mostly to tell you that nothing is really their fault. In *Fatal Addiction*, an absorbing tape of Bundy's last interview before being put to death, he blames his actions on pornography. Right to the very end he eschews responsibility, as they all do.

I would love the opportunity to talk with one of these killers (in a safe situation, of course), but I suspect that I wouldn't discover much more than I have through reading about them.

Naturally, all villains do not fall in the above category. In most books, if the author isn't writing about a psychopath/sociopath, the villain's motive has to do with money or property. The jewel or art thief, the forger, the blackmailer, the bank robber are all such types. As well as the killer who knocks off his or her spouse/relative for an inheritance or insurance money.

In these novels, I believe, the plots are usually more interesting than the characters. Exceptions to this can be found in the books of Patricia Highsmith and Margaret Millar to name only two. Donald Westlake also creates engaging thieves.

One of the most well-known writers in the field, James Cain, created several books where the killers were seemingly ordinary people who, had they not met each other, (a *folie à deux*), might never have committed their crimes. At least the men might not have. In *The Postman Always Rings Twice* and *Double Indemnity* the main villain is the woman who seduces the poor besotted male into killing her husband, respectively, for love and financial gain.

In creating a villain of any type, motivation is essential. Even a sociopath can have a delusional motivation. In *Donato and Daughter* Russ Lawrence believes the murders he commits are totally justified. In *A Creative Kind of Killer* the motive is greed, and in *Razzamatazz* it's revenge. In the crime of passion, killing because he loves her so much (and it usually is a man) is, as I said earlier, a narcissistic motivation. Nevertheless, it is a reason, no matter how misguided and distorted.

So understanding your villain is essential. Although I never outline a book, I do write biographies of my main characters. Even if I'm never going to go into the mind of my killer, before I begin writing the novel I know everything about him, from where he was born, to how he did in grade school, his hobbies, what he eats for breakfast, what newspapers he reads, and even what deodorant he uses. Doing this, I also come to know his parents and siblings and his relationship to them. Writing this kind of biography can sometimes give you your motivation if you don't have one to start with.

I wouldn't be playing fair if I didn't say that sometimes my villains are based on real people, real cases. Newspapers and magazines are great sources for finding fascinating killers. I've spent hours in libraries looking at microfilm of old newspapers, searching for just the right killer. When I find him I make adaptations. Occasionally, I will even base his physical description on a friend. Once I was caught doing this, and my friend wasn't too pleased!

To sum up, villains can be based on anyone. We must make our villains believable and not too sympathetic.

One caveat: Whatever you do, don't make them more interesting than your protagonist. If you do, it will make your novel lopsided and might even sink it.

In Search of
a Novel

■ *George C. Chesbro*

Writing a novel is a long-distance run of the imagination and will, an arduous exercise, a quest, requiring stamina, discipline, confidence, patience, courage, technique, and perhaps not a small amount of cunning in order to compete with that most problematic opponent of all, oneself. Writers need all the help they can get, wherever they can get it, especially when it comes to the critical preliminary phases of a novel when one is plotting the story line and planning the structure. It is folly to believe in, or profess, a single prescription for success in any phase of the essentially dark art that is the writing of fiction. Consequently, what follows is not a prescription, but a description of how this particular writer goes about the complex business of plotting and structuring; perhaps others will find the same approaches useful.

Plot is arguably the most essential ingredient in a mystery novel, which is the focus of our discussion here; a story must be told. Every story has a beginning, and the beginning of a mystery novel is an idea. Therefore, the mystery novelist begins her or his quest by coming up with a single notion that can be squeezed, patted, poked, and fondled by the mind (a process I call noodling) to see if it might possibly yield up that spectral entity we call a plot—the conceptualization of a series of dramatic events that is the nourishment that must sustain the straining muscles of the imagination for weeks, months, sometimes years.

Writing is dreaming; anyone can dream, but not every dreamer can cause a dream to materialize by way of words on the printed page, strings of letters that may eventually entertain, enthrall, or even terrorize countless readers. A plot is simply a writer's dream that has been noodled, conjured up, from an idea. But where do these rich ideas that can cause altered states of consciousness in both writer and reader come from?

I have a boxful of them.

With very few exceptions, the plots for my short stories and novels have started out from a single item cut from some newspaper or magazine, or a scribbled note made while reading a book or watching some television documentary.

Somewhat of a news junkie, I read two newspapers daily, subscribe to a host of magazines and newsletters, and watch a great deal of television on PBS. Hardly a day goes by that I don't read or see something that pokes my curiosity and makes me think there just might be something there that could be noodled up into a novel. Over the years I've discovered that an initial idea can be more or less than it first appears; only time and wide-awake dreaming will tell. Since, as is often the case, I'm already at work on a novel when I come across such an item, I file it away for future reference.

Now, my filing system for notions is amazingly simple—a large cardboard box in my closet. This is my "boxful of ideas" into which I drop each day's collection of news clippings and notes, and it has been of inestimable value over the years in supplying material to stoke my imagination.

When I have finished a novel, recuperated, and am ready to begin another, I drag my boxful of ideas out of the closet, dump its contents on my office floor, and begin rummaging through this small mountain of paper. The only thing all of these pieces of paper have in common is the fact that at one time or another the information printed there caught my interest. Now it is time to noodle those notions, to see if any one or a combination of several will yield a plot that will sustain me on the new quest I am beginning, the new novel I wish to write.

This dreaming, these flights of the imagination off the launchpad of a single idea, can, of course, be great fun. But an idea is not a novel, and at this point it should be stressed that creating a *plot* from an idea can be, and usually is, extremely stressful, difficult work. Authors who tell you about the book that "wrote itself" usually fail to mention the many hours, perhaps weeks, or even months, they spent *thinking about* the plot and planning the structure of the book that "wrote itself." While in the beginning noodling from a single notion may be entirely free, this thought process must eventually become more and more focused; the purpose of our flights of fancy is to finally catch *one* flight that will take us where we want to go: the land of the published author.

To help me focus my dreaming, I always keep "production notes," organized memos to myself concerning possible twists and turns a particular plot might take, names, titles (personally, I always find it useful to have a working title for my book in progress, since it gives me the feeling at a very early stage that I've at least accomplished *something*, but this is a personal quirk), casts of characters, locales, whatever.

In any case, write down everything that occurs to you, *as* it occurs to you; do *not* trust memory.

Eventually, if I am lucky, this increasingly focused *thought* process will lead to the *writing* process, the first step for me being a plot *outline*, a step-by-step description of how my story will unfold. I try to make this outline as detailed as possible, for I have learned that, for me, at least, the more effort I put into these preparatory phases, the fewer problems I will have in actually writing the book.

However, I have also learned that there is only so much planning I can do before I actually begin to write the book (by which I mean the first *draft* of the book; one should always bear in mind that rarely is anything of value merely written, it is *re*written, increasingly refined and polished through subsequent drafts). After all, we are talking about a *creative* act, which implies a certain amount of spontaneity, which by definition cannot be completely thought out in advance. I will begin my first draft when my plot outline has become a kind of map, however rough, that will at least get me from one end of the land of my story to the other; I know the terrain at the beginning of my journey, the landscape at the end, and have some idea of the mountains I must cross, the rivers I must ford, in between.

Having done this, I am now in a position to receive one of the greatest thrills a fiction writer can experience: *discovery*. In the process of discovery, the writer begins the actual writing of a novel only to discover that all is not exactly as she or he had planned; the actual landscape of the novel is incredibly richer, more complex, than could have been imagined from the mere map, the plot outline, that has been made—this despite the many hours that have gone into drawing up that map! New characters appear, or characters you thought you understood suddenly acquire new personality traits. A path you thought would be easy turns out to be particularly treacherous, or vice versa. Of course, you continue to take production notes all through the writing of this first draft—a note to yourself that something will change at the beginning, plans for a different ending.

A dark art indeed! Let's examine how these processes I have described actually come into play in a specific example.

In the recently published *Second Horseman Out of Eden*, Mongo, my dwarf private investigator, and Garth, his big big brother, battle a very dangerous band of murderous religious fanatics for the body and soul of an abused child who has written a letter to Santa Claus to ask him for help.

I've always been fascinated by the inextinguishable propensity among human beings for superstition, and by fanatics of all flavors, and so I didn't need any further stimulation in that area. But the real genesis for that novel came while I was sorting through the contents of my boxful of ideas and came across a yellowed clipping (it had been stuck to the bottom of the box, perhaps for years). The article described how, each year at Christmastime, the main post office in New York City puts all the thousands of letters addressed to Santa Claus it has received in cardboard boxes and places them on counters in the lobby for the public to browse through. Interested New Yorkers may take up to five letters each, the idea being that these people will express their holiday spirit and goodwill by responding to the requests in the letters, either by buying gifts and distributing them, or providing some service requested by the children who wrote the letters. In effect, these people celebrate Christmas in part by playing Santa Claus.

Fiction writers' dreams are made of such stuff, and novels noodled.

Mongo and Garth are New Yorkers, I said to myself, and, good men that they are, it wouldn't surprise me at all to find out that they are among the thousands of New Yorkers who select letters and play Santa each year at Christmas (I am constantly finding out new things about Mongo and Garth as I write about them, and am frequently surprised and delighted by the things I unearth about their characters in this long-range process of discovery). Now, what if one of the letters they select is from a little girl who is obviously being abused, and who is asking Santa to help bring her release from her pain and misery? . . .

Another news item, this one from *Newsweek*, another idea to weave into the dreaming generated by the first. This clipping concerns a biological super-project, an attempt by an idealistic billionaire philanthropist to build totally self-contained environmental modules that might be used to house colonists on the moon, or even the other planets in the solar system.

What if our religious fanatics, who control the fate of the little girl in distress, are attempting to build such a structure, not to colonize the moon or other planets, but to be a refuge for themselves in the "final days," Armageddon, which they believe are upon us? Indeed, what if they have made plans to nudge Armageddon along by wiping out millions of people? . . .

Noodle, noodle . . .

And what if the child, in her letter, says that she is being held captive in a "secret place"? What if there are traces of soil inside the envelope, dirt that only comes from the Amazon rain forest? . . . And what if? . . .

But you get the idea.

While news articles may provide a rich lode of ideas, they are not, of course, the only source. Overheard conversations, incidents in one's own life, a fleeting thought that seems to have come unbidden . . . Virtually *anything* can provide an idea that, with patience and hard work, may provide the genesis for a plot, the waking dream that becomes a novel.

After one has found a story to *tell*, the next problem that looms is one of structure, or how to actually *write* it. Specifically, who will be telling the story? One person, or several? From whose point of view does the reader view the action? This decision as to what voice to use can be crucial, especially in the mystery novel, since it may largely determine the sequence of action, what information is given to the reader, and what information can be legitimately withheld in order to create an air of mystery and suspense.

Perhaps the easiest way to tell a story is through the "eye in the sky," omniscient speaker, who is never named. This voice is not a character in the novel, but solely a narrator of events. Of course, the advantage to using an "eye in the sky" narrative is that the author may arbitrarily switch locale at any time, probe all of the characters' minds for their deepest secrets and darkest motivations, and provide any and all information at any time so as to keep the reader up-to-date on events.

Alas, the easiest way to tell a tale is not necessarily the best; the best way to tell any story, *particularly* in a mystery novel, is that which will generate the most suspense in the mind of the reader, compelling her or him to keep turning pages to see what will happen next.

For my novel *Bone,* I employed a multiple-point-of-view technique, a structure in which the case is always third person, but the reader experiences events through the eyes, and in the mind, of one character at a time throughout any chapter, which can be of arbitrary length. This is the structure that seemed best suited to what was to be a psychological novel of suspense requiring the reader to know what was going on in the minds of a number of characters.

However, in all of my Mongo novels, I use the "classic" structure of the detective mystery, the first-person narrative. It is Mongo himself who is telling the story, and so the reader experiences events, thoughts and emotions *only* from Mongo's point of view, and discovers things only as he does. While the use of first-person narrative may be a more difficult literary device (if you want the reader to know what is going on in another locale, you must find a way of getting your narrator there, and, of course, it is impossible for the narrator to know *precisely* what is going on in anyone's mind but his or her own), I believe it particularly lends itself to the mystery novel.

The use of a first-person narrative structure requires considerable discipline on the part of the writer; the reader cannot simply be *told* things by the author, but must discover—or deduce—them along with the narrator. However, if the reader can be made to care about the narrator, and if the puzzle the narrator must solve is a good one, the reader will be compelled to follow along through the pages, since first-person narrative encourages close identification of reader and character, and this empathy, this sharing of peril in the reader's mind, is the key ingredient in the generation of suspense.

Yet another factor an author must consider in structuring a novel is the question of what *tense* the narrator will speak in. Most mystery novels are written in the past tense, with the narrator describing events that have supposedly already happened. However, some authors have successfully used the *present* tense, which tends to make the action seem more "immediate." In my two novels involving Veil Kendry, *Veil* and *Jungle of Steel and Stone*, I have employed *both*, using the present tense to indicate that this brain-damaged painter and "street detective" is dreaming.

There are no surefire recipes; indeed, there may be almost as many ways to plot and structure a mystery novel as there are mystery writers. The point is that attention *must be paid* to these two key ingredients if you hope to transport a reader into the world you have created for the few hours or days it will take to read your novel. A thoughtful disciplined approach to both plot and structure can make all the difference between a "good story" you might tell around a campfire and a published book that people will pay to read.

BUILDING WITHOUT
BLUEPRINTS

■ *Tony Hillerman*

In thirty-seven years of writing, I have accumulated two bits of wisdom that may be worth passing along.

First, I no longer waste two months perfecting that first chapter before getting on with the book. No matter how carefully you have the project planned, first chapters tend to demand rewriting. Things happen. New ideas suggest themselves, new possibilities intrude. Slow to catch on, I collected a manila folder full of perfect, polished, exactly right, pear-shaped first chapters before I learned this lesson. Their only flaw is that they don't fit the book I finally wrote. The only book they will ever fit will be one titled *Perfect First Chapters*, which would be hard to sell. Thus Hillerman's First Law: *Never polish the first chapter until the last chapter is written.*

The second law takes longer to explain. When I defend it, I'm like the fellow with his right arm amputated arguing in favor of left-handed bowling. However, here it is: *Some people, sometimes, can write a mystery novel without an outline.* Or, put more honestly: If you lack the patience (or brains) to outline the plot, maybe you can grope your way through it anyway, and sometimes it's for the best.

I was in the third chapter of a book titled *Listening Woman* when this truth dawned. Here's how it happened:

I had tried to outline three previous mystery novels. Failing, and feeling guilt-ridden and inadequate, I finally finished each of them, by trying to outline a chapter or two ahead as I wrote. I had tried for weeks to blueprint this fourth book, sketching my way through about six chapters. At that point, things became impossibly hazy. So I decided to write the section I had blueprinted. Maybe then I could see my way through the rest of it.

I wrote the first chapter exactly as planned, an elaborate look at the villain outsmarting a team of FBI agents on a rainy night in Washington, DC. I still feel that this chapter may the best 5,000 words I've ever written. By the time I had finished it, I had a much better feeling for this key character, and for the plot in which he was involved. Unfortunately, this allowed me to see that I was starting the book too early in the chronology of the story I was telling. So this great first chapter went into a manila folder (to be cannibalized later for flashback material). Then I planned a new opening. This one takes place now on the Navajo Reservation at the hogan of an elderly and ailing Navajo widower named Tso. It is mostly a dialogue between him and a shaman he has summoned to determine the cause of his illness. The chapter was intended to establish time, mood, and the extreme isolation of the area of the Navajo Reservation where the novel takes place. It would give the reader a look at Tso, who will be the murder victim, and intro- duce the shaman, who would be a fairly important character. Fi- nally, the dialogue would provide background information and— in its discussion of Navajo taboos violated by Tso—provide clues meaningless to the FBI, but significant to my Navajo Sherlock Holmes. Again, all went well, but as I wrote it I could sense a flaw.

It was dull. In fact, it was *awfully dull.*

I had planned to have the second chapter take place a month later. In the interim, Tso has been murdered offstage, and the killing is an old unsolved homicide. Why not, I wondered then, have the murder take place during the opening scene? Because then either (a) the shaman would see it, tell the cops, and my novel becomes a short story; or (b) the murderer would zap the shaman, too, messing up my plot. At this stage, a writer who specializes in Navajos and has accumulated a headful of Navajo information searches the memory banks for help. Navajos have a terribly high rate of glaucoma and resulting blindness. Why not a blind old woman shaman? Then how does she get to the isolated Tso hogan? Create a niece, an intern-shaman, who drives the old lady around. The niece gets killed, and now you have a double murder done while the blind woman is away at a quiet place having her trance. You also have an opportunity to close the chapter with a dandy little nondull scene in which the blind woman, calling angrily for her newly deceased niece, taps her way with her cane across the scene of carnage. The outline is bent, but still recognizable.

Early in chapter two, another bend. The revised plan still calls for introducing my protagonist, Navajo Police Lt. Joe Leaphorn, and the villain. Joe stops Gruesome George for speeding, where-upon G.G. tries to run over Joe, roars away, abandons his car, and eludes pursuit. Two paragraphs into this chapter, it became apparent that Joe needed someone in the patrol car with him to convert the draggy internal monologue I was writing into snappy dialogue. So I invent a young sheep thief, handcuff him securely, and stick him in the front seat. He turns out to be wittier than I had expected, which distorts things a bit, but nothing serious goes wrong. Not yet. Leaphorn stops the speeder and is walking toward the speeder's car. As many writers do, I imagine myself into scenes—seeing, hearing, smelling everything I am describing.

What does Leaphorn see? His patrol car emergency light flashing red reflections off the speeder's windshield. Through the windshield, he sees the gold-rimmed glasses I'll use as a label for Gruesome George until we get him identified. What else? My imagination turns whimsical. Why not put in another pair of eyes? Might need another character later. Why not put them in an unorthodox place—peering out of the backseat of the sedan? But why would anyone be sitting in the back? Make it a dog. A huge dog. In a crate. So the dog goes in. I can always take him out.

Still we seem to have only a minor deflection from the unfinished, modified version of the partial outline. But a page or two later, in chapter three, it became obvious that this unplanned, unoutlined dog was going to be critically important. I could see how this ugly animal could give the villain a previous life and the sort of character I was planning to hang on him. More important, I could begin to see how Dog (already evolved into a trained attack dog) could be used to build tension in the story. As I thought about the dog, I began to see how my unblueprinted sheep thief would become the way to solve another plot problem.

Since that third chapter of my fourth mystery novel, I have honestly faced the reality. For me, working up a detailed outline simply isn't a good idea. I should have learned that much earlier.

For example, in my first effort at mystery fiction, *The Blessing Way*, I introduce the Gruesome George character in a trading post on the Reservation. He is buying groceries while my protagonist watches, slightly bored. I, too, am slightly bored. So is the reader. Something needs to be done to generate a bit of interest. I decide to insert a minor mystery. I have the fellow buy a hat, put his expensive silver concha hatband on it, and tell the storekeeper that someone had stolen the original hat. Why would someone steal a hat and leave behind an expensive silver hatband? My protagonist ponders this oddity and can't think of any reason. Neither can I. If I can't think of one later, out will come the hat purchase and in will go some other trick to jar the reader out of his nap. But the hat stayed in. My imagination worked on it in the context of both the Navajo culture and my plot requirements. It occurred to me that such a hat, stained with its wearer's sweat, would serve as the symbolic "scalp" required at a Navajo ceremonial (an Enemy Way) to cure witchcraft victims and to kill witches. When my policeman sees the stolen hat (identified by the missing hatband) in this ritual role, it leads him to the solution of his mystery. (And the author to the completion of his book.)

I have gradually learned that this sort of creative thinking happens for me only when I am at very close quarters with what I am writing—only when I am in the scene, in the mind of the viewpoint character, experiencing the chapter and sharing the thinking of the people in it. From the abstract distance of an outline, with the characters no more than names, nothing seems real to me. At this distance, the details that make a plot come to life always elude me.

Another example: In *Fly on the Wall*, the principal character is a political reporter. He has been lured into the dark and empty state capitol building in the wee hours on the promise that doors will be left unlocked to give him access to confidential tax files. He spots the trap and flees, pursued by two armed men. Before I began writing this section, I had no luck at all coming up with an idea of how I could allow him to escape without straining reader suspension of disbelief. Now, inside these spooky, echoing halls, I think as my frightened character would think, inspired by his terror. No place to hide in the empty hallways. Get out of them. Try a door. Locked, of course. All office doors would be locked. Almost all. How about the janitor's supply room, which the night watchman uses as his office? That door is open. Hide there. (Don't forget to dispose of the watchman.) A moment of safety, but only a moment until the hunters think of this place. Here are the fuse boxes that keep the hall lights burning. Cut off the power. Darken the building. Meanwhile, the readers are wondering, what's happened to the night watchman? Where is he? That breathing you suddenly hear over the pounding of your own heart, not a yard away in the pitch blackness, is the watchman, knocked on the head and tied up. Check his holster. Empty, of course. So what do you do? The hunters know where the fuse boxes are. They are closing in. Feel around in the darkness for a weapon. And what do you feel on the shelves in a janitor's storeroom? All sorts of stuff, including a gallon jug of liquid detergent. You open the door and slip out into the dark hallway, running down the cold marble floor in your sock feet, hearing the shout of your pursuer, dribbling the detergent out of the jug behind you as you sprint down the stairs.

In an outline I would never have thought of the janitor's supply room, nor of the jug of liquid detergent. Yet the detergent makes the hero's escape plausible and is a credible way to eliminate one of the two pursuers as required by the plot. Even better, it is raw material for a deliciously hideous scene—hero running sock-footed down the marble stairway, liquid soap gushing out behind him from the jug. Bad guy in his leather-soled shoes sprinting after him.

Except for describing the resulting noises, the writer can leave it to the reader's imagination.

A big plus for working without an outline, right? The big negative is that I forgot Hero had removed his shoes and had no way to recover them. The editor didn't notice it either, but countless readers did—upbraiding me for having the hero operating in his socks throughout the following chapter.

I have learned, slowly, that outlining a plot in advance is neither possible nor useful for me. I can get a novel written to my satisfaction only by using a much freer form and having faith that—given a few simple ingredients—my imagination will come up with the necessary answers.

Those ingredients—not in any order of importance:

• *A setting with which I am intimately familiar.* Although I have been nosing around the Navajo Reservation and its borderlands for more than thirty years, I still revisit the landscape I am using before I start a new book—and often revisit again while I am writing it. And then I work with a detailed, large-scale map beside my word processor.

• *A general idea of the nature of the mystery* that needs to be solved, and a good idea of the motive for the crime, or crimes.

• *A theme.* For example, *The Dark Wind* exposes my Navajo cop to a crime motivated by revenge—to which Navajos attach no value and find difficult to understand.

• *One or two important characters* in addition to the policeman/ protagonist. However, even these characters tend to be foggy at first. In *Dance Hall of the Dead*, the young anthropology graduate student I had earmarked as the murderer turned out to be too much of a weakling for the job. Another fellow took on the role.

When I finish this, I will return to chapter eight of the present "work in progress." My policeman has just gone to the Farmington jail, where I had intended to have him interview a suspect. Instead he has met the suspect's attorney—a hard-nosed young woman who, as the dialogue progressed, outsmarted my cop at every turn. This woman did not exist in my nebulous plans for this book and has no role. But I have a very strong feeling that she will assume one and that it will be a better book because of her.

That's a good argument against outlines. Without one, I can hardly wait to see how this book will turn out.

OUTLINING

■ *Robert Campbell*

For years, before the advent of the word processor, I never out-lined my novels. Even when I was a screenwriter I resisted writing treatments. In both cases I preferred the method attributed to William Faulkner. When asked how he wrote his books he said something like, "I set my characters on the road and walk beside them, listening to what they have to say."

I've always strived for two sometimes seemingly contradictory qualities in my novels: the inevitability of the conclusion so that the reader, upon reflection, can see the shadow of the end suggested in the beginning; and the illusion that the writer and the reader are discovering the same things about the story and characters at the same time.

I try to include scenes or lines of dialogue or insights into charac-ter and motivation that will resonate throughout the book.

A man, when a child, has the courage to smash the life out of a fatally injured puppy suffering great pain. Years later, when he has the courage to assist a loved one out of the agony of a terminal illness, the reader will remember and understand. You as the writer will have made your case for the character's reasoning and philosophy in one place, saving the need for a too obvious explication in the later scene.

There's a great deal of difference for me in writing a book from an outline, which is, in a sense, the imposition of predestination on the characters and the plot, and embarking on a journey during which the book reveals itself or is discovered rather than being manufactured according to a blueprint.

This roving often leads to dead ends. To extricate myself, I am forced to retrace my steps to some fork in the road and set off on another path altogether.

But even such digressions prove valuable because I always get to learn a lot about my people along the path that didn't lead where I want them to go.

I think I might mention here that nothing is lost to the writer. Even discarded pages are useful, even if they've done nothing else but exercise the writing muscles.

Lately, I've come upon a technique that seems to offer the benefits of an outline and the freedom of the discovered way.

When I begin a novel I usually have a character or characters in mind. Not every one that will finally prove necessary to tell the story, but most of them. Not greatly detailed, for they are people just met who will reveal themselves to me as we get acquainted, but more than rough shapes.

Sometimes the initiating stimulus is a quote, a news article that engages my attention or a scene that for no reason I can usually understand has sprung to mind unbidden.

It used to be that I would simply begin to write, making a note now and then perhaps, pushing forward from front to back, wrestling the beast of form, listening sharply for the voice that would finally be the voice of the book, pausing, from time to time, in those terrible places where the writer wonders why in hell he or she had ever embarked on the project in the first place, the bones of the novel tottering, the language becoming as dry as dust, the whole effort turning into a disaster, yet somehow fighting on to the end of it, restoring order, polishing the words, refining the plot, getting it done as well as I was able.

Now I use the outline provision of my word processor to set up the document. If you haven't got such a facility, just make an outline as you used to do back in school or simply set down a line of numbers to represent the chapters you estimate the book will require.

I also create a number of documents. If your program has the capacity to create documents and stack them on the screen, it will prove invaluable. For those who handwrite or type draft material, these documents might be sections of a loose-leaf binder or separate file folders.

I create a Chronology, Cast of Characters, Address Book, Timeline of History, Notebook, and a document I call Agenda, which sketches the goals, desires, and probable actions of each principal character as I move along through the body of the book.

As a natural consequence of this last document the connections begin to form themselves, suggesting scenes and the flow of narrative.

Sometimes these documents can be placed between page breaks in separate sections at the bottom of the document that contains the novel.

If your program requires more than one document per book, simply move the information bits along from part to part as the book grows.

I tend to write chapters of ten pages, about 2,500 words, adjusting them for content, natural or dramatic breaks, tailoring them longer or shorter as I see the desirability of slowing down or speeding up the pace.

Once past the opening paragraph—the key in the lock to this house of history and wonders I'm about to explore—the outline usually grows rapidly.

Each time I introduce a character, I take a moment to do a very short bio in the proper document.

Each time I set a scene, I make a similar note locating it in a word map of the building, city, or countryside. For instance, in my books about Chicago I like to know what parish, political ward, and police district the building, house, or street corner is in, even if I intend to fictionalize the locality for some reason or other.

Often I set down in the proper document historical milestones that I may or may not include in the text but that will give me a context in which to have my characters operate and live.

I also keep a running record of how much time has transpired in each chapter, whether the book encompasses a day, a month, a year, or a decade.

I have a program that prints out calendars for every year for some decades in the past and some years into the future.

I print out the years and months encompassed in my story and mark the principal events of the book on them, accurately matching the day and date.

The notebook stands ready to receive little flashes and notions that will get lost forever in the heat of writing if memory alone is depended upon.

The document for each character's agenda grows in the same organic way.

All of that is largely recordkeeping.

At no time is anything considered engraved in stone. The whole idea is to remain flexible, closing off few options.

The flexibility of the system reveals itself in another way.

As I write I will have the thought that an object mentioned on page four may well be useful for the resolution of a problem, or even the central mystery itself, much farther along in the book. It may even be potentially important enough to bear notice once or twice before the denouement. Moving along the outline I make a notation of those places.

It may be that something about a character deserves development so that the character unfolds and changes before the reader's eyes rather than being offered all of a piece. Such opportunities become part of the expanding outline.

In one book I wrote, a character who is afraid of guns is given a political appointment in the sheriff's department in a job where a gun is not required. He places the gun that has been issued to him in a tin box and hides it on the top shelf of his closet. I had no specific intention of using that gun again, but not only might it figure in the accident that forces his medical retirement but might even later be used in the commission of a murder by his son. In the final polish, if I decide that there was no need for the gun I might simply leave it there as a character note or take it out altogether as being of no consequence.

I find that characters and situations suggest themselves as I work along. There is a theory of dramaturgy that has to do with the economy of the stage. That is to say: You don't want to create a character whose only reason for being is to walk on and deliver a single piece of information if another character already on the scene can do the job as well.

But at this stage of my novel I don't worry about such considerations. I just pop the characters in there. Later on, if they don't prove to have any purpose or function other than the small bits that thrust them onstage in the first place, I can easily give their lines to some other character and erase them altogether, or I might hold them in reserve as long as their continued presence doesn't distort the shape of the growing outline and narrative.

I find that by the time I'm a hundred pages into a four-hundred-page book, I have fleshed out a credible plot and have a very good idea of how I will proceed, what dangers to my protagonists will appear along the way, what villainies will impede their progress, and I even have a better than fair notion about who the killer will prove to be—if the book is a standard mystery—or how the book will end—if it is a book that doesn't require the classic revelations.

I have discovered through the years, and even now, that retyping pages over and over again to rewrite a paragraph or even a phrase is no longer required. Rereading the work over and over again to refresh my memory of the details and nuances that do not find their way into the outline or the supporting documents creates a condition in which the words become shopworn and the sinews of the plot are no longer a wonder of literary architecture but merely a cloth riddled with holes.

There's danger here of making changes not because they are better but merely because they are different and I have developed a craving for something green.

So, after each chapter is completed, I use the cut and paste function of my program and create a condensed version of it. Usually the first paragraph and the last, with a few significant paragraphs in between.

Then, when I want and need to get the threads of the story refreshed in my mind before the new day's writing session, I read the brief version, which is usually more than enough to do the job.

Of course the book will have to be read in its entirety more than once while it is in progress, but three or four readings instead of twelve or fifteen will keep it from going stale too soon.

Obviously this process of outlining might be done in the conventional way, thinking everything through and setting the scenes and characters down before the actual finished work is begun. But I find that by walking alongside my characters before they are fully formed I'm often pleasantly, even dramatically, surprised by conversations, actions, and philosophies that I could not have imagined. When deep into a scene, writing on overdrive as it were, something magical very often takes place, some hidden well of imagination tapped, and I find myself a passenger floating on the raft of what is sometimes called inspiration along a river of words in full flood.

Before I became a writer I was a painter. When in art school, we were told to go to museums and paint reproductions of the old and new masters.

It was astonishing how much could be learned in the process. In learning how to achieve results similar to those in those skillful paintings, the student learned how color worked, how complements properly mixed with black and white produced an extraordinary range of grays. We learned how to achieve certain textures, the richness of wool and the slickness of satin, by edge and highlight control. We saw that shadows contain the complement of the source of the light. But most of all, I think, we learned the conversation of painting, the interaction of one corner of the canvas with another, the far distance with the near distance, this color and value and texture against others.

So I suggest that you occasionally spend some time studying the anatomy of books you admire, breaking them apart into an outline and ancillary documents such as I have described. This method, like all writing methods, is an attempt to make a writer's life a little easier, a little more orderly. It may not be the best method for you, but I think that by altering and refining it to suit your writing temperament you may fashion procedures that will work best for you.

PERSPECTIVES ON
POINT OF VIEW

Loren D. Estleman

Aristotle said, "Give me a lever and a fulcrum and I shall move the world." The only problem was finding a place to stand.

Why he should have wanted to move our planet out of a perfectly sound orbit is Greek to me, but since his time, writers have struggled with the problem of where to stand when they're telling their stories.

Who is observing the details, an all-seeing god or a flawed mortal? If the latter, is he telling the story himself or is someone speaking for him, inserting *he* (or *she*) in place of *I*? Finally, is he allowed the occasional break while another mortal takes up the slack? Does it matter?

The last question is the simplest to answer, and the affirmative reply opens the way toward answering the others. An understanding of the strengths and shortcomings of the various points of view plays a crucial role in determining where one will stand.

1. First Person

First person is the natural way to tell a story, which may be why puritans in the woodpile of literature have ever been quick to warn against it. Fortunately, among those who didn't listen are Daniel Defoe, F. Scott Fitzgerald, Emily Brontë, Herman Melville, William Styron, Edgar Allan Poe, Daphne du Maurier, Ralph Ellison, Mary Shelley, E.L. Doctorow, Mark Twain, and Joyce Carol Oates, to name a dozen among the thousands. It's the choice made by the first communicating Stone Age man to relate the details of a momentous hunt to his listeners. It's the way your parents explained object lessons from their own pasts to prevent you from repeating their mistakes. It's the method you used to report to them what happened to you on your first day in kindergarten.

> I take up my pen in the year of grace 17—, and go back
> to the time when my father kept the "Admiral Benbow"
> inn, and the brown old seaman, with the sabre cut, first
> took up his lodging under our roof.

So begins *Treasure Island*, and from the moment the profane ancient mariner enters young Jim Hawkins's life, Jim's story is ours, and has been from age seven to seventy for 120 years. It's impossible to imagine the scene in which the boy clings to a crosstree high above the deck of the *Hispaniola*, fumbling to reload a flintlock pistol, while wicked Israel Hands scrambles nimbly up the mast with dagger in teeth and murder in his eye, told from any perspective other than Jim's. Certainly the cool distance of even third-person subjective doesn't answer. ("*He* felt a blow and then a sharp pang, and there *he* was pinned by the shoulder to the mast"? Please!) It's the wizard strength of first person that forces the reader to suspend knowledge that if the narrator has survived to describe his brush with death, he could not have succumbed to it.

The disadvantage is first person's confinement. Similarly harrowing experiences when the narrator is not present must be related to the reader at second hand; or, as Stevenson chose, by putting aside Jim's recollections during the "Narrative Continued by the Doctor" chapters in part four, wherein Dr. Livesey tells us what happened to Jim's fellow adventurers while the boy was absent. At this point—for this reader, anyway—the story loses steam and does not regain it until Jim returns to pick up the thread three chapters on.

Insofar as I may make suggestions to a departed master, I hold that this break in momentum could have been avoided had Stevenson jettisoned Dr. Livesey's narration in favor of a brief dialogue, Jim asking questions and the doctor providing answers. We care more what happens to Jim; we've lived with him longer.

The very confinement of this perspective is often one of its strengths. In expert hands, a narrative supplied to the protagonist from outside can heighten the drama, calling for the reader to supply details from his imagination. Consider Sherlock Holmes's remarks upon the death of Sir Charles Baskerville to Dr. Watson, Holmes's first-person biographer, in *The Hound of the Baskervilles*:

> "He was running, Watson—running desperately, running
> for his life, running until he burst his heart and fell
> dead upon his face."

Three pages of on-the-spot description would read no more chillingly than those brief lines.

I elected to write *Whiskey River*, the first book in my Detroit series, from the first-person point of view of Connie Minor, a tabloid journalist of the Prohibition era. The hands-on, I'm-the-hero reportage of the days of armor-plated Cadillacs and bootleg hootch was tailor-made for this highly personal story of violence, romance, and betrayal.

2. Omniscient

The omniscient voice is one that has passed nearly beyond the pale. George Eliot and other writers of the Victorian epoch wrote like God, gazing down upon and into entire casts of characters, so that every line provided total insight regarding the motive and behavior of each player. It's a difficult technique, requiring an even hand and absolute balance, like a teamster operating a twelve-horse rig. I employed it in my first novel, which my editors titled *The*

Oklahoma Punk (happily rechristened by me *Red Highway* in subsequent editions) and haven't used it since. I was twenty-four and encouraged by ignorance of the difficulty.

What's often called omniscience in today's writing courses—alternating perspectives between scenes, chapters, or parts of the book—is a considerably limited version of the original definition and will be dealt with later. True omniscience asks the reader to bounce back and forth between the innermost thoughts of several characters in the course of a scene, and sometimes within a single paragraph. Mystery is forfeit, since the reader is privy to everything. This, more than the difficulty, may be the reason true omniscience is almost extinct. One nontypical success is Larry McMurtry. Consider this passage from *Lonesome Dove*:

> "Call, if you want better food you have to start by shooting Bolivar," Augustus said, reminded of his own grievance against the cook. . . .
>
> Bolivar stirred his sugary coffee and held his peace. He whacked the dinner bell because he liked the sound, not because he wanted anybody to come and eat. . . .
>
> Newt laughed. Bol never had been able to get the war straight, but he had been genuinely sorry when it ended. . . .
>
> Pea Eye got interested for a minute. The beans and sowbelly had revived him. . . .

There you have four separate points of view within the space of a single page, without a break to clue us into the shift. (The ellipses are mine.) As a result, the transitions are unnoticeable.

Omniscience enables McMurtry to distill thousands of pages of American Western culture and history into *Lonesome Dove*'s brisk 843. At one point he shelves his entire cast and replaces it with another, cutting in and out of consciousnesses as easily as changing gears on a downgrade. Through this device he manages to encompass his vast subject. (It's interesting to note that a number of critics took him to task for thus "breaking the rules.")

3. Third-Person Objective

The most restricting perspective, third-person objective calls for the writer who writes for the printed page to surrender his greatest advantage: the ability to get inside characters' heads. Shorn of his best mind-reading tools, he must define character entirely through action. Screenwriters unwilling to exploit the hackneyed 1940s gimmick of voiceover narration are forced by their visual medium to work inside this straitjacket. When Christopher Walken enters and kicks a dog, audiences are conditioned to understand he's the villain. When Mel Gibson shinnies up a telephone pole to rescue a stranded kitten, they know he's the one they're supposed to identify with. The technique hasn't changed since the days of the silent cinema and is mandated by the limits of visual storytelling. Print writers, offered a smorgasbord of interior monologue, stream of consciousness, and backtelling, are better off giving third-person objective a pass. It's depressing, however, to note how many new writers, with their sights fixed on a quick sale to Hollywood, approach the narrative art as if they were writing a movie script. Let whoever adapts your story to the screen be the one who carves the guts out of it. It's his job.

Dashiell Hammett achieved a powerful result by telling *The Maltese Falcon* completely from outside the skull of his protagonist, detective Sam Spade. It allowed Hammett to keep the reader guessing as to Spade's motives and character until the denouement. But it worked only once. He used Spade in three more stories, which, after we knew what made the man tick on the basis of *Falcon*, tended to vanish from the page even as they were being read.

4. Third-Person Subjective

Not of the same species as its objective counterpart, the subjective third-person perspective provides us with a ticket into the thoughts and hopes of the protagonist but denies us the intimacy of the personal pronoun. It makes full use of the under-the-skin technique while maintaining aloofness: "This far you may go," our central character seems to be saying, "and no farther." Not for him the navel-gazing egocentricity of first person; its confessional quality repels him. By these lights, without knowing anything of this person's past or present, we begin to form an idea of him based solely upon the method his creator has chosen to tell his story. It's the most frequently used point of view in fiction.

One reason is the opportunity for commentary outside the immediate experience of the character. Less self-involved than first person, third subjective makes full use of one mortal's special knowledge of the world. Edith Wharton, writing of a New York society that had vanished by the time *The Age of Innocence* appeared in 1920, introduced both the city and her protagonist in one succinct paragraph:

> When Newland Archer opened the door at the back of the club box the curtain had just gone up on the garden scene. There was no reason why the young man should not have come earlier, for he had dined at seven, alone with his mother and sister, and had lingered afterward over a cigar in the Gothic library with glazed black-walnut bookcases and filial-topped chairs which was the only room in the house where Mrs. Archer allowed smoking. But, in the first place, New York was a metropolis, and perfectly aware that in metropolises it was "not the thing" to arrive early at the opera; and what was or was not "the thing" played a part as important in Newland Archer's New York as the inscrutable totem terrors that had ruled the destinies of his forefathers thousands of years ago.

Substitute "I" for "Newland Archer" and "he," and you will see why this passage is appropriate only to third person.

In establishing the character of Doc Miller, the ex-convict baseball pitcher who is the conscience of *King of the Corner*, the third book in the Detroit series, I selected third subjective for the same reason Wharton did: to create a disaffected hero who could pass judgment upon his city without appearing to climb on a soapbox.

It was as right for Detroit in grim 1990 as Connie Minor's first-person cant was to the jazz-age Detroit of sixty years earlier.

5. Shotgun

A term I invented, *shotgun* symbolizes the scattershot pattern of a story told by several characters, each in his own section, chapter, or scene. It's as close as modern writing comes to classic omniscient, yet it preserves mystery through the limited vision of the narrator of the moment. Both the subjective and objective third-person viewpoints may come into play, with the added advantage to the writer of being able to abandon one perspective when it begins to bore him and take up another. The effect can be stately—each character stepping up to tell his or her story at measured intervals—or frenetic, with many voices clamoring for scenes and fragments, some long and rambling, others short and explosive. Stephen King, who calls his books "fast food for the mind," often maintains the shock level crucial to horror fiction by serving up a family meal of frightened viewpoint.

When it came time for the Detroit series to visit the 1960s—the years of race riots, drug happenings, and political unrest—the decision to employ shotgun perspective required little thought. The psychedelic effect of a story told through the observations of a black numbers boss, his superior in the Italian mob, a white busted cop obsessed with muscle cars and speed, and a couple of dozen colorful satellites, captured the balloonlike dream quality of a Peter Max poster, the Beatles' *Yellow Submarine*, and an acid trip.

This perspective can support multiple first person (one narrator per portion) and mixing first with third, as long as the owner of the point of view is clearly identified in each case. It's a kind of controlled anarchy, and you may be surprised by how quickly it piles up pages without taking on fat.

Choose any of the above. Then pick your lever and fulcrum and move the world.

Good Books

Following is a recommended reading list beyond the examples already cited for mystery writers, classified by point of view. Although most are mystery titles, I include works from outside genre. Most of the true artists in this form read widely, in part because restricting oneself to one's own specialty is about as nutritious a practice as a shark devouring its own intestines.

First Person

My Antonia, by Willa Cather

The Big Sleep, by Raymond Chandler

The Murder of Roger Ackroyd, by Agatha Christie

The Last Good Kiss, by James Crumley

All the King's Men, by Robert Penn Warren

Omniscient

Suspects, by William J. Caunitz

A Tale of Two Cities, by Charles Dickens

Silas Marner, by George Eliot

Night and the City, by Gerald Kersh

The Godfather, by Mario Puzo

Third-Person Objective

The Glass Key, by Dashiell Hammett

To Have and Have Not, by Ernest Hemingway

The Friends of Eddie Coyle, by George V. Higgins

The Fountainhead, by Ayn Rand

The Hunter, by Richard Stark

Third-Person Subjective

Martin Eden, by Jack London

No Pockets in a Shroud, by Horace McCoy

Wise Blood, by Flannery O'Connor

A Demon in My View, by Ruth Rendell

The Daughter of Time, by Josephine Tey

Shotgun (Semiomniscient)

The Silence of the Lambs, by Thomas Harris
City Primeval, by Elmore Leonard
Appointment in Samarra, by John O'Hara
Dr. Jekyll and Mr. Hyde, by Robert Louis Stevenson
Law and Order, by Dorothy Uhnak

DRESS FOR SUCCESS: DEVELOPING YOUR PERSONAL STYLE

■ *Carolyn Wheat*

W hat is style? Is it something a writer can consciously enhance, or is it a mystical quantum leap that comes only after years of writing? Is it layering metaphors, juggling images, reaching for abstruse adjectives, decorating a wedding cake of words? Or is it the laconic "Just the facts, ma'am" prose popularized by Ernest Hemingway, Dashiell Hammett, and Sergeant Joe Friday?

What is style? And where do I get one?

"Fiction is like a dream," says John Gardner. Style creates that dream, keeping the reader's eyes glued to the page, hoisting him astride a steeplechase jumper along with a Dick Francis hero or trapping her, like Anna Pigeon in *Blind Descent*, deep inside a cave with an armed killer. Style gives life to two-dimensional words strung along a blank white page.

We know great style when we see it. It's as effortless as Astaire's dancing, as appropriate as black at a funeral, as organic as a mulch-grown tomato. Style makes us smile in appreciation of a well-turned phrase, makes our pulses race as action verbs hurtle us along a roller coaster of suspense. Style is what helps a good mystery writer conceal her clues and take us to places we've never been before.

We know bad style too. Maybe not consciously, but that thriller we put down and never picked up again probably had flat prose, talk-alike characters, mushy verbs, and too many adverbs. Or perhaps it had florid prose, overblown descriptions, forced metaphors—instead of creating the dream, the entire volume screamed at the reader: "You're reading a book, and look how cleverly it's written."

We don't want to read a book. We want to live an experience.

Style is to prose exactly what it is to fashion. We choose one set of clothes to wear to a job interview, another to climb Pike's Peak. Our clothes serve a purpose, and so should our writing style. Hard-boiled private eye fiction demands a different style from cozy mystery; though both may describe similar settings, they will be seen through very different eyes and the writing should reflect those differences.

An action book demands an action style. Here's T. Jefferson Parker in *Little Saigon*:

> Cops were all over the Asian Wind. Light bars pulsed, flashing against the building. Radios squawked. Two officers strung yellow crime-scene tape between sawhorses. An ambulance sped away.

The author evokes the controlled chaos of cops at a crime scene with five—count them, five—well-chosen sentences. Another writer might have taken five paragraphs to say the same thing.

And maybe the mythical other writer *needs* five paragraphs. Maybe he's writing not a suspense novel where the cops are walk-ons but a police procedural in which every detail of crime scene protocol will be included because that's what the reader wants in a police-oriented story.

Parker's purpose is to keep the story moving by getting the cops on and off stage quickly so he can focus on his main characters. His style fits his purpose, and so does that of the procedural writer, for whom the police are central characters. What cops do, how they do it, what they say while they're doing it—that's the dream he's creating for his reader, and his cops are therefore worthy of five paragraphs, or even five pages.

The classic detective story involves first the planting and then the concealing of clues. Style is an important aid here; if the reader's attention is drawn too pointedly to the grandfather clock in the corner, the reader will be unsurprised by the revelation that the killer hid the weapon inside it. On the other hand, if the writer mentions the grandfather clock for the first time in chapter twenty-seven, she's going to have angry readers complaining she hasn't played fair. Putting the vital clue in plain sight and then obscuring it is one of the most important tasks they mystery writer must master.

That's what style is. Now, how do we get one?

First, don't think about it. Just write the story. Let the events happen. Let the viewpoint character think and speak and act independent of your authorial voice. Tell your story simply, the way you'd describe a movie to a friend who hasn't seen it yet.

Your early chapters will be a mishmash of styles. You're writing your way into the story. Some passages will be too long, filled with backstory, because you're groping for the essence of characters you don't yet know well. There will be boring passages of exposition as you try to get the plot on paper. You'll probably write a few purple paragraphs as you imitate the latest best-seller.

Don't worry.

Somewhere around the first third to half of your novel, a style will begin to emerge, shy as a kitten at first, creeping onto the page almost unnoticed. You'll find your writing becoming consistent, reflecting a distinct viewpoint, whether that of your first-person detective or that of an invisible authorial narrator.

Problem: What about those early chapters, the ones with choppy style, lifeless passages, too much information, bloated prose? Answer: Rewrite, rewrite, rewrite. Empty that closet of anything that doesn't enhance the purpose you've chosen for this book. Pare down that verbal wardrobe and concentrate on quality. You have your style now; all you have to do is recast the opening chapters in the same mode.

Great style has two aspects: leaving out the bad stuff and enhancing the good.

Big problem: knowing which is which.

Elmore Leonard, when asked what makes his crime novels so exciting, invariably replies that he "just leaves out the boring parts most readers skip anyway." In general, this means exposition, explanations, repetition of things the reader already knows, and long unfocused descriptions without purpose. Leonard goes straight to the meat of his story and his characters; his uncluttered prose is a model of great style.

What else is better left unsaid?

Speaking of *said*, any and all verbs substituted for *said* must be words that can actually *be* said by the mouth of an actual living person. (I once heard someone "giggle" a word, and while I'm here to report it can be done, it wasn't a pretty sight.) Save the chuckling, snorting, snarling, bellowing, snickering, and huffing for the Bulwer-Lytton contest and you might win an award for worst possible opening line.

Adverbs get a bad rep for good reason. They usually serve to (a) repeat something the reader already knows, or (worse) (b) tell the reader something she should already know but doesn't because the writer hasn't told her in the most natural way.

Take *sarcastically*, a much-overused adverb. If my character has just said something that any reader would realize was sarcastic, I don't need the adverb. If, on the other hand, what my character *actually said* didn't sound sarcastic enough, I need to beef up the dialogue, not try a cheap save, such as telling the reader it was sarcastic.

Flab must go. Get the *had*s out as much as possible. "He had gone," "he had thought," "he had eaten" have us floating around in the nebulous and therefore uninteresting past. Bring the story as much as possible into the present with more active locutions—"he went," "he thought," "he ate." Similarly, phrases such as "he was eating," "he was thinking" clog the brain and deflate suspense.

Cut fillers such as "Joe began to run." Let Joe run. And if your "he began" was intended to show an awkward, ungraceful beginning to the act of running, describe that instead of shortcutting the reader's full experience with the meaningless "he began." Likewise, "the sky seemed prepared to rain" is better as "rain clouds scudded across the sky."

Whenever possible, let people and things *act* instead of being *acted upon*. Make these simple yet effective changes and your prose will be tighter, more muscular.

Simple words move us more than high-flown language. In *A Prey to Murder*, Ann Cleeves's amateur sleuth explains why he is driven to solve the murder:

> He had always thought revenge a misguided and destructive emotion, but having seen Eleanor lying on the grass amid the droppings, the dirty straw, the discarded pieces of fur and feather of the birds' prey, he felt angry and violent. *She was beautiful, he had admired her, and she had been killed.* [Italics added.]

Note the rule of three in the last sentence—three simple phrases, strung together, which add up to a powerful motive. Note also that each phrase holds up a different facet of the character's mood. Too many writers use the rule of three as a way of saying the same thing three different ways: "He was tired as a bear in winter, exhausted as a car out of gas, limp as an old dishcloth." This dissipates the point rather than building it. Pick one image that conveys tiredness and stop there.

Great style is organic. It doesn't reach; it uses material ready to hand. Here's T. Jefferson Parker again, describing his detective hero in *Little Saigon*:

> It was, in fact, a cave-house—with back rooms being nothing more than dark irregular caverns. But the living room, bedroom, kitchen and bath featured walls, electricity, and unimpeded views of the Pacific. *Frye's friends said that the cave-house was like Frye himself, half-finished, prone to dark recesses.* [Italics added.]

What better way to describe a character than by the house he lives in? There is no straining for metaphor here, just straightforward but evocative use of the organic material of the novel itself.

Making full use of setting is more than just a matter of relating description to character. Nevada Barr's *Blind Descent* takes park ranger Anna Pigeon into the depths of a cave—and the reader goes along with her every claustrophobic step of the way. At the climax of the book, when Anna is trapped in the cave with an armed killer, Barr uses every single aspect of the situation and the setting to the full, ringing all the changes on darkness, fear, trickling water, fissures, falling rocks, lost flashlights, dropped guns, pounding hearts. After reading these scenes, you *will* run outside and gulp large grateful breaths of fresh air. You have *been there*, even though you were only reading words on a page.

That's style.

Metaphor and simile are powerful tools of the writer's craft. In the hands of masters, these tools dazzle us with wit and precision.

Similies tell you they're coming by using the word *like*. Ross Macdonald, one of the hard-boiled school's most revered practitioners of the art, has a character in *The Underground Man* walking "like a caged animal that had paced out the short distance many times." Of the same character, Lew Archer says, "I caught a glimpse of the broken seriousness which lived in him like a spoiled priest in hiding." Kinsey Millhone, in *"H" Is for Homicide*, describes shots as sounding like "kernels of popcorn in a lidded saucepan."

Metaphors, on the other hand, sneak up on the reader without announcing themselves. Here's Michael Connelly in *Void Moon*:

> Karch waited for her to answer but nothing came over the line. His smile broadened. He knew he was cutting her right to the bone. And *the truth was always the best and sharpest knife to use for such a procedure.* [Italics added.]

Note that Connelly doesn't say, "The truth is like a knife"; he simply calls truth a knife and shows Karch using it as such.

A note of warning is in order here. Parody is just around the corner. Strained metaphors are a sure sign of an amateur private eye writer at work and, if the writer is not careful, will earn him a place in Bill Pronzini's hilarious compilation of bad writing *Gun in Cheek*.

To be effective, the simile or metaphor must arise out of the character's own sensibility and must not overpower the subject of the sentence. "She was nervous as a three-legged squirrel skittering along a hot tin roof" gives me a lot of squirrel, not much woman. As a reader, I'd be happier skipping the simile and reading a straightforward account of how this particular character looks, sounds, and acts under stress.

Humor is another powerful weapon in the writer's stylistic arsenal. In *The Galton Case*, Lew Archer arrives in a stuffy office and takes a seat in a Harvard chair. When, after a long wait, he is told the person he needs to see isn't there, he gets "up out of the Harvard chair. It was a little like being expelled."

Much of humor arises out of contrasts. Here's Kinsey Millhone again: "The air smelled of desire, like the sweet perfume of wet grass after a rainstorm. That or cat spray."

Like other stylistic tricks, humor is better when organic. Lawrence Sanders in *The Timothy Files*:

> It's a peppy August day, which does nothing for his crusty mood. So the sun is shining. Big deal. That's what it's getting paid for, isn't it?

Only a true son of Wall Street would view the sun as earning its paycheck by shining. In another passage:

> Cone plods down Broadway to Exchange Place. It's a spiffy day with lots of sunshine, washed sky, and a smacking breeze. Streets of the financial district are crowded, everyone hurries, the pursuit of the Great Simoleon continuing with vigor and determination.

How many descriptions of how many nice days have you skimmed in your reading life? How many have been this spiffy, this connected to the personality of the narrator, this good at contrasting nature with "the pursuit of the Great Simoleon"? We're talking style here, style that puts us smack into the character's worldview and leaves us wanting more. This grabs our attention just walking down the street.

Judicious use of jargon brings us inside worlds we've only glimpsed through thick heavy glass. A parole officer in Michael Connelly's *Void Moon* lectures her parolee in the following words: "You're down by law, honey, and you're under my thumb. You're only ten months into a two-year tail." We readers can figure out she means the parolee has two years of supervision, but isn't it both more authentic and more interesting to hear it described as a "two-year tail"?

The all-important opening line of chapter one is well served by an attention-getting statement. This one from Roger L. Simon's *California Roll* is classic: "I never sold out before because nobody ever asked me."

Put spin on the ball by varying well-known clichés. Archie Goodwin describes a woman baring her soul in Rex Stout's *Black Orchids*: "The seams had ripped and the beans were tumbling out and Wolfe sat back and let them come."

That's a lot zippier than saying, "She spilled the beans," isn't it?

Beware of copyeditors. Copyeditors are great people who know where the commas go and how to spell *oleaginous*. They are also good at pointing out that on page twenty-four the doorman had on a blue uniform, while by page eighty, he'd unaccountably switched to gray. They do not, however, appreciate style. They opt invariably for the bland, the predictable, the done-before. If their suggestions flatten your prose and take the spice out of the chili, *resist*. Your personal style is just that—personal.

Beware of what you do best. This is a toughie. You write the meanest metaphor on the block. Your dialogue snaps, crackles, and pops. Your descriptions are sheer poetry. So you use your strong points over and over and over, especially when you don't know what else to do with a scene. The result is overwriting, lack of balance, and prose no longer geared to the purpose of the book.

Like the man said, kill your darlings. Not all of them—just the ones that clog the story, murder true style by showing off, and kill the fiction dream by reducing it to a bunch of words on the page.

HOW TO WRITE
CONVINCING DIALOGUE

■ *Aaron Elkins*

Ⓗow-to books on mystery writing are nothing new. They've been
around since *The Technique of the Mystery Story* was put
out by The Home Correspondence School in 1913. The 1929 revision
of this estimable volume consists of 435 pages of sound professional
advice. There are 153 titled chapters or sections ranging from "Devious Devices" and "Remarkable Deductions From Footprints," to "Need
Love Be Excluded?" and "What Else to Eschew."

Not one refers to dialogue, even indirectly.

Neither do the five-hundred-plus entries in the index. The average mystery writer of sixty years ago, with a few towering exceptions, simply didn't worry overmuch about dialogue. Or characterization. Or setting. (Nope, those aren't in the index either.) A
mystery novel, or a detective story as it was then more often called,
was first and last a matter of ingenious plotting.

Well, things have changed. A good plot is no longer enough.
Unless it's acted out by plausible, rounded characters convincingly
portrayed, it's not going to make it with today's readers. And when
it comes to creating believable characters, nothing serves better
and more straightforwardly than dialogue, which is, after all, your

characters' only opportunity to speak for themselves. On the other hand, nothing will alienate, bore, and irritate readers faster than dubious, badly written dialogue.

Here then are some thoughts and cautions on the enjoyable, fascinating, treacherous craft of dialogue writing.

Speaking in Voices

A character's voice is the distinctive way he or she speaks: vocabulary, cadence, tempo, slang, subject matter, tone, and any other aspect of speech. Voice is the most direct way we have to flesh out our characters. In my own writing, one of the last passes I make through a manuscript is to review the dialogue sections to make sure that every line of speech seems right—that is, consistent—for the speaker. Is this the way Tony would answer that question, or does it sound too much like Ben? Would Anne really express anger like that? If not, what's wrong with it? How do I fix it? The point is, if I can't distinguish between the way my people talk, how can I expect my readers to?

Some writers' guides recommend that you differentiate your characters' speech patterns by assigning "types": having one character who speaks formally, another who's laconic, another who's meticulous, etc., and then making sure that you stick to that type when you write dialogue for them.

Personally, I don't think it's a good idea. People who respond predictably are tedious in real life and more so in books. What I usually do instead is model my characters' speech on that of real people—usually acquaintances (who never recognize themselves, by the way) or other people I've spent time observing personally, but often familiar public figures too. The question then becomes: Is this the way Dan Quayle—or Margaret Thatcher, or Cher, or Vince at the Safeway store—would probably say this? It's relatively easy, it develops the ear, and it's downright enjoyable.

It's Not What They Say, It's How They Say It

Most mysteries require a lot of talk. Complex information has to be brought out, and dialogue is often the best or even the only way to do it. Someone, most often the protagonist, asks questions . . . Who? Why? Where? . . . and someone answers. It's certainly efficient, but nothing is likely to put a reader to sleep quicker (or more deeply) than paragraph on paragraph of dialogue establishing dates, times, places, and prior events.

How do you avoid this and still present the needed data? You grit your teeth, gird your loins, and sit down and force content-heavy dialogue to do double or even triple duty. Can the conversation itself, aside from the necessary content, fill in important aspects of character, develop mood, reveal significant motives and perceptions? Ruth Rendell is a past master at this. Here is an early passage from *The Veiled One*.

"Yes, I go to Serge Olson. It's a sort of Jungian therapy he does. Do you want his address?"

Burden nodded, noted it down. "May I ask why you go to . . . Dr. Olson, is it?"

Clifford, who showed no signs of the cold his mother claimed for him, was looking at the mirror but not into it. Burden would have sworn he was not seeing his own reflection. "I need help," he said.

Something about the rigidity of his figure, his stillness and the dullness of his eyes stopped Burden pursuing this. Instead he asked if Clifford had been to the psychotherapist on Thursday afternoon and what time he had left.

"It's an hour I go for, five till six. My mother told me you knew I was in the car park—I mean, that I put the car there."

"Yes. Why didn't you tell us that at first?"

He shifted his eyes, not to Burden's face but to the middle of his chest. And when he answered Burden recognized the phraseology, the manner of speech, as that which people in therapy—no matter how inhibited, reserved, disturbed—inevitably pick up. He had heard it before. "I felt threatened."

"By what?"

"I'd like to talk to Serge now. If I'd had some sort of

warning I'd have tried to make an appointment with him and talk it through with him."

"I'm afraid you're going to have to make do with me, Mr. Sanders."

The essential data—time and place—are established, but how much more than that she tells us about the two people.

Move It Right Along, Please

For most of us, writing dialogue is fun, at least when it's rolling effortlessly along, which is precisely when it tends to get away from us. I wouldn't want to count the number of times I've had to delete five or six pages of dialogue—two or three days' work— not because it was badly written, but because I'd gotten off on a tangent that didn't take the story anywhere.

In some kinds of fiction this might be all right, but in the mystery you'd better keep that story moving along if you hope to keep your readers. When they start flipping ahead to get to the next place where something happens, you're in trouble. And they *will* start flipping if they sense that the plot's been put on idle. Fortunately you can sense it too if you read your own material with care. No matter how much wonderful mood or character development a dialogue scene may be providing, it has to get your story someplace. If it doesn't, then cut it, painful as it may be.

Sometimes, in fact, a scalpel-like approach to dialogue is in itself a tool for moving a story jauntily along. Here's an example from a book of mine called *Murder in the Queen's Armes*. The scene is a village museum in England from which a fossilized skull fragment of Poundsbury Man (familiarly, Pummy) has disappeared.

Professor Hall-Waddington thrust his face into the box. "Empty! Pummy . . . Pummy appears to have been . . ." He held the box in trembling hands and looked up at Gideon with wondering eyes. "But why would anyone steal a thirty-thousand-year-old parieto-occipital calvareal fragment?"

End of chapter one. I know, this may not be the kind of crisis that makes you clench your teeth with tension, but it does provide a nice, sharp close, right at the climactic moment, to an exchange that might otherwise have petered slowly out. It also ends the chapter with a question, always a nice idea for prodding a reader into turning the page.

And how does chapter two begin? This way:

> "Why *would* anyone steal a thirty-thousand-year-old whatzit?" Julie asked, her black eyes no less wondering.
> "Beats the hell out of me," Gideon said.

The dialogue begins as cleanly as it left off. And in so doing that wearisome bugbear of writers new and old—the transition from one scene to another—is sidestepped. No tiresome "After leaving Professor Hall-Waddington, Gideon walked thoughtfully along the High Street to the little park where he was to meet . . ." The new scene takes off from the old one, jump-started, so to speak, and in the doing there is even an opportunity for a little character development.

". . . ," He Ululated Menacingly

New writers seem to worry a lot—probably too much—about how often you can get away with writing *he said* or *she said*. There are two opposing schools of thought on this. One, subscribed to by some of the greatest writers in the English language, affirms that *said* is the only verb of attribution needed to identify who is speaking. The other school considers *said* colorless, preferring more spirited words like *mocked*, *bleated*, *gritted*, *rasped*, *ground out*, and *hissed*. This school is heavily represented in the formula romance racks of your supermarket.

Fortunately there is a sensible intermediate position (which I just happen to hold). I think that *said* functions very well indeed as the writer's standby, but that a little variety is not to be sneered at. There are other good speech descriptors too, all with their own nuances of meaning. *Asked, explained, mused, noted, whispered, cried, repeated, shouted, told,* and *informed* are examples of perfectly good variants, as long as they aren't used so excessively that they catch the reader's eye and thus disrupt the flow of the story. How much is "excessively"? My own rule of thumb is no more than once a chapter for any one of them. If I find two *whispered*s in a single chapter, I usually replace one with *said.*

There are other ways around the problem. An obvious one is to use fewer verbs of attribution altogether. A brief conversation between two people needs no more than a single *he said or she said* at the beginning to establish who is speaking. Longer dialogues can get by just fine with one every fifth or sixth time the speaker changes. And question-and-answer sessions, as in courtroom scenes or interrogations, can go on for twenty pages without a *he said* and still be completely clear as to who's doing the talking.

Ramona Sipped Her Strawberry Daiquiri (Toyed With Her Wedding Band—Pondered the Alternatives—Lifted an Eyebrow Imperceptibly), "Really, Darling . . ."

Another way to avoid an overabundance of verbs of attribution, and to enliven scenes as well, is to identify the speaker by action or thought, as in the following exchange:

> "Look, I wasn't even in Omaha last Wednesday." Lester stared sullenly at the paint-spattered floor.
> "Is that right?" Walter smiled pleasantly. "I'm afraid I don't believe that."
> Neither did Vincent. "Where, then?"

If you want to find examples of fine dialogue writing that goes on for pages without using a single *said,* read some Robert Barnard. On the other hand, if you need confirmation that one can write riveting dialogue while relying on nothing but *said,* try a Tony Hillerman.

While we're on the subject, still another way to eliminate verbs of attribution and also speed things up is to slip out of the dialogue mode for as long as necessary, then pick up the dialogue again when you're ready. Do it well, and the reader will never notice. This is an example from *The Killing Zone* by Rex Burns:

> "What was his schedule for Wednesday?"
> She told him, pointing to the calendar and explaining its abbreviations. In addition to routine committee work, meetings, and functions, he had a dozen-or-so visitors to talk to.
> "Is that usual?"

A lot of dull, nonessential material was deftly slipped by us there, without missing a beat.

Veracity Vs. Verisimilitude

> "You know how, how . . . but . . . some mornings the minute you walk in the door—"
> "Every morning."
> "Yes, that's how these, the way they, the way they . . ."
> "No, it's not. It's not the, the—"
> "Yes, it is, it is. Because if you, unless you—"
> "No, uh-uh, absolutely not."

Absolutely not what? What are they talking about? Would you keep reading a book with dialogue like that? Neither would I. Yet this is a snatch of authentic dialogue, the speech of real people; two intelligent, literate women engaged in an earnest discussion. I scribbled it down verbatim a few mornings ago on a Seattle-bound commuter ferry. Suppose that the next day I'd given them pens and asked them to write down their entire half-hour conversation. Would this particular passage show up?

Not a chance. People may talk that way, but they don't remember it that way. Which takes me to a critical point. Every mystery writer had better be concerned about writing realistic dialogue—but "realistic" isn't the same thing as "real." In writing realistic dialogue we're not trying to document authentic speech; we're trying to set it down as people remember speech, as they think it ought to have been. Genuine or not, a conversational passage like the one above has no place in mystery fiction unless it's there to make a point. Even then, it better not go on very long.

Realistic dialogue attempts to capture the flavor of real speech, but it does it selectively. Word repetitions, hesitations, stammers, and dead ends have to be ruthlessly pruned. So do many of the polite conventions.

"Hey, come on in, Hal, glad you made it. Care for a drink? Scotch? Coffee? Why don't you sit right there, Hal?"

In real life people do a lot of this. That's fine for them; they're not living out somebody's plot and trying to do it in 90,000 words or less. But your characters are. Everything they do—and most emphatically everything they say—must have a point, must take the story somewhere. Otherwise, out with it.

What Else to Eschew

Writing manuals are agreed in their advice on how to use dialect: Don't.

Generally speaking, I agree. There is little that is more awful to the sensitive and discriminating eye than clumsily done dialect, whether foreign—"Vat you vant, meesus?"—or regional—"Ah shore am hongry, chile, cuz ah hain't et mah grits." Dialect in your fiction is likely to make an enemy of your copyeditor and strain the patience of your audience, two things I don't recommend.

Still . . .

It can be done and done well. You don't have to traumatize the language to provide a flavor of foreign or regional speech. Sometimes a few simple adjustments will suffice. For example, an inoffensive sort of all-purpose foreign accent can be achieved simply by eliminating the use of contractions.

"Now, we'll see what's going to happen" sounds like an American speaking. But "Now we will see what is going to happen" sounds to most of us like a German. Or Frenchman. Or Russian.

It works because we know, even if we've never consciously noticed it, that many people who learn English as a foreign language never become comfortable with its frequent use of contractions.

You can dig deeper and show dialects through rhythm, vocabulary and syntax. Here is a typical passage from Stuart Kaminsky's *A Cold Red Sunrise*:

> "What do you want?" Rutkin said.
>
> The creature said nothing.
>
> "Are you drunk?" Rutkin went on. "I am a Soviet Commissar. I am conducting an important investigation and you, you are in my way."
>
> The creature did move now. It moved toward Illya Rutkin, who stepped back, clutching his briefcase protectively to his chest.
>
> "What do you want?" Rutkin shouted. "You want trouble? You want trouble? That can be arranged."

Not a mutilated word in there; no *nyet*s or *da*s either, but Kaminsky, with his good ear, shows Rutkin talking in a way that fits our notion of what a Russian would speak like (if he were speaking Russian in English, of course).

And what if you don't have a good ear? Then go to the language section of your library or a school language department and get help. And if you still feel insecure about it? Then give it up. Just write:

"I am Sigurd Asbjornsen," he said, his Norwegian accent almost impenetrable.

And let it go at that. It will get you by satisfactorily, it won't make you look silly, and your copyeditor will love you.

I Was Not Moving My Lips

The critical test of dialogue is how well it stands up to being read aloud. There is just no better way to show up awkwardness or artificiality in written speech than trying to say it. Another one of the final passes I make through my manuscripts is a read-the-dialogue-out-loud exercise. It never fails to turn up some spoken lines that seemed fine when I wrote them but that don't work now. I don't always know what's wrong technically; sometimes all I know is that something is "off." But trying it a few different ways—out loud—almost always gives me something better.

Moving your lips while you read is not to be encouraged. Doing it while you write is.

PACING AND SUSPENSE

■ *Phyllis A. Whitney*

The best lesson I've ever received on pacing came to me from Farnsworth Wright, editor of *Weird Tales*. This was several lifetimes ago in Chicago, before I had written a full-length book. The few stories I had sold as a beginning writer were to the pulp magazines. No paperbacks in those days, so we learned in the pulp field.

Weird Tales was an elite member of the pulp group, and highly respected. I had sold them one story but was having no success with others I'd submitted. Mr. Wright was kind enough to send me a criticism that has forever proved useful to me: I must not try to keep everything at high pitch all the way through a story. Excitement, if too steady, can be as boring as having nothing at all happening.

This was when I first recognized that a reader's attention could be as easily lost by too much as by too little. There can be a strong buildup to a dramatic scene, after which we must allow for a letdown, a rest, before we start building up all over again. That is what pacing is.

There is another aspect that is worth considering. If a writer piles on endless defeat and discouragement, the reader may find the story too unpleasant to read. The mystery writer is first of all an entertainer. While the main character's course should never be easy, hope can be laced into the action, and there can be small "wins" along the way. Please, Stephen King, don't kill off all the good characters!

For me, suspense is the fun part of writing. It is the game I most like to play—a game that readers are sure to enjoy when it is handled successfully. The development of suspense should affect every phase of our writing.

In my own novels I start first with a setting that I am able to visit. I want a place that will give me fresh and interesting material that will furnish good scenes for a mystery. One needn't always travel to a distant country. If I look at my own home locale with a fresh eye, I'm likely to find just what I need.

In my fourth book (my first adult mystery) I had only to visit Chicago's Loop and get behind the scenes in the window-decorating section of a big department store. There were wonderful mystery settings I could use, the story developed well, and *Red Is for Murder* got good reviews. It sold about three thousand copies and I decided (with Mystery Writers of America) that crime certainly didn't pay enough. I returned happily to writing for young people—in which field I eventually learned the craft of mystery writing. Years later, when I had been "discovered," my adult mystery was reprinted many times in paper, and is still selling as *The Red Carnelian*. Styles in titles can change. So take heart if your first novel doesn't succeed. Earn your stripes and all the old titles will be reissued.

Once I visit a new background, I look deliberately for scenes that will trigger my imagination. In St. Thomas, Virgin Islands, I immediately noticed the "catchments" on every hillside. These were huge, steep, concrete constructions that caught rainfall and sent the water into containers at the bottom. When I climbed up to see what one of these looked like from the top, my first reaction was, "What a wonderful place for a murder!" So I used a catchment in *Columbella* to good effect. Suspense grows out of our own reactions first of all.

Writer's block is unlikely to occur if we find new experiences and impressions to feed into the creative right brain. Each new place or subject requires library research, and this in itself will provide fresh ideas that we can use.

Once I have my setting, I search for a main character who will be driven to solve a life-or-death problem. Little difficulties don't build high suspense. The more serious and threatening the problem, the higher the reader's interest. No strong drive for the main character will result in a weak story.

We need to think about this powerful drive in our planning stages. It is easier to build this quality into an action story than into something more quiet. Yet the latter can create just as much page-turning suspense, if the writer remains aware of the character's desperate need to reach an important goal. Taking action needn't always be violent.

In the beginning the main character may not know what action is needed. Sooner or later, however, he or she must decide to *do something*. This is the point where the story really begins. Until this happens, it's all preparation. It is all too easy to mark time and let a character drift along for too many chapters without making a decision to act. He may be caught up in other characters' problems, and the writer may need to pull up short and face what must be done to hold the reader.

Giving my character a purpose—something she must strive for in every scene—is not always a major problem, but at least something that will lead into the main goal of the character. Sometimes there may really be a situation in which my heroine can take no action on her own. Then I bring on another character who has a strong drive, and perhaps a very different goal, so that she is forced into taking action. Suspense results.

In any piece of writing we can count on reader curiosity to carry the story for a time. Providing, of course, that we furnish something to be curious about. We need story people who are interesting enough to make readers wonder what they will do next. What are these strange goings-on, and what is this person hiding? Curiosity serves us well in the beginning, and from time to time thereafter.

Long ago, in writing for young people, I learned the value of the eccentric character. These are always fun to do, since they are dramatic, flamboyant, out of the ordinary. Such characters furnish suspense by doing the unexpected and perhaps messing everything up. The reader stays to see what on earth will develop next. It's advisable not to have more than one eccentric character per novel. Overdo this and the reality is lost.

Writing from a single viewpoint happens to be my choice. It isn't always easy to achieve, but I like its special advantages. Most writers seem to prefer the multiple viewpoint, since it enables them to skip around into the minds of various characters. There may be added suspense when the reader knows something the character doesn't and can see danger coming. One of the handicaps in using different viewpoints lies in the letdown that can result when the reader must leave a character in whom a strong interest has developed, to move to someone unknown, or about whom we may not care. This requires a quick new buildup of interest and suspense, or the reader is likely to put the book aside.

For me, the strong suspense that results from immediacy—that sense of everything happening *now*—is increased when I stay in the thoughts and feelings of one character.

Whether I write in third or first person, emotion can be more readily felt by the reader when I stay in the single viewpoint. Emotion is always an important ingredient. The reader who feels nothing, because the character feels nothing, is quickly bored. We do need to care. Worry and fear can be more intense when we follow the fate of one character. Breaking viewpoints can dilute.

If you do use several viewpoints, however, don't skip around into more than one mind on a page. It's much safer to use one viewpoint per chapter—unless confusion is your aim.

A major objection to the single viewpoint is that the writer may want to show events at which the main character can't be present. I have always found a way around this—perhaps through another character's report, which can be dramatized.

Describing the main character can offer some difficulty in the single viewpoint. We can't step outside and objectively look at this person. Once a pulp editor asked me to stop standing my heroines in front of mirrors. That is certainly a hoary device, yet I'm still guilty at times when it seems appropriate. Working a bit harder, I can usually find ways to give bits of description through other persons in the story who talk to the main character. In my experience the single viewpoint is apt to build intense suspense.

Of course the basic idea of plot must never be forgotten. I bring this up because of my years of experience in working as a teacher with beginning writers. Too often a string of incidents is regarded as a plot. I've often used Forster's example: *The king died and then the queen died.* This is a string of incidents. But if you say, *The king died and then the queen died of grief,* you have a plot. Cause and effect. Whatever happens grows out of what happened before and results in future happenings.

Another useful element in building suspense is to do the unexpected. If a reader can guess what is going to happen, we lose him. So we push ourselves to discard easy approaches and try to surprise with the astonishing, but logical. In *Woman Without a Past* my main character finds herself alone and abandoned at three in the morning in the dungeon of the Old Exchange Building in Charleston, South Carolina. She has arrived there through surprising but logical circumstances. There is some suspense, but I needed more. So I even surprised myself. While my heroine is groping her way blindly in the pitch dark among the brick pillars of this echoing place, her outstretched hand rests suddenly on the warm human flesh of a face. This gave me new action that I hadn't figured on ahead of time. No one will stop reading at that point.

At the end of a chapter it's advisable to use the carryover of suspense. If you want to receive letters telling you that readers stayed up all hours reading one of your books—this is a good way to accomplish that. Most readers have the neat habit of setting a book down at the end of a chapter. So we prevent this in our own sneaky way.

Time is another important aid we can use in building suspense. If there is a threat that depends on time, the reader is held. Remember the movie *High Noon* and the inexorable hands of the clock? It isn't always possible to achieve that tight level of danger and suspense, but I find that when I can move my action along from day to day, this will give the reader a sense of being carried swiftly toward impending disaster. When there are lapses of time between scenes or chapters, there can be a slowing of interest. The necessities of plot govern this to some extent. When I was writing a Civil War novel, the events of history dictated the passage of time. When it's possible, the shorter time space lends its own momentum to what is happening.

A reader once wrote to me that my heroines were always changing their clothes and taking showers. That's what happens if you write from hour to hour. There are meals to eat, times to sleep—though no one wants too many details along the way. (I *have* cut down on the showers.) However you may use the time element, it needs to be considered in the building of suspense.

Another useful device to think about in the planning stage is to give every character a secret. As a writer you need to know about the hidden goals, the past guilts of every character. Such secrets can be used to make your story people behave in mysterious and suspense-building ways. As we think about and develop these secrets, the characters become more real to us, as writers, and thus to our readers. Conflict is likely to grow out of these concealed matters, and of course this is a main weapon in our suspense arsenal.

Car chases and fistfights aren't the most interesting type of conflict—Hollywood to the contrary. Holding a reader doesn't depend on violent action. It depends on *people action*. Is our sympathy engaged so we care enough about what is happening to the main character? Psychological conflict is the most interesting kind of all.

Two or more people sitting in a room talking can give us strong suspense and be far more interesting than slamming into something physically. Conversation that builds and makes a reader curious is likely to provide surprise and hint at action to come. Suspense is not always achieved by jumping off a cliff. (Though that may be a culmination of all these other elements!)

Conflict grows out of well-conceived characters and strongly opposing goals, which brings us back to that life-or-death problem our main character started out with. It's time to give that problem the ultimate test. What are the terrible penalties for failure? What are the satisfying rewards for success? If *happiness* is always the goal of the main character—to quote my favorite writing teacher, Dwight Swain—then let's build up the failures and rewards. It's a good idea to set these down on paper, and then consult what we've written from time to time—to keep us on the right track. The easiest thing the writer does is fool himself. So let's look at this in one of our more left-brain states when we can be critical and objective.

Happiness may be the overall goal, but what is it *specifically* that will make the main character happy? If you don't know, you are fooling yourself and your story will collapse.

Danger should be a main ingredient in a mystery novel. Sometimes it may be only a threat, but it must always be real. We dare not threaten the main character with something false that is supposed to scare the reader but adds up to nothing. *It was all a mistake* is fatal to the writer. We try not to annoy.

Danger is of course easier to provide in an action novel when the main character is a man. The frailer sex (physically) had better not plunge into an obviously dangerous situation that she probably can't handle. Better not go walking down a dark alley alone when danger threatens. It's not very bright, and the reader will notice. Male characters too sometimes plunge into such situations, but they're more apt to get away with it.

There is a way around this for either sex. We must build up specific reasons why the main character is *forced* into danger. Because of these reasons (this and this and this—know what they are) the character *must* put himself or herself in jeopardy—and then has to be pretty ingenious to get out of it.

In a mystery novel, where there is certain to be a murderer and a death threat, how do we furnish an assault that won't be that overdone bop-on-the-head? Sometimes a threat can be as scary as an open attack. In my Charleston novel, my main character is backstage at night in a huge warehouse that has been turned into a theater. There are props all around, aisles of them, piled on shelves, tables, the floor. She stumbles up some unexpected steps when she hears someone creeping about, and falls, banging her head on an iron stove, knocking herself out. A self-imposed variety of the bop-on-the-head. When she comes to, she finds that someone has placed an unusual weapon beside her—a long medieval halberd, with its axe head turned toward her. Its presence is creepy and threatening. And perhaps more effective at this point than if it were used against her. It will turn up later!

The halberd is there because *I* found it in the cavernous backstage area of a theater in Charleston. It caught my imagination, and I took a flash picture to remind me. This is what can happen when you get out into the field and do active research. The more fresh impressions we put into our minds, the more we have to work with.

In the creation of suspense our choice of words is endlessly important. John Ciardi once wrote that words can have an emotional vote. So we must choose carefully. Not the trite and obvious that come so easily to mind, but words that will spring into life on their own and move the reader . . . to alarm, to astonishment, to delight, to terror. It's all done with the right words.

Verbs, of course, are important. Though I don't shun those adverbs and adjectives that we're sometimes told to avoid. Just don't overdo. I keep a book of synonyms at hand. *Roget's Thesaurus* has served me so well that I've worn out several copies. Endless pains may bring bigger checks in the long run.

Reveal new turns of the story and new information about the characters gradually. Hold out. Build curiosity and milk it for a while. Tantalize, but not to so maddening a degree that the reader throws your book across the room. Pacing again! Feed in with partial answers, and then bring up new questions. The tempo should always rise and fall and rise again. The fall is that necessary rest period. Even slower scenes, however, can hold their own milder surprises and revelations.

As we near the climax, the threat of danger becomes more imminent, and we'd better handle this in an action scene. No more do we sit around a drawing room with our clever detective questioning and exposing suspects.

Emotions run high, possible avenues of escape are cut off—and there is no way out. How the solution is managed, and who is revealed as guilty, should surprise the reader. Most readers love to be fooled and are disappointed when they guess the ending. Satisfaction is important. An ending doesn't necessarily have to be happy to satisfy, but it has to be right.

At the end we *stop*. We stop because there is no more suspense, no more curiosity. We don't go on for pages boring the reader with explanations that should have been worked in earlier. This isn't easy. Perhaps we hold out the answer to one important question until the last paragraph—to pull the reader along. That easily read conclusion has often been rewritten a dozen times.

The greatest sigh of relief and satisfaction comes from the writer. All our travail, our brain-searching, our tired backs at the typewriter have paid off, and we've done it one more time.

I manage to feel quite giddy and free for about a week. Then I start searching so I can begin all over again. The writer is the one who never finishes the story.

DEPICTION OF VIOLENCE

■ *Bill Granger*

The depiction of violence in novels is difficult for two reasons. The violence itself is both external and internal, objective and subjective; and the nature of the violent act described can impede the flow of narrative when the writer hopes that it will increase the flow.

External violence depicted in narration, oddly enough, is always in danger of becoming tedious.

How does a man shoot his victim? He pulls the trigger. The victim receives the bullet. The victim cries out or does not cry out. The victim falls, or the victim stumbles and falls, or the victim is thrown back by the force of the round. It is all anticlimax, in any case; the narrative tension has been used up in setting the final act of the scene. There are only so many ways of describing violent death, and they have all been done before.

Or, if the violence is short of dying, what makes it interesting as objective narration?

Like a barroom brawl in a John Ford Western, smaller acts of violence—a sock to the jaw or a blackjack to the noggin—seem so predictable in fiction that the eye of the reader glazes over when he comes to it. This impedes the flow of the narrative, the second problem of depicting violence.

The wider world of fiction—movies, television scripts, et cetera—has inured us to shock at seeing violent acts. How much more difficult to portray violence in words? When cars crash into fireballs of death (something that can be seen nightly on the tube), the special effect is no longer special and has limited effect, except as punctuation at the end of the chase. And the punctuation is as muted as a period.

There are three good ways to describe external (or objective) violence in prose.

First, slow it down to the point of absurdity. Or, second, hide the act of violence in an empty bracket separating the before and after of the violence. Third, hide the horror of the act of violence (and all acts of violence rendered should be horrible) by deliberately underplaying the prose.

Here is an example of the first point.

> He fired. The round caught Henry below the right eye.
> A moment after the lead punctured the flesh and
> cracked the bone beneath the eye socket, Henry heard
> the sound of the gunshot and his eyes widened. He did
> not feel the impact of the bullet at all. The shooter stared
> at Henry's staring eyes while the round lost its velocity
> tearing up through the skull, through bone and brain,
> until it was stopped by the top of the skull. Henry was
> dead but his eyes remained wide open, still registering
> the sound of the gunshot in the closed, damp room.

Another example:

> The left front wheel of the Buick leapt the curb a moment
> before she felt the plastic steering wheel twist away
> from her grip. The wheel had developed a life apart from
> her intent. Two thousand pounds of Detroit machine
> hurtling sixty-one miles an hour down Garcia Road had
> entered a curve that could not be exited on mere wet

pavement. The left front tire clawed at the sod and exploded over the neat row of hackenberry bushes and
the rest of the automobile followed, the tires crying pro-
test louder than Lydia's screams. A picket line of two-
hundred-year-old oak trees waited for the car just below
the crest of the drive. The left front tire exploded when
the rubber was pierced by a jagged stone but, by then,
the rest of the automobile encasing Lydia Holman's
body, was already being crushed by the unyielding trees.

In both illustrations, the moment of violence is just that but,
because words dawdle at the pace of the reader, the writer has
made them dawdle even more, to force the reader into the action.
It is the writer's equivalent of Sam Peckinpah's celebrated slow-
motion scenes of death without the worry of rendering the violence
either beautiful or less horrifying (traps that Peckinpah let himself
fall into).

Second point: Hide the external (objective) depiction in an empty
bracket. The size of the bracket is determined by what went before and what comes after. The reader's eye is then forced to con-
front the empty bracket and *fill* it with his own invention of imagination, which is generally more graphic than the writer's.

Example:

Ninety-one minutes after takeoff from the wet, bumpy
runway at Heathrow, George C. Scott stood in front
of a giant American flag and pretended to be General
George S. Patton addressing soldiers during World War
II. Of the 197 persons in economy class, 59 were watching Scott on the small movie screen at the front of their
section of the cabin and twenty-three were asleep. Two
of the four small, plastic washrooms were occupied by
men who had whiled away the hour before boarding in
one of the airport bars. Everyone in the overpacked
economy class was uncomfortable but only two children,
both too young to understand the silent endurance necessary for flight in the cheap seats, expressed their frustra-

tion by crying aloud. The Scott movie was also being shown in business and first-class sections where drinks were served in real glasses. Scott said all Americans love to fight. A man who sat in the aisle seat in first class opened his Zenith laptop and turned it on. The pilot told the navigator the one he had heard that morning over coffee in the Hilton, not usually a time of day for good or even funny jokes.

A moment later, the radar screen of Air France 121 trailing eleven miles behind made the green dot that was Flight 901 disappear. The Parisian navigator looked at the screen, blinked, turned a knob, and said something to the captain. Both men looked out the windshield. The day was full of sun and all the clouds were beneath their wings. Between the clouds were patches of the blue Atlantic. They were four minutes south and east of Iceland. "Mon Dieu," the captain said. He blessed himself; he was from Marseilles. He saw nothing in front of him but the long, clear day.

Another example:

"Please take your wallet back." The smiling man extended the wallet. He had taken only the money. James did not move.

"Please." The smiling man held the wallet out only a few inches from his chest. James had to take a step nearer to grasp the wallet he had surrendered a moment before. The man made his smile wider and more sincere. There was no one else on the subway platform, as though the throbbing night city above had suddenly forgotten all the trains and stations and miles of track below. James touched the wallet. Then he saw the knife. The knife had been there all along but James only now saw it.

The first policeman knelt on one knee on the subway station platform. He was careful not to kneel too close to the body. The policeman said, "He must have been very strong."

The second policeman said, "You can't just cut like that. He cut all the way across. Nobody cuts like that."

The kneeling policeman said, "His wallet. He's got his wallet in his hand. Why didn't he just give him the wallet? Money isn't that important. Christ, he must have been strong, whoever did it, to cut like that. It must have been a helluva big knife to get that much cut in it."

Third point: Underplay the prose. This is still most effective in police procedurals, but it can be used in all categories of the thriller. The narration of violence does not have to be coplike or even acquire a Joe Friday monotone. Understatement is the key to making this approach to depiction of violence successful.

Here is a rape scene. The rape scene is graphic, but it has two inherent problems common to all depictions of violent sexual assault. It must not be prurient. It must not excite any feeling except horror. On the other hand, if it is too graphic, it will turn off readers and destroy the narrative flow, at least temporarily. The third approach to depiction of objective violence is the most useful (although the second approach—the empty bracket—might be preferred by some writers. The first approach—slowing the action—cannot be used without falling into the traps set by the inherent problems described above.).

The two men followed her to the C level of the empty garage. She dropped her keys and bent to pick them up. Her hands were shaking. Her heels clicked loudly on the cement and she fumbled with the keys in her hand, trying to find the door lock key. They were so close to her now that she couldn't turn around. Maybe they were kids, just kids. The first man stood behind her and the second man went to the driver's side door. He looked at her. She did not look at him. She put the wrong key in the lock.

He hit her very hard across the face and she screamed.

He hit her again and told her not to scream. She saw the knife. She started to speak and he hit her again.

The second man laughed and grabbed her shoulders. The first man pushed her down on the cement. She turned her head and saw an oil spot on the floor of the garage beneath her car's motor. She stared at the spot. Her ears rang from the force of the blows. The first one forced her legs apart and then it began. She bit her lip and closed her eyes. When she opened them again, she had drawn blood from her lip and the oil spot was on the cement below the motor housing. Maybe there was something wrong with the car. She smelled them but she couldn't look at them.

She felt one and then the other and then the second one hit her again and she began to cry. The first one said something to her and then hit her again and she kept crying. The second one said to stop hitting her. The first one stood over her and said they ought to kill her. She heard that above the ringing in her ears. The second one said he was going to split. The first one lifted her purse and opened it. The second one said he was going to split. She said nothing. She turned her face toward the car and saw the oil spot on the cement just as it had been a moment before. She was crying but she didn't hear it. She didn't hear them running down the ramps to the street. She just saw the oil on the floor of the garage and had to keep staring at it.

There is a touch of Hemingway in using the third method in depiction of objective violence but that is simply because Hemingway did it better than anyone else. Simple sentences or long sentences connected by strings of *and*s and *but*s and deliberately stripped of descriptive language are very powerful instruments in writing about violent acts. The understated approach borrows a little from the "empty bracket" way by bringing up irrelevancies and giving them prominence—the victim of the rape stares at the oil spot on the garage floor. There is no hidden meaning in that focus but it carries weight simply because the writer (and reader) are imagining the action so bleakly described.

Incidentally, there is no point in slowing down detail (or stripping detail of description) to the point of giving an anatomy lesson. A graphic rape description would be unbearable (note Garp's first chapter of a proposed novel in John Irving's book; it is so long, horrible, prurient, and unbearable that the editor can't believe it's only the first chapter). Anatomy lessons almost always deaden narration, if not at the time then in everything that follows.

Back to the third method of depicting objective violence. Here is another example, about death on an army firing range.

> The instructor in the tower was shouting into the microphone. While he shouted the instruction to lock and load one clip into the rifles, Tommy Leary shoved the butt on the M1 into the hollow between his shoulder and his rib cage. He sighted the rifle and saw a deer on the slope beyond the paper targets. The deer stared at the tower, at the row of soldiers sprawled in the prone firing position on the red clay. Tommy Leary dug his elbows into the ground and he was staring at the white-tailed deer.
>
> The word "Fire" was followed by a chorus of shots. Some of the men fired very quickly and some of them fired in careful steps, first one and then another and then another, the shells flipping up from the firing chamber and to the right, out of the way. The left-handed soldiers had a problem because the rifle was designed for right-handers and the spent shells flipped across their line of vision. Tommy was right-handed. He fired twice and then he shifted a little and brought the rifle around and Sergeant Mackelson was at the end of the sights, fixed vertically on the front hair and horizontally on the rear sight, about halfway up his belly. Tommy Leary fired twice and Sergeant Mackelson leaped out of sight and fell down the firing line ridge. Tommy Leary turned the rifle back to the target line by rolling on the flat of his

belly and the deer stood still on the slope the way deer
do and Tommy lobbed a shot over the target line towards
the slope. The deer didn't move. He was too far away.
'Cease firing, cease firing' the instructor was screaming
into the microphone but some were still popping shots
at the targets. Tommy released his finger from the trigger.
He had two rounds in the clip left.

Depiction of violence subjectively is, on the face of it, easier. But
it is actually much more difficult if done well enough not to interrupt the narration. Take the rape scene earlier. It can be rendered
subjectively but how do you do it without falling into clichés or
falling into the trap of prurience?

Subjective depiction, to be successful, uses a small brush on a big
canvas that is never filled. It is concerned with detail and the
shock that external violence has on the subject. For example, a
person who has been shot or stabbed rarely sees the objective
horror of what was done to him (her). I once talked—with
detectives—to a man who had been stabbed twenty-three times
in the chest by his girlfriend. He was hooked to syrup and plasma,
he had been slightly doped, and some of his wounds were superficial but . . . twenty-three times is twenty-three times. The cops
wanted to know who did it (the girlfriend part came later), and
the guy kept saying he had cut himself in the bathroom shaving.
He just couldn't believe he had been stabbed twenty-three times.

Gunshot victims say the same sort of thing in real life. Days or
weeks later, they reconstruct the narrative of the violence done
them from an external (objective) point of view because that is the
context everyone else has dealt with and they have learned it the
way Americans learn French in Paris—in self-defense in the war of
communications.

In short, the act of violence is usually a period in punctuation
whereas everything leading up to it is exclamation.

This example is from one of my novels. I've edited it a bit using
the ellipsis method to get to the core of the illustration:

She stepped out into the bright October light. The sunlight was fragmented against the golden maples behind the apartment complex. . . . Rita Macklin stepped onto the new gravel on the lot, stopped, smiled at the sky and trees. The bad thoughts about Devereaux had left her; she would be all right the rest of the day. . . . She fumbled for her car keys in her purse and pulled them out. The car was a five-year-old Ford Escort, a minimal sort of car. . . . [A long passage describes the car, her lifestyle, her job, her attitude, a sort of going-nowhere stream of consciousness, and then] . . . She had her keys in hand as she reached the car. In the next moment, she was on the ground. She had fallen, she thought. She felt a dull sickness in her stomach and wondered if she had broken the heel of her right shoe. The shoes cost $125, which was obscene, but she had loved them when she saw them in the store on L Street. She thought her skirt would be soiled by the gravel and the dirt in the parking lot. A stupid fall and she had ruined her clothes and would have to change and miss the next flight. . . .

Rita has been shot, but not until a neighbor tells her she has been shot do we know it, though obviously something has happened. The point is, Rita—like most of us—is finding it hard to connect her world of interior monologue with what is happening around her, or, in this case, to her.

The subjective side of depiction of violence is most useful when it underscores the violence by ironic understatement or misstatement. Rita thinks about her shoes, her clothes, the reason she owns a car, thinks about falling down and missing her plane . . . all of it faintly comic in its triviality weighed against the gravity of the violence done her. Sympathy for the victim can be evoked subjectively very well by using a sort of stream-of-consciousness narrative that runs parallel and counter to the objective action.

Let's say a man is shoved in front of an El train in Chicago. Try it this way:

The train suddenly rounded the curve between the apartment buildings and the crowd along the narrow wooden platform stirred. Steve took a half step closer to the edge, looked at the train, looked down at the tracks above the street, looked at his shoes, clenched the *Tribune* in his hand, looked up again. The train rattled the wood-and-steel structure of the elevated line.

The tracks were wet from the morning rain and the third rail threw up showers of sparks. It was beautiful and dramatic and Steve smiled because it reminded him of the old man on the day the old man had taken him for his first El ride.

Steve's father had told him about the third rail, had told him that he would be dead in an instant if he ever touched the third rail. He had been so solemn that little Steve almost did not believe him until he saw the sparks showered up by a passing train.

And, in that moment, he fell.

He was on his knees on the tracks, the street was visible below between the ties, he could see the top of a green-and-white bus.

Steve blinked at the train screeching fifty feet in front of him. He stared at the double headlights. It was wasteful to have them on in broad daylight, it was broad daylight, he was going to QEM Productions and the El would be quicker and cheaper and he saw his father telling him about the third rail and the possibilities of violent death on the El, about a man who had fallen from a train, about a train that had once fallen from the tracks in the Loop . . . his sweet, cautionary father and all the sweet times of his life and the sweet, sweet smell of early summer when the grass was first cut and the third rail, he must never touch the third rail, but his father was not always right about everything and Steve had to grow up and get a job and live alone and take the El to QEM and the noise of the train screeching was even louder than his scream.

(I apologize to every English teacher for that sentence but I liked it anyway.)

I like the disjointed narrative in subjective depiction because it resembles, for me, the random, rimfire shooting of dreams during REM sleep and the victim feeling you have when you are caught in a dream and cannot move or speak or act.

> He knew it was dangerous. He was frightened all the time, even when he slept and he was safe and there were locks on the door. He thought about Sheila in that bed that one time when they had locked all the locks and taken off each other's clothes and not said a word as they got on the bed. On the bed. And then the shooting stopped. Just like that. He blinked to hear it better but it was definitely quiet, very quiet, too quiet, quiet like the grave the way Healy would say. Sheila never said a word. He was on his knees and that meant he had been shot. He didn't feel pain and he knew that they did not always feel pain at first, that some of them in the hospital said they never felt pain until the surgery was over; in any case, he had been shot. Sheila opened her legs and smiled and he slid onto her lap and into her.
>
> There was absolutely no pain at all and Sheila never said a word, it was so quiet, just like now, the silence had a sound to it because it was so intense and it would be all right to lie down now, Sheila said it was all right, and the ground was as soft and yielding as a bed, as laying down in Sheila's lap in the dark silence of the locked room.

Finally, the question to be asked of violence in narration is what purpose it will serve. Violence in itself is a willing character and this sometimes fools a writer into thinking the amiable clod can do everything he claims. Violence as character is deceitful to the writer and can lull the writer to laziness. If the narration is slowing down, violence suggests a shot of itself will pep the thing up; in most cases, it merely points out how weak the narration has been up to then and how weak it is following the pep pill of violence.

The world is violent, so violent that we become inured to depictions of violence. The coin of violence has been debased by screenwriters who patch up leaky TV and movie scripts with violence that is merely routinely spectacular. The clichés of TV and movies make it much harder for novelists and short story writers to convey the suspense and horror of violence.

The writer should remember the old newspaperism that violence only counts when it touches home. A ferry overturning in India in which a thousand died does not move the heart as surely as the death of a boy trapped in a well in Texas or the murder of a grandmother down the block. Tragedy is personal, and violence, tragedy's sister, best serves the writer when it is personal. The best way to make it personal is not to stage John Ford fights in saloons but to bring the haunting finality of tragedy to it.

If you do not believe in the violence—if you are not affected by it at the moment you write it down—then you are a hack and do a disservice to your reader or are really engaging in comedy. Life is not all Ingmar Bergman but it isn't all Roger Rabbit either; the bigger the paintbrush of violence, the less real it is. Depictions of violence are miniatures.

CLUES, RED HERRINGS, AND OTHER PLOT DEVICES

■ *P.M. Carlson*

"But I want *you* to be the victim. And the person who kills you can be Deirdre Henderson. The repressed plain girl whom nobody notices."

"There you are, Ariadne," said Robin. "The whole plot of your next novel presented to you. All you'll have to do is work in a few false clues, and—of course—do the actual writing."

—Agatha Christie,
Mrs. McGinty's Dead

"All you'll have to do is work in a few false clues. . . ." Yeah, sure. Anyone who's ever tried to plot a mystery knows that Robin's careless words to Ariadne Oliver gloss over one of the most difficult and most important aspects of plotting.

My own books generally start with a complicated cluster of an unusual motive or an unusual murder method with a setting that I find interesting and a character or two whose problems I want to explore. Even at this primitive stage it's almost impossible to answer the cocktail-party question, "Where do you get your ideas?" because a lot of sources have already fed into the cluster. But once this cluster of "ideas" has jelled into the basic triangle of victim, murderer, and detective, the hard work of plotting begins.

A logical story of the murder must be laid out early, of course, even though it will be revealed in a less logical order and won't be seen in full until the end of the book. Signs of this logical story must be thought out carefully for the detective (and reader) to discover as the story progresses. At this early stage I try not to tie things down too much. My notes are full of question marks—maybe this, maybe that—but it's important to me to get a rough sketch of the true direction to be tracked. I'll be subjecting my detective to plenty of distractions and agonies, but this is the trail my hunter must ultimately follow. As Watson writes of Sherlock Holmes in "The Boscombe Valley Mystery,"

> Men who had only known the quiet thinker and logician of Baker Street would have failed to recognize him. His face flushed and darkened. His brows were drawn into two hard black lines, while his eyes shone out from beneath them with a steely glitter. His face was bent downward, his shoulders bowed, his lips compressed, and his veins stood out like whipcord in his long, sinewy neck. His nostrils seemed to dilate with a purely animal lust for the chase, and his mind was so absolutely concentrated upon the matter before him that a question or remark fell unheeded upon his ears, or, at the most, only provoked a quick, impatient snarl in reply.

The metaphor of detective as hunting dog hot on the scent has been with us for a long time. And it's useful to remind myself that readers too are hot on the scent, a whole pack of eager hounds chasing after my foxy murderer. Some readers are wily old hunters who know all the tricks and keep up with the detective or even surge ahead for a few pages; others are mere pups, easily distracted by the scenery. All of them enjoy the chase, and all of them deserve a good hunt.

Enter the red herring.

The original red herring was a smoked herring, actually more brownish than red, with a powerful scent very attractive to hunting dogs. It was dragged across the true trail to try to distract the hounds from their real objective. In a detective story, the distraction must be similarly powerful.

So once I've outlined the basic story of the victim and the murderer, together with the unusual motive or unusual murder method that links them, I go back to the victim and think about him or her. Who else might want this person murdered, and why? Several more stories have to be outlined about people who have good reasons to desire the victim dead and who have the means and opportunity to kill the victim. At this point I often start grumbling that a mystery writer's lot is not a happy one, and why didn't I decide to write the kind of novels where one plot is enough?

But I plug away, thinking up more stories, still with lots of maybes and question marks. The task is harder because, like the original red herrings dragged across a trail, these extra stories should cross the true murder story from time to time.

For example, suppose we want to write a story that includes a gourmet cook—we'll call him Dan. In a gourmet shop window we notice a handsome marble rolling pin, used for French pastries. We, of course, are not attracted by the thought of crisp, airy napoleons and éclairs. Well, okay, we *are* attracted by the thought, but even more by the thought that this is the ideal blunt instrument for the plot we're hatching. It's unusual and distinctive, and heavy. It can definitely be a clue on our true trail. So, first, we make sure that our murderer is able to lay hands on our (now fictional) marble rolling pin in time to do the murder. If Dan the gourmet cook is the murderer, we may decide that this distinctive weapon will be the decisive clue—he is the *only* person who has access to it. In this case, we'll probably want to have it disappear from the scene of the crime, hidden somehow by clever Dan. Throughout the book, then, the detective, the police, and (we hope) the readers will be wondering about the weapon used.

Now, how do we confuse the trail? One way is to give our red herring characters access to similar objects. Perhaps one character is remodeling a room, and has a tool chest with a variety of hammers and mallets. Another character may be a golfer with a handsome trophy that has a cylindrical, heavy pedestal base. But only our detective notices that Dan the gourmet cook has recently rearranged his collection of expensive kitchen implements to mask the absence of a rolling pin.

On the other hand, maybe we don't want Dan to be the murderer. We can still provide false weapons to various characters as above.

Or we may want the true weapon to be identified early in the story. Now the game is to provide access to the weapon for several red herring characters. Dan owns the rolling pin. Let's suppose he keeps it in his kitchen, in full view. In that case his family and guests have access to it. When? We can narrow down the time to the few minutes of a visit, or expand it. For example, Agatha Christie has a crucial weapon turn up in Suspect A's house—but it turns out that it was purchased at a church sale, donated by Suspect B, and no one can remember if it was the sale preceding the murder or the sale following the murder. Furthermore, Suspect A's house is a boardinghouse and is never kept locked, so the entire village may have had access to the weapon at the time of the murder.

We can also narrow the field of suspects to a few who had opportunity to steal the weapon, and then widen the field later in the book. For example, let's suppose that the owner of the lethal marble rolling pin, Dan, cooks a gourmet meal for several suspects—Ann, Jan, and Fran. Naturally the rolling pin disappears at this time. We know that Stan and Nan have never been near Dan's kitchen. Now, after much detective work, we learn that in fact Ann is the one who took the rolling pin from Dan's kitchen, but she claims she lost it. Things are looking bad for her, when—aha!—our detective remembers that Stan or Nan could have stolen it from Ann's bag when they met her on the way home from Dan's.

A truly foxy murderer will probably create false clues too. In that classic maze of false trails, *The Five Red Herrings* by Dorothy L. Sayers, the murderer provides himself with an alibi using a complicated bucketful of false clues including meals, bicycles, painting techniques, clothing, and most notoriously, train schedules. Luckily for Lord Peter Wimsey, the murderer makes one small mistake in his haste, so that after the lies are stripped away from the stories of the five red herring characters, Wimsey is able to reconstruct the crime and cover-up in almost every elaborate detail. When I'm sketching in my alternate stories, I often find it useful to lay out a big chart showing each character's activities at the crucial times in the narrative. It boggles the mind to think of what Sayers's chart for *The Five Red Herrings* must have looked like.

One device Sayers did not use in that book was the frame—the situation in which the true target is not the murder victim, but someone who will be falsely accused of the crime. In a case like this, the detective's usual starting point—the victim's life—may turn out to be largely red herrings, and there will be many circumstantial clues pointing to the wrong person. It is not until the investigation turns to the accused person's life that progress is made.

Since my books are often fair play whodunits, I've been concentrating so far on the kinds of plots that are used in such books. In the classic fair play whodunit formula, there are perhaps half a dozen suspects, and the clues and false clues point first at one, then at another, in an evenhanded way.

Clues and red herrings may be handled a little differently in the classic quest formula, typical of many private eye books. While the same kinds of misdirections that I've been talking about will work, and many private eye plots involve wondering which of several suspects may be behind the gore, there is often a shift of emphasis. The trail may occupy a smaller proportion of the book, for many reasons. In a country house whodunit, for example, the world that led up to the murder is given from the beginning. But a private eye in Sara Paretsky's Chicago, or Robert Crais's Los Angeles, or Sue Grafton's Santa Teresa lives among wide-open possibilities. The first task is often to discover which of the many worlds inhabited by the victim is the one that got him into trouble. Did he do drugs? Did he embezzle from his firm? Did he have gambling debts? Did he cheat on his wife? While all of these questions may eventually arise in the closed world of classic puzzle mysteries, a private eye often has to do extensive preliminary work before the appropriate set of suspects even appears. To use the foxhound analogy, the detective has to hunt through several fields before he even picks up the scent of the true fox.

A quest plot may also give more emphasis to the final overcoming of the quarry. Once the fox is found and cornered, there's a bigger fight—as though the fox turned out to be a wolf pack that outnumbered our lonely private eye. Several chapters may be devoted to the excitement and danger as the detective uses all her intelligence and physical ability to plan and carry out the defeat of the awesome adversary.

Because the private eye may need more chapters to find the correct trail and more chapters to overcome the villain, the actual trail-following aspect of a quest plot may end up being considerably shorter and more straightforward than that of a puzzle plot. Weapons tend to be guns rather than unknown blunt instruments that turn out to be gourmet kitchen implements. Progress along the true trail may be blocked by simpler means than the elaborate counterplots of Wimsey's or Miss Marple's adversaries: A bureaucrat refuses to release needed information, or the villain's henchmen beat up the detective and make off with the only known clue, or the client gets cold feet and tries to stop the private eye from proceeding.

My favorite obstacles are those that grow from character. My detective Maggie Ryan is a loving parent and sometimes has difficulty believing evil can be done by others who love children. Keith Peterson's tough investigative reporter in *The Trapdoor* is haunted by his only daughter's suicide, and must courageously overcome enormous psychological obstacles to discover the truth about a rash of teen suicides. Even Lord Peter must struggle occasionally to go on with the hunt because he is shattered at the thought of the punishment the murderer must undergo. There are many possible plot devices like these to intensify the interest of the story even while blocking progress toward the solution.

"All you'll have to do is work in a few false clues." It's a long and sometimes painful stage of mystery writing—but as things fall into place, as our stories full of question marks and maybes are braided into a fine wriggly plot, it's a matter of fun and even pride. And when you're done? Well, as Agatha Christie's character says so offhandedly, we must, of course, "do the actual writing." But someone else can tell you about *that* little difficulty.

THE BOOK STOPS HERE

■ *Lawrence Block*

It's the most mysterious thing. You're working on a book, plug-ging away at it like The Little Engine That Could, turning out a page a day or five pages a day or ten pages a day, watching those finished pages pile up, and beginning to see the light at the end of the tunnel. You don't want to get too cocky, don't want to get the Big Editor in the Sky mad at you, but, by George, it certainly looks as though you've breezed past the halfway mark and are closing fast on the three-quarter pole. All you have to do is keep showing up for work every day, keep putting your behind on the chair and your fingers on the keys, and it's just a matter of time, and not too much time at that, before the book will be finished.

Oh, you may still have work to do. Some light revision at the very least. Maybe a formal second draft. No matter, that's the easy part, what the military would call a mopping-up operation. When your first draft is done your book is written, and you can jump up and down and call people and celebrate and even take that shower you've been promising yourself for so long. And the first draft's almost done, it'll be done any minute, all you have to do is keep at it and—

And, all of a sudden, kablooey.

You're stuck. The book's going nowhere. It's dead in the water, finished, kaput.

Now what?

The conventional wisdom holds that what I've just described is a disaster, and it's not terrribly hard to guess how it became the conventional wisdom. The conventional wisdom goes further to suggest that the thing to do when a book gets stuck is to lower your metaphorical head and charge forward. (It helps, I suppose, if you're wearing a metaphorical helmet.) By pushing on, by damning the torpedos and going full speed ahead, you can go right through whatever's impeding you and get the book finished as planned. You can turn a deaf ear to the voice that keeps telling you there's something wrong. You can brush all those doubts and anxieties right out of your mind. Casting them as the road and yourself as the chicken, you can Get To The Other Side.

Well, sure. And sometimes that's exactly what you ought to do. And sometimes it's not.

When a book grinds to a halt, it may have done so for a reason. To avoid looking for the reason is a little like overlooking the trouble lights on a car's dashboard. You can run the car when those lights go on, and you can even do as the previous owner of my car seems to have done, disconnecting a wire so that the lights won't bug you like some sort of mechanical conscience. Maybe you'll wind up all right, but there's a good chance that sooner or later they'll come for you with a tow truck.

A couple of examples. Several years ago, I was writing the fifth volume in a series of mysteries about Bernie Rhodenbarr, a burglar and bookseller by profession, a solver of homicides by circumstance. I was 180 pages into what looked likely to be a 300-page manuscript, when Something Went Wrong. I spent a day staring at the typewriter without getting anything done. I took a day off, and another day off. By the end of the week I realized that I was in trouble. I didn't know what was wrong, but I knew something was wrong.

Now I could have barreled through it and forced the book over the finish line. I knew who the killer was, and how and why the crime had taken place. I had not painted myself into any impossible plot corners. But there was something wrong, and I couldn't see how to fix it, not least of all because I wasn't altogether sure what it was.

I still don't know exactly what was wrong. I think there was something gone off-stroke in the book's timing. I can't tell you how or why I screwed it up in the first place, or just what enabled me to fix it. I know what happened—I moped around for a few weeks, during which time I despaired that the book would join the great body of manuscripts I've abandoned forever over the years. While this was happening, I suspect a portion of my unconscious mind was playing with the problem and looking for a solution. One evening I had a long conversation about the book with a friend of mine. I don't recall what either of us said, or that a specific solution came out of our conversation, but I walked away from it somehow knowing how to proceed. I started the book over from the beginning, using most of the scenes I had written but fitting them together somewhat differently, and running the whole thing through the typewriter again. This time, everything worked. I finished the book without a snag, and I think it's the best one in the series.

I probably could have finished the book by just staying with it and forcing myself to write. And it probably would have been publishable. But I'm sure it was better for my having had trouble with it, and for having surrendered to the trouble instead of trying to ride roughshod over it.

More recently, I settled in and went to work on a new Matthew Scudder novel. I'd spent half a year thinking about the book and felt ready to write it. I had no trouble getting started, worked at a fast clip, and had 200 pages written in a couple of weeks. The writing went well, and I was pleased with the scenes and characters that I had developed.

But, by the time I was a little ways past the halfway mark, I realized that I'd managed a kind of reverse synergy—i.e., the whole of what I'd written was rather less than the sum of its parts. The book was taking too long to get going, and it was wandering off in far too many directions. Some of my best scenes and characters were just marking time, doing nothing to advance the plot. And the plot itself was unwieldy and unworkable. I was going to have to start over. The story I wanted to write was in there somewhere, and I had a feeling I could find it, but all of that would have to wait. I needed time away from the book, and eventually I would have to scrap 90 percent of what I'd written and start over from the beginning.

This didn't mean what I'd written was a waste of time; it was all part of the process, and I evidently had to go through it in order to find the story I'll eventually write. (At least I hope I'll eventually write it, if all of this is to have a happy ending.)

Again, I could have forced myself to keep writing, could have overruled my own doubts and anxieties. And I could have finished the book that way. It wouldn't have been very good, and I'm not sure it would have been publishable, but you never know what is or isn't publishable these days. It certainly wouldn't have emerged as a book I would have been pleased with.

The implication would seem to be clear: If you get stuck on a book, there must be something wrong with it. Set it aside or fix it.

But I could furnish other examples that would seem to prove the opposite. I have had books stall in much the same fashion, have pushed on and seen them through to completion, and have had them turn out just fine. Some years ago, when I was writing a series of paperback suspense novels about a sort of freelance spy named Evan Tanner, I noticed that I always seemed to hit a bad patch somewhere around page 125. (The Tanner books ran around 200 pages in manuscript.) I always stayed with what I was writing, and the books always worked out all right, and when I read them over afterward there was no evident sag or quagmire around page 125.

I suspect what happened was that I tended to have a sort of failure of confidence at around that point. Once I got a chapter or so further along in the work, my confidence returned of its own accord and I felt capable of completing the work. I don't know the source of this, but I have a hunch it had more to do with me than with the work. Years later, during my career as the world's slowest but most determined long-distance runner, I experienced a similar sinking feeling at about the same stage—say, six miles into a ten-mile race. There would be a point at which I felt I really ought to drop out of the race, that to go further would only result in injury, that I couldn't possibly go the distance. I never did quit a race short of the finish (although there were times I probably should have), and once I got a kilometer or so past that crisis point I always knew I would make it. The two processes are vastly different, and none of my runs were the athletic equivalent of publishable, but I don't think it was coincidental that I tended to feel on the verge of failure at the same point in books as in races.

On the other hand, maybe I only noticed crises of this sort when they came at that particular stage, a little past the halfway mark. Maybe I had comparable crises, comparable failures of nerve, at other points along the way—but I didn't recognize them for what they were.

I was packing my office not long ago and I came across two 30-page chunks of manuscript, one written two years ago, the other a little older. Each was the opening of a novel about Bernie Rhodenbarr, and each had been forever abandoned around the thirtieth page. I had stopped working on them because they just plain weren't working. The writing felt labored, the dialogue seemed flat, and I wisely stopped work on them and said the hell with it.

Well, I read both of those chunks of manuscript, and I was amazed. I don't have a clue what I thought was wrong with them at the time I stopped work on them. My writing seemed as spritely as it ever gets, my dialogue was as crisp and lively as I could have wanted it, and all either manuscript lacked to be perfectly publishable was another 270 pages in the same vein. Looking back, it strikes me as highly probable that I would have been incapable of producing those 270 pages back then, and an unconscious recognition of this fact soured me on what I was writing. Not really wanting to go on, I decided that the grapes I'd already reached were sour.

The point, though, is that in neither case did I feel I'd hit a snag. Instead I just figured I'd had a false start, and one that only represented the work of a couple of days. I have tossed off and subsequently tossed out a chapter of a book or a few pages of a short story on more occasions than I can remember, and so have most writers I know, and so what? You can't expect the world to salute every time you run one up the flagpole. Often the only way to find out if something is going to work is to try writing it, and to drop it if it fizzles out.

You can avoid this sort of false start if you never write anything without having it clear in your mind, but you might miss out on a lot of stories that way. Donald Westlake wrote an opening chapter once because he had this image of a guy crossing the George Washington Bridge on foot. He didn't know who the guy was or why he was walking across the bridge, but decided that he (like the guy) could cross that bridge when he came to it. The book turned out to be *The Hunter*, the first of sixteen books (under the pseudonym of "Richard Stark") about a professional criminal named Parker, who the guy on the bridge turned out to be.

And if it hadn't worked out that way, if Parker, upon crossing the bridge, had turned into a drugstore instead of turning into a terrific series character, well, so what? Don would have wasted a day's work, and we all do that often enough, don't we?

You might think that outlining could make a difference, especially in avoiding snags late in the game, where the book is two-thirds written and you can't think of a thing to have happen on the next page. If you've got a detailed outline, all of those problems are presumably worked out in advance. The book can't hit a real snag because you always know what's going to happen next.

Sure you do.

Although I haven't outlined anything in quite a few years now, I used outlines on many occasions over the years, some of them sketchy, others more elaborate. And it's unarguably true that a writer working from an outline always knows what he originally intended to have happen next.

But there's no guarantee it'll work. Sometimes the novel proves to have a will of its own and veers away from the outline. This isn't necessarily a bad thing, but it does mean that you have nothing but your imagination and your vocabulary to help you figure out what happens next.

And, even when the plot hews close to what you've outlined, there's no guarantee that what worked in outline will work in manuscript. Sometimes, indeed, a novel will stall out around the two-thirds or the three-quarters mark because the outlined plot just isn't working and the writer's unable to loosen up and make the necessary departures from it.

So what's the answer?

Beats me. Every book is a case unto itself, and every time we sit down to write one we take a plunge into uncharted waters. It is a hazardous business, this novel-writing dodge, and it doesn't cease to be so after long years in the game. Novelists who have been at it since Everest was a molehill still find themselves leaving a book unfinished or finishing an unpublishable one. (Sometimes a good writer gets away with a bad book and publishes it, and sometimes it sells as well as his good books, but only one's accountant is gladdened when that sort of thing happens. The object is not to sneak by with a bad book; it's to write a good one.)

So, when a book hits a snag and the sun goes out and the moon turns black, do you:

1. Keep right on going and finish it? or

2. Figure out where you went wrong and make it right? or

3. Decide that it doesn't say Purina, and bury it in the yard?

The answer, I guess, is:

4. Any or all of the above, depending.

All you have to do is figure out which, and you have to figure it out anew each time it happens.

Look, I never said this was going to be easy.

IN THE BEGINNING
IS THE END

■ *John Lutz*

"Of course!" you think, as you read the last paragraph or sentence of a successful mystery short story or novel, "this is how everything *had* to turn out." The ending does more than simply surprise you. It seems not only possible but plausible. That's because the writer knew from the beginning where the story was going.

Writing is an extremely individualistic endeavor, so none of the rules apply to everyone. There are a few writers who sit down and begin a tale without a scintilla of an idea as to where it's headed. Most of these writers never sell anything. Some do, and some of them are superb writers, but they're members of a small minority among the professionals I know. If you're sure you're one of these rare and wondrous creatures, move on to another section of this book, and good luck.

Still with me? Good. I think the odds are better for our kind of writer. Beginning a work of fiction without having at least some idea as to the ending is something like jumping into your car and driving away without any idea as to your destination. It's true you might arrive someplace interesting, but you're sure to meander getting there and spend time driving through plenty of not-so-interesting places. And meandering, digressing, is fatal to good fiction.

As in taking a trip by car, you need to know your destination before you set out. And, in fiction, the trip should be at least half the fun. When you and the reader reach the destination at the end of the story or novel, the reader will remember how the two of you got there, and the more direct, memorable, and plausible the journey, the better. The techniques of foreshadowing and the planting of clues are invaluable in creating the above qualities, in preparing the reader for the destination only you know about.

To write good mystery fiction, you should know the difference between these two techniques, keeping in mind that while they are, by definition, different elements of fiction, the distinction isn't always clear, and there is some overlapping.

The planting of clues is exactly what the term implies. Let's say you're writing a short story wherein Colonel Mustard has been found dead in his study, a knife wound in his chest but no weapon in the room. All doors and windows have been locked from the inside, and there are no hiding places or hidden passages. There are no footprints in the freshly fallen snow beneath the windows or surrounding the house, and all of the house's occupants have ironclad alibis.

Now, let me explain the missing weapon. Fortunately we're not really writing this story, because I have no idea how to explain the rest of the circumstances, as I had no idea how to explain them when I sat down and wrote this. Do you have any ideas? See what I mean about how this can get you into trouble?

The missing knife, as many of you have no doubt guessed, was fashioned from a blade of ice which, after being wielded as the murder weapon, melted. Now, if you were to create a blood-tinted puddle near the body, which your detective will later determine is the melted weapon, you would be creating a clue. The reader, as well as your detective, would know about this puddle and have a chance—a slim one, if you've written this correctly—to figure out what it means. At tale's end, the detective could point out the presence of this puddle to some of the other characters, as well as to the reader, as evidence leading to his or her conclusion about the method of murder. And of course method often leads to opportunity, motive, and suspect. So, a clue.

If you were to make the colonel's study uncommonly warm, mention that the eventually-to-be-revealed murderer was seen getting a midnight snack from the freezer, drop the fact that one of the suspects was earlier leaning out a window (above which, icicles hang) and wearing gloves (needed to wield the icy dagger), you have foreshadowed.

The puddle next to the corpse was certainly made by something, is tangible and remarkable, and *must* mean something, even if it isn't relevant to the murder. It requires an explanation, if the writer is to keep faith with the reader. But the above mentioned circumstances don't necessarily mean anything other than what they appear to mean. It might well be that the murder simply occurred on a relatively warm day, that the suspect raiding the refrigerator merely had an attack of the munchies, and certainly there's nothing unusual about wearing gloves in winter; the writer might well be remiss in *not* mentioning gloves in a description of the suspect's outdoor attire. Yet because these elements are part of the story, when the reader gets to the final paragraphs, he or she will find the explanation of the frozen weapon plausible. Committing murder this way is certainly possible, and the puddle as *clue* will lend the impression that if the reader had been just a bit sharper in regard to that in particular, he or she might have figured out this entire nasty business a few steps ahead of your detective.

Notice I said "impression." You shouldn't actually give your readers a chance to be a jump ahead of your detective, or those successful in doing so will be disappointed at not being fooled, and reviewers who manage to figure things out prematurely will impolitely suggest that maybe you should give up writing and sell insurance, or perhaps surrender your firstborn and slit your wrists for wasting their time and straining their eyes.

Okay, we've taken care of both possibility and plausibility: The puddle as clue, since its presence from the beginning suggests some explanation is needed, and that explanation falls solidly within the realm of possibility. And as foreshadowing we've pro-

vided weather, snack, and gloves; they don't necessarily mean anything unusual, but at the end of the story they do add up to
plausibility.

Clues provide the eventual explanation of the crime, and it must
be a logical explanation. Foreshadowing is what makes that explanation, the outcome of your story, seem in retrospect not only
plausible but inevitable. Not only should the reader have figured
out this foul matter, but it *had* to end this way as surely as the last
domino in a row is fated to fall once the first is toppled. Fate
seemed to decree it. Your foreshadowing has created this impression. There's that "impression" business again—we know not too
many things in real life fall as predictably as dominoes. But in fiction
they do, so you must topple your first domino in the proper
direction.

Some examples:

In my short story "The Real Shape of the Coast" written for
Ellery Queen Mystery Magazine, the detective, an inmate of an
insane asylum, eventually reaches the inescapable conclusion that
he himself is the murderer. In the first paragraph is the sentence
"There are twenty of the sharp-angled buildings, each rising bricked
and hard out of the sand like an undeniable fact." This isn't in any
way a clue, but in a subtle way it foreshadows the ending: Eventually the detective's investigation will build what even he must
acknowledge, the undeniable fact of his guilt. This domino, nudged
to fall at the correct angle, was made possible because when I
began the story I knew where I wanted the final domino to drop.

Consider the opening of "The Day of the Picnic" published in
Alfred Hitchcock's Mystery Magazine:

> "South into the hot barren country of Southern Califor-
> nia, east all the way into Arizona, that's the range of
> the California Condor."
> "Those birds fascinate you, don't they?" Judith asks.
> It is another of her stupid questions that are beginning
> to annoy me more and more.

Oh-oh. Know where this one's going? I did when I sat down to write it. I knew Judith had a date with a condor. And the reader, at least on some level, suspected it, so that when it happened it seemed all the more plausible as well as possible.

One trick in planting clues is to integrate them in the text so they seem incidental, or perhaps seem to be there for some other, obvious reason (that overlapping mentioned earlier). The reader might not find it unusual that there is a puddle in Colonel Mustard's study, for instance, if clutched in the colonel's dead hand is a plastic drinking straw. No drinking glass in the locked room, though, so maybe the reader should be wondering about *that*.

Another effective way of planting clues is through dialogue. One of your characters ponders aloud about the meaning of this or that, perhaps the fact that the straw is unbent and looks new, and has no liquid trapped in it by air pressure. A second character might explain why this is so. Perhaps the colonel used the straw only to stir his drink, not to sip it. But, as it turns out, the explanation will be inadequate. The straw had nothing to do with the puddle, which had nothing to do with anything the colonel was drinking (the colonel was using it as a bookmark, and it's had time and resilience to spring back to perfect roundness). Still, the reader will assume that he or she had the opportunity to agree with the first character. The choice was there to be made. The fact that the straw appeared unused *was* mentioned. Being fair within limits, yet deceptive, is part of the game; an obvious clue doesn't always have to be relevant to the crime itself and turn up as Exhibit A later in court.

Which brings us to yet another effective way of planting a clue: We can obscure it in a parade of possibly significant facts. The puddle and unused straw might be mentioned along with an unusual hat on a hook, an open ledger book on the colonel's desk (foreshadowing the explanation as to the use of the straw), a fishbowl containing a piranha (a possible source of the puddle, even though the fish isn't a red herring). None of these other than the puddle is important, and can later be explained away—perhaps the colonel was a cruel and stingy slumlord who kept the books and collected hats and vicious fish—but the reader is likely to fix attention on any or all of the more bizarre possible clues. Just as a solitary duck in a flock being shot at by hunters has a good chance of individual survival, your clue will probably fly by unnoticed only to touch down at the end of the story.

Foreshadowing requires equal subtlety. It should register more on the reader's subconscious than conscious mind, be more emotion than fact, so that at the end of the story the neural connections are made, and possibility and plausibility merge and become indistinguishable.

A good way to foreshadow is through character. In the opening paragraph of my story "High Stakes" from *The Saint Mystery Magazine*, a man checks into a sleazy hotel with one suitcase, tips the teenage bellhop a dollar, and is sneered at. Is it a complete surprise that he's a luckless petty gambler who commands no respect, is visited by mob enforcers, and at the end of the story is treated with disdain? His stay at the hotel doesn't turn out to be a pleasant one, which seems plausible to the reader, because in the first paragraph it's been established that he's down on his luck and is the sort of person who evokes a teenage bellhop's open contempt.

Life is a random adventure, but fiction isn't. Everything on the page means something, and often more than one thing. If in the final paragraph of your story your main character, an undercover policeman, is going to be killed with his own gun, there is no problem about convincing the reader that he'd be carrying a gun. Everyone knows undercover cops usually are armed. But the ending would pack more punch if earlier in the story you described him slipping the gun into its hidden holster, or described the gun itself, or even merely established the gun was there by having him adjust it beneath his clothes as he stepped down from a bus. That way, at the end of the story, he's using a gun that has already been made real in the reader's mind, a gun the reader can see and hear when the trigger is squeezed. Since the gun is more real, when it's used the action will seem more real, and the accompanying vicarious emotion in the mind and soul of the reader will be more real. And that's what fiction's all about, engaging the reader's emotions. If you don't do that, you are simply using words to convey information, and you might as well be writing instruction manuals, where the twist ending is that the manufacturer left out a screw.

One of the main pitfalls to avoid when writing an ending is what I call The Horse Nearing the Barn Syndrome. Writing fiction is satisfying but hard work, and the tendency is to hurry things along when you know you're approaching the end of a story or novel. You want that feeling of accomplishment, and the sooner you type "The End" the sooner you'll experience it. But you haven't done your job if the reader senses this impatience in the work. The story's pacing should remain firmly under your control, so that the ending seems a natural outcome of what went before. No inconsistency should jar the reader from your fictional world, or put him or her outside the story looking in, rather than experiencing on a vicarious level what your characters are experiencing. It's comforting to know the reader's cooperating with you in achieving this mesmerizing effect. Even rooting for you. Nobody begins reading a story or novel wanting to be disappointed.

The writer's job is to create a thoroughly wrought and believable fictional world, weave a seamless illusion, and to draw the reader into that world. In most cases, it should be a world that ends not with a whimper but a bang. And the bang has to make sense.

The next time you read a story whose twist ending leaves you breathless with envy and admiration, ask yourself, Is it possible the writer isn't really all that clever, but only seems so because he or she knew from the first word where the story was going?

Of course!

REVISION

■ *Jan Burke*

I can't write five words but that I change seven.

—Dorothy Parker

As frustrating as writing the first draft of a manuscript may be at times, we who write also often experience exhilarating moments along the way. Those moments when we say just what we mean, just as we'd like to say it. Those moments of discovery—when we walk into a room with a protagonist and are surprised at what we find there. Or turn our heads to hear the distinct voice of a character who is speaking for the first time. Moments when the characters take over and scenes seem to write themselves. Some theorize that the compulsion to write is rooted in our addiction to such moments—we tough out the worst times because we know how good life can be when the writing is going well.

Revision is seldom embraced with the same joy. Some new writers fantasize never having to revise all, others accept the inevitability of revision but don't look forward to it, and even experienced novelists begin to add expletives to their working titles as they grow weary of rereading a work they've spent months or years creating. You'd be surprised how many famous novels have lived a good part of their histories being known as *The *&$#! Book*.

And no wonder. A first draft is a courtship—terrifying and stimulating. Infatuation is allowed. Revision is noticing your lover's voice is a little grating when she gets excited, or finding his car blocking yours in the driveway when you're late to work, or discovering a receipt from the local No Tell Motel in your lover's pocket—and you've never been to the No Tell. Revision tests what the book is worth to you, how much you believe in it, and whether it's time to move on to something that holds more promise.

Revision also tests our ability to be honest with ourselves about our strengths and our weaknesses. Who enjoys that sort of honesty, really? Yet for all but a few enlightened geniuses, who probably aren't reading handbooks or worrying enough about being crazy, revision is an integral part of the writing process. For most of us, rewriting will be necessary for the good of the book.

Right? Well, now for a confession. I've come to like it!

These days, I think of revision as one of the great job benefits of being a writer. Commercial airline pilots do not get to make a complete hash of their daily work. No one wants a brain surgeon who's just going to take a stab at it. And I'd prefer my tax accountant did not create a return that was "not quite there yet." But I'm a writer, so—hooray!—I get to revise.

It would be a miracle if I created a perfect manuscript on the first try. I don't expect this of myself. Instead I do my best without worrying if it is indeed the best I can do. Knowing I will be able to work out problems in revision is freeing rather than confining. I tell my inner critic, one of my creativity's worst enemies, that it will have to step aside and wait its turn.

When to Revise

When does that critic get its turn? Should you begin to revise your manuscript during the writing of the first draft? Only after the entire manuscript is finished? Or should you set a manuscript aside for five weeks before beginning to revise?

I would love to be able to tell you that manuscripts are like loaves of bread and all you need do is set the oven at a certain temperature and bake them for a given amount of time. "Wait fifteen days, four hours, and thirty-three seconds, then begin revision. It works the same for everyone." Alas, writing is not a one-recipe-fits-all endeavor. This is probably for the best—otherwise the result might be uniform but dull bread.

Revision is one more process through which each writer must find his or her own way, and while it may take some time and experimentation to learn what method works best for you, mastering this part of the craft of writing will be well worth it.

Some writers find it best to move through the first draft of a manuscript without pause. Once the story gets going, they don't want to halt the process. If they come across something that may be a problem, they dog-ear that page corner or place a note in their manuscripts, but they don't do any correcting until the book is finished. They find this method allows them to focus separately on the tasks of creating and revising. Some say this method makes it easier for a writer to find his or her voice. If you allow yourself to simply enjoy telling the story the first time through, anxieties about pacing or grammar won't get in the way of your style. You can delay worrying about perfection and write. By insisting that your inner critic must wait its turn, you may find the process of creating a manuscript more enjoyable.

Other writers, however, would be driven crazy by this approach. Instead, they do at least some revising as they go along. Some begin each day's work by lightly revising the previous day's output. Those who favor this style find that going back over these earlier pages allows them to "warm up" while they write, and to once again immerse themselves in the fictional world they are creating. I've met writers who tell me they aren't able to go on to the next page until they review the page they've just finished.

Some writers begin revising a manuscript almost immediately after the first draft is finished. Many others wait two to six weeks (or longer) before attempting any revision, allowing the manuscript to rest, so that when they look at it again, they are seeing it with a little distance, or at least at a point when they are refreshed and able to change gears for this different task.

Whether you do all your revising at once or revise to some degree as you go, sooner or later the entire manuscript must be considered as a whole. If you're writing your novel on a computer, print out the manuscript—don't attempt to read for revision without a hard copy of your work. You will see things in print that will escape your attention on a screen.

What to Look For

Most writers make more than one pass through a manuscript for revision—there are many aspects of a manuscript to be considered, and sometimes it is easier to focus on these a few at a time. Even if you revise as you write, some problems can only be discovered when the manuscript is read from start to finish rather than piecemeal.

As you read, watch for any writing that calls attention to itself, writing that takes the reader out of the imaginary world you've created and dazzles him with your prose. You'll sometimes have to cut passages that please you, ridding the manuscript of what feeds your ego but is not good for the book. Leaving something in just because it demonstrates how clever you are is something like giving chocolate to a dog. Understandably, it gives you pleasure, but it's not good for the dog.

Here are some elements of crime fiction you should consider while reading for revision. You may find it easiest to evaluate these aspects of your manuscript in separate readings.

The Opening

Are we plunged into the problem facing the protagonist early on, or is so much time spent setting up the story, we're in the middle of the book before anything begins to happen? Is the tension between antagonist and protagonist present from the start?

A strong opening is important, but lately I've heard editors complain that some writers put so much effort into a strong opening, the next few chapters have little to recommend them. New writers also run the risk of polishing the life out of a first chapter.

A friend who served on an award committee once told me that she received an overwhelming number of books that began with the protagonist waking up in the morning, or with a weather report.

If your first chapter starts with an alarm clock ringing on a rainy day, consider trying a more refreshing approach.

Structure, Pacing, and Logic

Does the story build from a strong beginning toward an inevitable end? Does the protagonist's problem get worse by the middle of the book, or is all the shouting over at the end of chapter two?

While you were trying to create twists, did your story become disjointed, or do you play fair with the reader, with the groundwork for the solution laid all along the way? Does the reader know everything your protagonist knows? Has the reader seen all the protagonist has seen?

One of the best ways to examine your manuscript's pacing is to read it aloud, whether to a listener who can offer constructive criticism or simply to yourself. You'll usually hear when a chapter is dragging or if a scene is redundant. You'll also hear which words are repeated too often and probably recognize the places where your beautiful prose sounds stiff or pretentious.

Ask yourself questions along the way. Does *every* scene move the story forward? Have the characters revealed themselves or changed in some way by the end of the scene? Does description or dialogue bring the action to a halt? Do characters give long, unnecessary lectures based on the fascinating research you did on a subject? Do we really need to know what your protagonist ate for breakfast?

Do things happen for a reason in the book, or do coincidence and accident rule the day?

On a second read-through, you may want to look for the smaller logic and consistency problems. I find some of these in almost every manuscript I write—for example, I once discovered that I had a character without keys enter through a locked gate. If your character parks ten blocks away, does his car stay ten blocks away or drive itself much nearer when he's ready to leave? Have you kept track of the days that have passed in the story so that it isn't suddenly Wednesday in the middle of Thursday? So that your character isn't calling someone at a government agency on a weekend?

Characterization

Will the reader believe that these characters would behave exactly as they do, based on what has been revealed about them?

Do you tell where you should show? (Do we read, "Catherine was a selfish little girl," or do we see her smile to herself just before she eats the candy bar she was supposed to share with her sister?)

Are we concerned about the protagonist? Are we rooting for the protagonist? Does the protagonist actively detect? Does our hero think out the solution, or does he stand on the railroad tracks of the plot and let it hit him like a train?

Do we meet the villain early on? Is he or she a worthy opponent? Do we believe the villain's motivation?

Are the secondary characters brought to life, or are they mere props? Are they real or cliché?

Dialogue

Reading aloud may be of help here, too.

Do the characters all sound alike? Do they all sound like you? Do they all seem to have the same level of education? Do they come from the same part of the country? Does a character start out sounding as if he's a high school dropout from the northeast and suddenly transform himself into a Southerner with a college education a little later on? Do the characters talk to each other or lecture one another? Can you picture a real human being speaking in the way this character speaks? Are the characters' voices distinct so that a reader might know which character was speaking even if you didn't add an attribution? Are dramatic attributions (*he wailed, she growled*) being overused or used to shore up weak dialogue?

Dialogue has an impact on characterization and pacing. Read dialogue with an eye toward both.

Point of View

If you are writing third person, are you consistent in point of view, or is the reader jerked back and forth between third-person privileged and omniscient? Within scenes, are we tossed back and forth between the minds of two different characters?

If you are writing first person, does anything become known without the protagonist learning of it? Similarly, what the protagonist knows must be revealed to the reader—does the reader see what the protagonist has noticed, how the protagonist has analyzed information, how the protagonist has been misled?

Typographical, Spelling, and Grammatical Errors

Another reading can be used to copyedit the manuscript. This time through, look for misspelled words, missing words, poor grammar, and awkward syntax. Most editors and agents will be more interested in your story and style than in nitpicking your grammar—but they'll tire of reading a manuscript that is peppered with misspelled words and other errors. Too many of them, and you will seem to be a careless writer. Since your manuscript will be competing for attention with thousands of others, you'll want it to look its best.

If you're using a computer, make use of your word processing program's spell checker—but beware. Most programs won't detect misused words or inverted word order, and sometimes they can be downright dangerous to proper nouns. A friend of mine had already called FedEx to pick up her manuscript when she decided to give it one last look—to her horror, she realized that a character named "Brian" had been rechristened by her spell checker and was now known as "Brain" throughout the manuscript.

Look for the most common grammatical errors, including mixups with *it's/its, you're/your, their/there/they're, who's/whose, lay/lie.* Any number of excellent grammar handbooks are available to you, among them Edward D. Johnson's *The Handbook of Good English* and Patricia T. O'Conner's accessible *Woe Is I: The Grammarphobe's Guide to Better English in Plain English.* When shopping for a grammar text, don't just grab one off the shelf and head for the checkout counter. Open the book and read an explanation or two. If they aren't clear to you, this is not the grammar book for you. Also, examine the book's format, including its table of contents and index. Is the book organized in a way that will make it easy for you to look up your questions about grammar? One of the great ironies of life is that the rules of grammar, provider of clarity in language, are so often presented to us in books that are indecipherable.

Sometimes another pair of eyes is needed—you may not be able to see errors that will be obvious to another reader or feel confident about your use of grammar. For this specific purpose, if you don't have a knowledgeable friend who will help, it may be worth your while to hire someone who is well versed in such matters to help you produce a clean manuscript. But who else should be reading your work in manuscript?

Showing the Manuscript to Others

Remember that recipe for bread? Few questions divide writers as much as that of when and how to get feedback. Some believe strongly in writers groups and courses. Others believe that writers groups and courses are more likely to end careers than boost them. Whether groups and courses will be useful to you depends in part on how you write, and how well you choose those who will comment on your manuscript before submission. The short test: Avoid anyone who makes you feel as if you no longer want to write.

Sometimes members of groups and instructors have their own jealousies and agendas. Some enjoy the process of talking about writing more than writing itself. Try to be a wise consumer if you go this route. Some courses may help you to develop discipline and a better sense of your strengths and weaknesses. On the other hand, procrastination by enrollment is a common ailment among new writers.

Ultimately, a writer must learn to rely on his own judgment— and to develop judgment on which he can rely.

You'll find many writers—myself included—who are opposed to "book doctors" and agents who ask for fees. If your goal is to get someone to buy your work, don't begin by paying someone to read it. Reputable agents make their money solely by the sale of their clients' manuscripts. For more on this subject, see the excellent Writer Beware Web site operated by Science Fiction and Fantasy Writers of America, at www.sfwa.org/beware.

Usually, your friends and family members will not be able to be objective readers. They tend to love unconditionally, lie to avoid complicating a relationship, or brutally criticize in a misguided attempt to spare you public humiliation. Ask them instead to read it if they'd like, but please pass it along to another person—someone unknown to you who enjoys reading this type of book—for comment. You may want to include a form that asks for specific kinds of feedback. If ten of these forms come back saying your book drags in the middle, you might want to take another look at the middle of the book. If one comes back with this comment, and you think the middle of the book is just fine, you may want to learn the useful art of shrugging off criticism.

If you include scenes that involve firearms or some area of specialized knowledge with which you are just finding your way, you may want to let someone with expertise read those pages. If one of your characters takes the safety off a revolver, you may lose some readers. If you put your protagonist on a yacht and you've never sailed, you may want to ask someone who has done so to read those passages before you drift off course.

At the end of the day, though, you are always the one who must decide what stays and what goes in a book. This is one of the terrible things about writing fiction. The author has control over everything that ends up in the manuscript. This is also one of the greatest things about writing fiction. Very few people work at creating anything over which they have as much influence as a writer has over his or her work.

When Should I Stop Revising?

When it comes to revision, you're the doctor.

If the patient is dying of a heart attack, don't spend all your time and energy perfecting his big toe. Focus on the most vital aspects of revision first. Don't wear yourself out changing the name of the protagonist's apartment building if the problem with the book is that there is no suspense after the opening scene.

I've known authors who operated on healthy patients. Don't bleed the life right out of a story trying to make it flawless. There are almost always other ways in which to write a book. One reason writers are often the worst critics of other writers' books is that they so easily see other ways to tell a story or handle a scene. A writer's imagination will allow him to picture revising a book until it is a book that *everyone* will love. Forget it. Even the Bible isn't universally loved.

If you've lain awake all night with visions of brutal rejection letters dancing through your head, it will seem so much easier to do a little more polishing than to risk being turned down. I've never understood why people who fear negative comments want to be published. I can only imagine they've never had a job that brings them into contact with the public. Once you're published, any clown with a library card can tell you what he thinks of your book. To get almost anything worthwhile done in this life, you have to risk disapproval. Writing is no different.

Sometimes, Dr. Reviser, you must stop operating because the patient is dead. Naturally, you don't want to pronounce it dead if it can be saved, but sometimes, no matter what you do, a manuscript just can't be fixed—or you decide you just can't live with the stench. If this happens to you, my sympathies—I've had to bury a few myself. Sometimes I've been able to use old manuscripts as organ donors, taking from the dead what could be used by some other story. But not always.

This may seem like the worst outcome, but it isn't. You haven't wasted your time—you've learned something more about the complex task of writing a novel.

A writer never wastes time by writing—only by not writing.

May the Muse be good to you.

HOW TO FIND AND WORK
WITH AN AGENT

John F. Baker

The classic scene in the old movies about a writer's career comes
when he goes to the mailbox one day (we're talking way
back before e-mails, and probably even phone calls) and finds there
a letter from an editor at a big New York publishing house. "They
love my book!" the writer cries ecstatically. "And they're going to
publish it!"

These days an updated version of the scenario would show an
excited would-be author getting an e-mail or phone call from a
literary agent. "I think you might have something here I could sell,"
it would say, far more cautiously. "I'd like to represent you, and
will send you my standard author contract."

For the fact is that it's the agent, rather than the editor, whom
the writer must pursue in the current state of the book business. Editors are no longer the prime talent spotters. It's the agents who are
the ace screeners today, who cull from the countless thousands
of would-be authors (and it sometimes seems as if every other American has a book in him or her) the comparative handful with real
talent and storytelling ability and help launch new careers. The
agents are the ones who pore through the slush pile of unsolicited

manuscripts in search of the often elusive jewels and then make it their business (literally) to get them published. And by and large the editors, who tend nowadays to restrict their tasks to acquisition and some line editing, and spend much of their time trying to fire the sales and marketing people with enthusiasm for their purchases, have been willing to cede the thrill of discovery of new talent to the agents.

So it is to the agents that the contemporary writer must look for his first hope of recognition—and the hunt for an agent willing to work for a specific writer has now replaced the eager pursuit of a receptive publisher.

But where to find the right one for you? Too often it seems to the budding author that he is caught in a kind of Catch-22 situation: The editor insists that she reads only works sent in by agents, and the agent demands proof that an author can attract, or has attracted, a publisher before she will agree to take him on.

It's not quite that hard. Most agents today, particularly the small entrepreneurial ones rather than the big companies with a staff of a dozen agents, still read unsolicited material because that's where their clients, and ultimately their income, are going to come from.

Looking for an Agent

There are several ways of setting about the hunt for an agent: in the books, on the ground, or by networking.

In the books is the least expensive and time-consuming approach, and it's where many people start. There are extensive listings of agents, for a start, in a hefty annual publication called *Literary Market Place* (*LMP*), which can be found in the stacks, or in the reference room, at any public library worth its salt. It lists about seven hundred agents, by no means all of them in New York, with their salient details, an idea of the kinds of books they're looking for (and are *not* looking for), and, most important of all, how they prefer to be approached.

Most of them say, in their listings and in person, essentially the same thing about the approach. They *don't* want to be sent manuscripts. And they *don't* want to be called cold on the phone; in fact, most agents won't even take calls from people they don't know. They want to be queried first and have a chance to decide whether they even want to look at your manuscript. A query letter should be an author's masterpiece, representative of absolutely the best he can do: brisk, to the point, challenging, vivid, readable, persuasive, making the best possible case for the book you want to send. Some agents want you to send postage, in the form of stamped self-addressed envelopes, so they can reply without having to spend their own money—but you can be quite sure that if your letter has piqued their interest they won't worry about postage but will get right on the phone or e-mail to make sure they nail you down before another agent can do so.

There's a reason they should worry about that if you're really promising, because you'll probably approach more than one agent at a time with your query. But if you do, be sure to tell them you've done so. Maybe, if you feel you have somthing particularly strong to offer, you can offer an agent an exclusive look for a limited period of time before you send the material elsewhere; a couple of weeks is about right. On the timing of a reply, by the way—a subject I know authors think and worry about a great deal—an agent should be able to respond to a query letter in not more than six weeks. If someone takes longer than that—and after all, she's reading only a page or two, not an entire manuscript—then that agent is probably not for you.

Don't feel insulted or angry if you just receive what is obviously a printed or mass-produced rather than a personal reply. Agents get dozens, some of them even hundreds, of query letters a week, and to reply personally to them all is out of the question.

There are two circumstances when you should expect to receive a few personal lines, however: (1) if the agent thinks you're promising but perhaps not quite ready yet and wants to make some suggestions on improving your offering, and perhaps hold out some future hope, and (2) if the agent has already encouraged you, on the basis of your query letter, to send some material and has then decided not to pursue it after all. In that case the writer deserves a few lines of explanation as to why the requested material didn't make the grade. (And if material has been requested, it's not a bad idea to mark "requested material" on the envelope to distinguish it from all that other stuff that hasn't made it that far.)

There's one way of approaching an agent, by the way, on which the jury is still out. Very few, as noted, will accept phone calls from unknown parties, but what about e-mail? Some agents simply don't read unsolicited e-mails and delete them just as if they were junking unwanted snail mail; others can't resist opening them for a peek, so that just might be a way in. But don't, whatever you do, accompany a pitch letter with a long e-mail enclosure containing all or even part of the manuscript. That clutters up an agent's system and will certainly irritate her.

For other guides to agents, check your local library or go to the Writing and Publishing section of your bookstore. You'll likely find two or three sources that are useful. There's one published by Writer's Digest Books and updated annually; one by Jeff Herman, himself an agent, on agents and editors to consider; and, with luck, a small book by me called *Literary Agents: A Writer's Introduction*. Writer's Digest *Guide to Literary Agents* and Jeff Herman's *Writer's Guide to Book Editors, Publishers, and Literary Agents*, though offering fewer listings than the *LMP*, are more personal, in that they attempt to get from agents and editors a fairly specific notion of what they're looking for and how they like to work. These listings are based on questionnaires, to which some agents reply and some don't. My own book offers interviews with fifty or so independent agents as to how they started in the business, how they work with their authors, some of their better-known clients, general observations on the state of publishing today, and the outlook for new writers in the current marketplace. It also has a general introduction to the agent world, offering the same kind of advice I'm giving here.

Hunting down an agent on the ground is usually done in the context of a writers conference. There are dozens of these scattered around the country, many of them advertised in *Writer's Digest* magazine, and they are of varying degrees of usefulness. Most of them offer a sprinkling of editors and agents who give presentations and, in many cases, offer brief consultations with the attending authors about their work. It's not unknown for an author to be discovered at such a conference (Jean Auel, author of the series of superselling novels beginning with *The Clan of the Cave Bear*, was one of them), but in most cases, although authors may well receive some good advice, they will simply be asked to send some material as if they had written successful query letters.

Though an expensive and time-consuming way to make contacts, networking with other authors can be a valuable part of the writers conference experience too. Many attendees feel they get more out of conferences in this way than from their necessarily brief contact with editors and agents.

Which brings us to the whole question of networking. This is really the most promising approach of all to getting on an inside track with agents, for they're far more likely to give a sympathetic read to something that comes personally recommended than to anything that simply descends out of the blue. So if you know a published writer—perhaps you share a writing support group with one—ask for an introduction to his agent. It's also important, when seeking an agent, to find one who represents an author you particularly admire; in fact, to tell an agent in your query letter that you chose her because you knew she represented so-and-so is likely to inspire sympathetic interest right off the bat. And how do you find what agent represents what author? Well, in my book the agents I interviewed say whom they represent. But there's another way to find out. Most books have acknowledgments pages in which the authors thank various people who helped get their books written and published, and almost invariably they mention their agents; so there's your answer. I'm often surprised by how few people think of that.

Agents vary as to what they regard as the normal cost of doing business. And, most important, they will *not*, absolutely not, ask an author to pay for reading his work, or editorial suggestions, or any of the traffic that might be expected to pass between author and agent. Any agent who asks for money up front, before a sale has been made, should be avoided like the plague. (There is a professional agents association—the Association of Authors' Representatives, or AAR—to which many agents belong and that specifically prohibits its members from indulging in a number of questionable practices, of which "fee reading" is the foremost. Most directories indicate which agents are members and which are not, so an author can choose accordingly, always bearing in mind that nonmembership is not necessarily sinister.)

Working With an Agent

Now that you've found an agent who's ready to work with you, what should you expect of this exciting new relationship? Well, much of it will be spelled out in the brief author contract you'll most probably be asked to sign (I say "most probably" because a handful of older agents still work on the basis of a handshake, but in this litigious era that's become increasingly uncommon). The contract will usually say that the agent will take 15 percent of the moneys she makes off the book sold on your behalf—and 20 percent on sales of foreign rights, which takes more time in terms of postage and phone calls, for example. The contract will usually also spell out what other expenses the agent may claim; many will bill authors—as deductions on their statements—for sums in excess of what are regarded as normal for items such as multiple photocopies of a long manuscript, extensive long-distance phone calls or faxes, and the like.

In return for taking a chunk of your advance and royalties, agents do an enormous amount for authors. For a start, it is up to the agent to find the right editor for your book, one who will publish it with fire and zest and who will line up the all-important marketing and promotional heft behind it. The agent will get the most money possible for you, perhaps by encouraging editors to bid against each other in an auction or by persuading them to make their "best bids." An agent will negotiate your contract for you—a terrifying document that can be up to twenty pages long and is full of daunting and threatening legal boilerplate that an experienced agent can tame with a few strokes of the pen. The agent will handle your finances for you, prying the money loose from the publisher as soon as it can possibly be done; and that is by no means an easy task, since a publisher who will gladly messenger over a catalog will delay sending a check as long as humanly possible, and will then normally send it by surface mail timed to land after the bank closes on a Friday afternoon.

You don't actually pay an agent, by the way. She becomes your financial officer and accountant, and all checks for you from a publisher are sent by way of her. She then deducts her commission and necessary expenses, if any, and sends the balance along to you.

There are many other ways in which your agent is useful, even valuable, to you. She, far more than anyone else in the publishing world, has your best interests at heart and will do everything she can to make your life easier. The agent will try to guide your career; she will work with you on your prose; she will lend a sympathetic ear to your troubles (of which all authors have more than their share) even outside normal office hours; she will seek other authors to blurb your books; she will help you fight for the right title and the right cover; and she will even work with your publisher on your publicity campaign. What usually develops between an author and agent—and is invariably there in the best of these relationships—is a lasting friendship, even if, as is frequently the case, they have never met in person.

It is therefore strange, but perhaps only human, that one of the most frequently asked questions about the author-agent relationship I get asked when I speak on the subject at writers conferences is, How do I end the relationship if it isn't working out? Obviously not all such arrangements work out as well as the parties originally hoped, but the author-agent contract will spell out how you can end a relationship with three months' written notice to the other. In such cases, the agent continues to receive commission on work she sold for the departed author but, obviously, not on new work.

But this is all about finding an agent and working happily with one; let's not be thinking of separating so soon!

DIAL M FOR MARKET

Russell Galen

Before you can market your mystery manuscript, you must figure out if it is:

• a mainstream mystery, which contains elements designed to attract readers who usually don't read mysteries, or

• a category mystery, which is the classic mystery story aimed at mystery fans.

There are many smaller divisions within the genre, and to publishers these distinctions are as important as the ones between mysteries and, say, romances or Westerns. But for our purposes, we'll focus only on the divisions between category and mainstream mysteries.

The Mainstream Market

Mainstream mysteries possess elements, as important as the mystery story itself, that appeal to a wider audience. Sometimes these books aren't thought of as mysteries at all, though you and I know that's what they really are.

The elements can include humor; hipness or trendiness; a distinctive prose style or an unusually appealing or memorable lead character; and settings that give the reader an opportunity to learn about another way of life, culture, or profession. The elements give the novel a larger scope by making the mystery one aspect of a plot in which the issues at stake are greater than the identity of the murderer. Or, they can turn a mystery into a mainstream thriller by concentrating on fast pacing and on creating suspense by putting main characters in jeopardy.

These mysteries are marketed to publishers like any other mainstream commercial novel . . . with a special trick. You must decide between approaching houses with mystery programs or mainstream houses that publish no category mysteries at all.

At a mystery-oriented house, you'll be talking to people who may hunger for out-of-category success, but are also proud of their association with category mysteries. Stressing the mainstream appeal of your book tactlessly, or too much, can do more harm than good. Saying "This is more than *just* a mystery," will get you kicked right out the door.

At a mainstream house, the *mystery* label can be the kiss of death. While you shouldn't insult an editor's intelligence by saying "This is not a mystery" when it clearly is, your pitch should concentrate on elements other than the mystery plot.

The Category Market

A category mystery must be offered to a house that has a mystery program. Check the bookstores and libraries, read the reviews in the Crime section of *The New York Times Book Review* and the mystery reviews in *Publishers Weekly* for a full list of which publishers have a mystery program. The publication of two or three mysteries a season signifies a house that only occasionally publishes mysteries; more than that denotes a house with a strong mystery program.

You also need to compile a list of editors who acquire mysteries;

this is a specialized taste, and a submission to an editor who doesn't acquire mysteries can result in a manuscript languishing unread for months.

Don't just call the switchboard at a publishing house and ask for the mystery editor. Some houses have an editor specializing in mysteries who might not want his name given out to unknown callers. In that case you may be given a fake name or be simply brushed off. Other houses have several editors who read mysteries, and the operator may not know who to forward your call to. You can get editors' names from other industry newsletters, by checking the acknowledgments or dedications in recently published books, and from references such as *Writer's Market* and *Literary Market Place*. If there's a recently published mystery you admire, call the publisher and ask for the editorial department, then ask for the name of the editor who worked on that book. If you have some professional credits in the field you can also join the Mystery Writers of America [17 E. 47th St., 6th floor, New York, NY 10017, (212) 888-8171] and get market information as well as other useful tips.

Then determine whether the house is acquiring the type of mystery you've written. Just because you've written a mystery and sent it to the mystery editor at We Publish Lots of Mysteries Press doesn't mean you've made a smart submission. A house's interest in a particular type of mystery will fluctuate, sometimes rapidly. Check the house's recent publications of books by new authors. (Ignore the backlist of classics or longtime best-selling authors; these reflect tastes fixed long ago—not, perhaps, what the house is looking for right now.)

If you're checking paperbacks, bear in mind that some are *paperback originals*—books acquired and developed by the paperback house—and some are *reprints* picked up from a hardcover house. Paperback editors often look for different kinds of originals than they do reprints, so if you're studying the taste of a paperback house, check only its originals. Look at the copyright page (the page to the left of and facing the title page). If it's a reprint, the original hardcover house will be mentioned.

Category publishing is much more open to new, even unpublished novelists than mainstream, and mysteries are among the most open of all categories. The field has a dazzling tradition of brand-new writers selling novels to prestigious houses, and doing so without an agent. If you demonstrate a minimum amount of savvy in your submission, you can get even a top mystery editor to take a look-if you also follow these steps:

• Complete your mystery. (You'll need to send it quickly if your query attracts interest.)

• Submit to an editor who buys mysteries and who has recently bought other novels of the same type as yours.

• Send a short query consisting of one to three paragraphs describing the book and what is unique or distinctive about it; one paragraph listing your credits, if any; and one paragraph listing your personal background if there's a connection to your subject matter (you're an expert rock-climber, say, and the mystery is set in the world of rock-climbing).

• Wait for an invitation to submit the manuscript, and then send it with a brief cover letter.

The same steps can be followed to query agents. Many mystery markets, unlike most mainstream markets, accept unagented submissions if the above procedures are followed. Having an agent puts you at a great advantage, but if you're having trouble finding one, you may be better off going directly to editors. Then have an agent negotiate the contract after you've found a publisher. (Few will turn you down at that point.)

Making the Deal

A first mystery won't bring much money; the key to making money in this genre is to develop an audience by producing new books regularly. This is not a field in which it makes sense to dabble. An editor won't be interested if he or she suspects you're not planning to continue writing mysteries regularly. If you have a track record in another field, be sure to say that your hope and intention is to stay with mysteries.

Should you seek a hardcover or paperback deal?

Hardcovers are more likely to be reviewed and to sell to book clubs. If all goes well, they can produce more money in the long run. You'll receive royalties on the hardcover, a share of the book club income, and, if the hardcover publisher sells reprint rights to a paperback publisher, a share of that income as well. But your hardcover might never become a paperback; those houses are plenty busy with their own new authors and buy only a fraction of those published by hardcover houses. In that case, your hardcover sales of 4,000 to 5,000 copies won't be enough to spread any serious word of mouth and build your audience for the future.

A paperback original, however, might sell 30,000 copies or more, and then you'll have 30,000 people across the country telling their friends about you.

Another advantage of paperback originals is that 100 percent of the royalties go into your pocket, and if the book stays in print for many years, that can add up. If the book is first sold to hardcover, the hardcover house will keep 50 percent of your paperback money for as long as the paperback stays in print.

Both hardcover and paperback have their advantages. Anyway, it's more likely you're mainly worried about getting a sale. If you have a book suitable for Scribner's or St. Martin's (which are hardcover houses), try them first and don't worry about whether you'd be better off with a paperback original. If you think a paperback house like Pocket or Bantam is your best shot, worry about getting into hardcover later. All the paperback mystery lines are divisions of larger companies with hardcover imprints, and if your paperbacks sell well, eventually your new books could be published by the hardcover imprint. (In that kind of deal, where the hardcover and paperback are published by the same conglomerate, you get the best of both by keeping 100 percent of hardcover and paperback royalties.)

Breaking and Entering

Plotting mysteries is like composing music in sonata form or poetry in rhyming meter: you have limitless freedom in some areas but also must follow certain rules. If a mystery doesn't contain a murder in its first third (in most cases it should come as early as possible), and if the identity of the murderer isn't revealed as a result of an investigation, it's not a mystery. It may be a crime novel or a caper novel or a thriller, but it's not a mystery.

But to break in, a new writer must offer something beyond the basic mystery plot. A new writer *must* offer something new, and the pressure to do so has produced a number of exciting new writers with unique, individual voices and themes in recent years. They range from brilliant exponents of the classic category mystery to experimentalists and trendsetters.

Variation within restriction is the rule of thumb for a new writer trying to break in. If you ignore the restrictions, you risk creating an unpublishable mystery. If you fail to create an original and unique variation, you'll have a book that, whatever its sheer quality, can't compete against the hundreds of other new mysteries being published every year.

Before composing a new mystery, try this test. See if you can, in 50 words or less, summarize the distinctive qualities of this story. If you can do it in a single sentence, so much the better. Keep that summary around, because this—the novel's "hook"—will be the basis of your query letter when the time comes to market the manuscript. In one form or another it could end up in the catalog and jacket copy of the printed book, and be the main factor in bookstores', libraries' and readers' decisions to investigate the book further despite your unknown byline

The variation can be anything so long as it's something that might sound like fun and can be said about no book but yours. Something general, such as "What's special about this book is its humor" or "The writing is exceptionally good" or "It's unusually fast-paced and suspenseful," isn't enough to make a place for an unknown author: there are plenty of established authors already out there who are as funny, distinguished or suspenseful as you. Buyers will choose them over you every time.

(Also, if you put *too* much emphasis on other elements, what you wind up with is a gimmick, something so outrageously clever and odd that it puts off traditional mystery fans, who are a rather conservative audience.)

The mere existence of a fascinating variation is no magic key to salability. It's simply the ingredient that must be added to the traditional strengths that have given mystery writing a century of unbroken popularity and made it the preeminent field for the discovery of new writers.

Surviving in the Magazine Market

To sell short stories, follow the advice of writer Jo Gilbert:

> Finding a magazine to publish your short mystery could be the easiest case you ever solve—if you're willing to do the detective work needed to analyze your manuscript and the market, searching for clues to a perfectly molded submission.
>
> One thing to remember when marketing your mystery is that, generally, your story should be just that . . . a mystery. No mainstream stories with just a hint of crime. No romances on the side. Because of space availability, editors want short, but fully developed, category mysteries.
>
> These simple rules will also help:
>
> • Study market information. Reading the market list-ings will tell you the length requirements. (Many maga-zines average between 2,000 and 4,000 words per story. Most magazines require those numbers for a maximum length; a few list 10,000 as a word maximum and even fewer go higher.) You will also find out what types of mysteries are wanted and what the magazine's submis-sion standards are. Don't send the complete manuscript if editors prefer to see a query or outline.

• For information on specific markets, consult *Writer's Market*, *Novel & Short Story Writer's Market*, monthly market listings in *Writer's Digest*, and Mystery Writers of America newsletters.

• Once you've identified your suspects, request the writer's guidelines for additional information. Include a self-addressed, stamped envelope (SASE) with your request. The guidelines will usually go into detail regarding submission standards, word length, audience profile, and so forth.

• Prepare a readable manuscript. Your submission may not be read if the editor has to use a magnifying glass. The black ink should be *black* and on white paper. On the first page, type your personal identification information—name, address, telephone number—in the upper left-hand corner. In the opposite corner, put the approximate word count (round it to the nearest hundred).

• Double-space with one-inch margins all around. If you're sending photocopies, make sure they're clear, too. (Photocopies *are* acceptable; never send your only copy of a story.)

• Most important, *always* include a SASE with your query or manuscript. You'll look more professional and editors will be more likely to give you a quicker response. If your submission doesn't draw a reply by the magazine's stated response time, wait an additional two weeks, and then send a brief note (with a SASE) asking for an update. If you have not received a response within three weeks after sending your note, call the editorial office.

Picking up these simple—yet important—clues could put you on the trail to getting your short mystery published.

THE MYSTERY NOVEL
FROM AN EDITOR'S POINT OF VIEW

■ *Ruth Cavin*

L urking under that title is another, more straightforward one.
To paraphrase Papa Freud, it's "What does an editor want?"

That's an easy one. What editors want, of course, is a wonderful crime novel that will get terrific reviews, sell thousands and thousands of copies, and make everyone rich and happy.

That's not very helpful, however.

Unfortunately, there is no step-by-step program that, if followed faithfully, will culminate in a finished work that every editor is guaranteed to love and want to publish. All I can do here is describe to you what an acceptable, buyable, publishable mystery looks like to me.

Manuscripts from agents and authors come to me on an average of about five a week, and that is the rate for most of my colleagues as well. Editors must do a million other things involved in getting out a list and still find time to consider all those submissions. We simply can't afford to plough through ninety very ordinary pages because there might be a real gem on page ninety-one.

So you must learn how to Grab The Editor. Authors too often misunderstand the nature of what grabs an editor. It's *not* having

bloody mayhem on the first page. Nor is it that (perhaps unconscious) scam that puts a dark, ominous prologue in front of what
is a perfectly pedestrian story.

No.

What I want is a beginning that excites my interest and makes me
want to read on, and that shows me that the author has a unique
and personal way of seeing things and writing about them. Most of
the literally hundreds of manuscripts that come across my desk are
pretty good. But they are, many of them, ordinary—there is nothing
special about them. By "special," I don't mean two-headed serial
killers or neckties that strangle people of their own accord (I had a
proposal like that once, honest). I mean special in the sense that the
author is able to make the story stand out from the crowd because
of a fresh approach, a noticing eye, an able pen.

Before you rise in rage and get me blackballed by Mystery Writers
of America, let me be quick to say that I don't mean I read only the
first paragraph of a submission. I give it much more of a chance
than that. But over the years, I've found that the unusual, the
extraordinary signals itself pretty clearly very early on. And the
unusual and the extraordinary are what this editor wants.

If *you* had forty or fifty manuscripts waiting to be read and
chronic guilt about not being able to get to them—or through
them—fast enough, which of the opening paragraphs below would
encourage *you* to take the manuscript home to read that evening?

> The phone shrilled and Joe rolled over and glanced at the
> clock. Two A.M.? Who the hell would be calling now?
> But he was afraid he knew. It had to be little brother.
> "For Chris'sake! What kind of trouble are you in
> now?" he growled.

and

> Joe looked at the pile of case files on his desk. Victor had
> a football game, and to a high school kid it was urgent
> that his dad be there to see it. Especially a kid whose
> Mom had died just six months earlier. Who knows—

maybe Coach would get him off the bench this time. Joe sighed, and said "Homicide can wait."

Contrast those with these openings, each very different from the others, but each with a freshness the ones above do not have:

When the lefthander found me, I was sitting in my usual chair in front of the fire, trying to stay warm. The calendar said April, but April in Paradise is still cold enough to hurt you, and I could still feel the sting of it in my hands and on my face. I sat there by the fire, watching the baseball game on the television over the bar, nursing a cold Canadian beer, as the lefthander made his way in the darkness. He knew where he was going, because he had a hand-drawn map in his back pocket, with a little star on the right side of the road as you come north into Paradise.

—Steve Hamilton,
North of Nowhere

and

"The Chemin des Dames, that's the name," said Charles. "Do you know that in 1917 the whole French army was in revolt because of the terrible deaths on the Chemin des Dames? That wonderful army that Napoleon built, reduced to chaos and despair . . . that's the mood I want to create with our bombs. Then we can rebuild society."

Not me, thought Jerry. I'm a soldier. I get instructions from above, I do the job, and walk away. Also, I get paid.

—Gwendoline Butler,
Coffin's Game

and

They started with the boots, which looked new. They tried to hurry, but their fingers were already stiff and

clumsy with cold and the buttons were troublesome. The
second boot was particularly difficult. She was curled
up on her side against the fence, and the leather had fas-
tened to the earth in an icy bond. It book both of them
to get it off, one holding to the frozen leg, by now stiff
as stone, the other tugging until the boot came away.
Next was the waist, a decent black sateen, but in their
haste they pulled on her arm too sharply, and they
heard the bone snap as the elbow dislocated. "Be more
respectful," said the younger one.

—Maureen Jennings,
Except the Dying

and

Whoever dines at Amsterdam's pricey restaurant, The
Plumgarden, set off by palm trees in brass buckets under a
cupola ceiling where angels make music, whoever enjoys
nouvelle cuisine dishes there sprinkled with rare wines,
hardly expects the gent at the next table to fall over and
die.

—Janwillem van de
Wetering, *A Law Student*

All four of these will tell you something new and interesting and
promise more. The two earlier openings are examples of the way
too many hopeful—and sometimes published—books begin.

Occasionally an agent or author will ask me whether I have any
"guidelines" to give writers who aspire to be published by St.
Martin's. Yes, indeed, I do. Here they are:

1. Double-space your manuscript.

2. Use one side of the paper only.

3. Number the pages consecutively, not chapter by chapter.

4. If the submission is directly from the author, enclose return postage.

Those are my guidelines.

What did you expect? "The detective should be between twenty-seven and forty years old?" "The murder should happen on page fifty-two?" Uh-uh.

I don't want mystery novels that are written to a formula. The good mystery novel is, first of all, a good novel. It is a mystery because it is built around a crime and (with variations) the search for the perpetrator of that crime. I want a solid story with a life of its own, not a written-by-the-numbers tale that seems to have bored its author as much as it will bore me.

To my mind, the most important element of the mystery novel is character. I want to believe in the people in the story. Readers of mysteries must be able to involve themselves in the goings-on to the extent that it matters very much what happens to the people in them. I can't really care what is about to happen if it's going to happen to some two-dimensional puppets, paper dolls stuck together with Elmer's glue and pushed through a series of actions. Develop your characters, and you'll find that they do half your work for you in return.

• In a play (or movie or TV drama) the writer has only three ways to "describe" the people in it:

By what the character says.

By what the character does.

By what others in the work say about the character.

You, however, can tell the reader anything you want to: what kind of person the character is, his or her weaknesses or strengths, whatever. There's nothing wrong with taking advantage of that freedom, but the more you can work within a playwright's restrictions, *showing* rather than *telling*, the more effective your character will be.

• Don't regard your characters as being there simply to act out your story. It's really the other way around. There's a fair amount of talk about "character driven" vs. "plot driven," which can be misleading because even the most intricate plot events happen *because that is what the character(s) would do.* Imagine yourself an actor preparing to play the different parts, and do some thinking about each one. What is the person's history? How would that character react to situations other than those in the story? What are his or her fears? Fantasies? Hopes? Even though these enriching details never appear in the finished manuscript, they will have a positive effect on what you do put down on paper.

• Observe everyone—relatives, friends, Romans, passengers on the bus. Borrow mannerisms from real life—*but only those that tell us something about the character you have created.*

It's amazing to me how often otherwise good writers have their characters doing absolutely unreal things. If a character's behavior is so bizarre that no human being would ever act that way, it means the writer hasn't really thought of the character as a person. Here's an actual example:

A woman detective is back home after a stormy, cold night of trying to stop a serial killer, and failing. With her is a new colleague. It's 5 A.M. and they are both exhausted, depressed, wet, and muddy. Does she offer the guy a drink? A hot chocolate? A shower? A bed on her sofa? No. She says, "Would you like to see my house?" and takes him on a tour of the rooms. Whatever got into that author? What was he thinking? (*Was* he thinking?)

I've said this next so often that it's now a cliché that I have a patent on. If the characters are believable, the background and atmosphere real and interesting, and the writing smooth and accurate (I'll give you my definition of "accurate" writing later on), I'm not going to worry too much about plot problems unless the basic premise is irretrievably flawed. They're usually quite fixable. If the plot is neat and logical and the characters are wooden, the prose is clunky, the atmosphere nonexistent—then there's little, if any, hope of salvaging the story.

You notice I don't say, "Plot doesn't matter." It matters very much in a mystery. Regardless of how far today's mysteries have departed from the strict puzzle and become bona fide novels, the story is still vital. What I do say is, "It can be fixed."

Plot generates its cousin, suspense. It is suspense that keeps you reading and wanting to know what is going to happen.

What creates suspense is a threat. There must be the prospect of something really bad happening *unless* . . . Unless the crime is solved. Unless something intervenes between the villain and his or her intention. This is what gives your sleuth a solid motive for pursuing the matter, and you need that motivation. I see too many manuscripts that don't give the detective any reason but curiosity for trying to solve the case. I call that the Nancy Drew Syndrome. Adult readers have gone beyond Nancy Drew; curiosity is not enough. (It's pretty silly, too.) You need the threat of another murder, or of having someone we like suspected of the crime or arrested for it. Or a sympathetic character marked for extermination by the criminal. A police officer must have some stronger motivation than just the requirements of his or her job: rivalry in the department, the desire to "show" a superior, a fixation that justice has miscarried, a question of career advancement or failure.

If you read a lot, and read different kinds of writers, notice what you're reading, and do a good bit of writing on your own, chances are you'll develop your own prose style. You won't do it by trying to copy a writer you admire; you'll do it, in part, just by noticing what other writers do as well as what they don't do.

A while back I mentioned accurate writing. I assume you know you should get the facts straight. I'm talking about saying exactly what you mean to say and not some approximation of it.

"He looked up to see the back of silky brown hair, gently curling three inches below the collar of her blouse."

Obviously, "He" didn't see the back of silky brown *hair*, he saw the back of a head covered with silky brown hair. As in "She had her back to him; her silky brown hair curled gently below the collar of her blouse."

That is a rather startlingly clear example of inaccurate writing. Watch out for more subtle ones in your own work.

Notice details and use them—but use them wisely. Details that tell the reader something about the character or the situation, or that enhance the atmosphere of the story are the secret of vivid writing. Details just sprinkled about for no particular reason except that some book on writing tells you to use details are what one of my professors called "deadwood."

"He turned toward the left and rested his arm on the back of the bench."

Who cares? Get on with the story.

Have faith in yourself and your readers. They'll understand what you're saying very well without your having to spell everything out for them. I see this kind of thing so often; it pains me to see it.

"He got up from the couch, walked to the TV, and switched it off. Then he went over to the kitchen. He opened the door and went up to the table where Jane was making sandwiches."

I made that one up, but it's hardly an exaggeration of what I come across. In fact, come to think of it, it's no exaggeration at all.

"He turned off the television. In the kitchen, he found Jane making sandwiches."

That's all you need or want. Say what you have to say as clearly and straightforwardly as possible and your own style will emerge and keep refining.

Don't misunderstand me. I'm not advocating that everyone go in for sparse, Hemingway-like prose. If your sentence is thirty words long, just be sure that every one of those thirty words is there because it has something specific to do, and that the total effect is one of total communication.

Where's the action?

I'm not looking for a crap game; I'm talking about a sense of place. Your story is not happening in a vacuum; I want details that make the setting real to me—details that evoke the locale: the weather, the buildings, the interior, whatever. Places have characteristics of their own, and a writer should be able to convey that.

Take advantage of our collective semiconsciousness when you can. Here's an excellent example:

> Roberts walked down the ramp and stood on the hot tarmac, breathing diesel fumes. He was sweating heavily and his shirt was soaked through to the skin. The sky was like a fiery kiln of clay glaze, smelling of sulfur and charcoal smoke. He looked at the low airport complex, sets of concrete buildings with tin roofs, a long hedge of cactus separating the runways from miles of confused, jumbled slums. In the west, high brown mountains rose into crabbed valleys and wrinkled ridges, then a slash of green. All around him the Haitian passengers were lugging their packages and bundles toward a tin customs shed located at the far end of a concrete building with several broken windows and an air conditioner leaking water.

> —Gaylord Dold,
> *Samedi's Knapsack*

It's a real plus if, in your story, you can use some special knowledge you have. Readers love it—they're getting a bonus. Gideon Oliver's physical anthropology. Lovejoy's phenomenal knowledge of antiques. The Navajo lore from Hillerman's Joe Leaphorn and Jim Chee. If you can work it into your story as an integral part of the action and not just something that's stuck in awkwardly, go for it.

Finally, I have to go all psychic on you. An editor will leap for joy to find a writer with what we call "voice." It's what we always hope for in a manuscript; it's what we find to a greater or lesser degree in the better ones. Occasionally it will be present in such force it stuns us. It's a quality in the writing that's hard to define, but when you come across it, you *know*. It is clear and unequivocal and unique to that writer, setting him or her apart from all others. From two different authors:

Amelia, the new heifer named for Amelia Earhart, one
of Ruth's heroines, was in heat for the first time. She
was humping the other cows and they were humping her.
A child would have thought they were playing leap
frog. It was early, though, for Amelia to breed, she was
not yet six months old. Now she was in a standing
heat, remaining immobile while one by one the other
cows mounted her. She was enjoying it, Ruth thought,
looking through the barn window—Ruth who hadn't
made love with a man since her husband Pete went off
with that actress, leaving Ruth with three children, one
of them a ten-year-old.

> —Nancy Means Wright,
> *Poison Apples*

The routine at Collins House was lax and lazy. The sisters
got up when they wanted and meandered as they
pleased. They stayed up way past their usual bedtime.
The summer days were warm and dry. They walked,
read, rested and played croquet on the side lawn. The
younger ones tried badminton, but found it difficult,
wearing veils. They did not swim in the lake but they did
take off their shoes and stockings to wade in the rock-
bottomed pool below the small waterfall that was the
entrance to Collins House.

> —John R. Hayes,
> *Catskill*

So now I've come full circle, haven't I, with my dissertation on
voice. I said something very much like that when I was talking
about openings—about grabbing the editor. I can't tell you how to
get it; it comes of writing a lot and loving to write—*having* to
write. Of being self-critical, of knowing what you want to have
happen in your work, of reading, reading, reading. And of being
lucky enough to have what the Wagnerian tenor Lauritz Melchior

once called "a little touch of God's finger." Old unbelievers like me call it less poetically "a special talent."

There it is—this editor's "want list." I would guess it's very much like the want lists of most editors. Recently one of my first-time authors called me when he got his manuscript with all my editorial notes on it. This man has a great pair of detectives, fine secondary characters, a solid familiarity with an interesting milieu, and a good ear for dialogue. His prose, however, overall, was still rough. It needed, shall we say, polishing.

I polished. I cut out all the "he walked to the television"'s and that mark of so many new writers, the "then"'s—"He got up, then left." "She spotted her father, then waved." I cut lines and lines of deadwood detail. What was left was fine, and the author, far from taking umbrage, was delighted.

"I learned more about writing in a week from your criticisms than I learned in two years from books," said he. I was grateful, but it's a dubious compliment, really. I'm not all that sure you can learn from books, where there's no one going over your own material with a fresh eye. (I'm a great believer in writing groups for that reason.) One learns to write by writing, but it's true that someone can steer you in the direction you should take, rather than your having to flounder about at the crossroads. I hope I've done that, if only a very little bit. Once your feet are on the road, it's up to you. Happy journey!

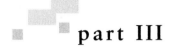

part III

Specialties

WRITING MYSTERIES
FOR YOUNG READERS

■ *Joan Lowery Nixon*

Do you remember the excitement you felt when you read your first mystery novel? The overwhelming awe that such a marvelous form of storytelling had been invented? You shivered, you jumped at a sudden noise in the hall, you moved to sit close to your father, but you kept reading as though you were under a spell, hoping that no one would remember it was past your bedtime. As soon as you finished reading the last page of the book you immediately searched for another mystery to read. And another. And another. You were hooked.

Juvenile mystery writers often find their books on lists for reluctant readers; teachers and librarians will tell them how kids who won't read anything else devour mysteries; and the young people themselves will write letters such as these: "I hate to read, but I read one of your mysteries, and now I want to read everything you've ever written." "I'm fifteen. I'm in the ninth grade. I never read a book in my life until I read your mystery novel, and I loved it. Our librarian promised to give me some of your other books."

Why do kids of all ages love mysteries so much? Why do they demand them and buy them and read them in such quantities that almost all publishers of juvenile books carry one or more mysteries on each list?

Reader Identification

Children of elementary school age are great at identifying wholeheartedly with the main characters of the books they read. When young readers dive into mystery stories they *become* the main characters—the persons who are brave enough to tackle something strange or mysterious or frightening—and through these vicarious experiences they grow a little in independence. They prove their bravery. They tackle a situation far beyond their own back-and-forth-to-school routines, and they conquer it. Bring on the next challenge! A mysterious box? A ghost in the attic? A mummy in the basement? Just watch how fast the reader becomes involved in the next story and—with a little help from the main character—again faces danger and solves the mystery!

Character rapport is the key here. The main character of any mystery story should be likable, with a few welcome faults (such as procrastination, forgetting homework, losing patience with a pesty little brother), which call on the sympathy of young readers. Characters' actions should be well motivated, consistent, and believable so that readers can easily step into their shoes. But "can" is not enough. Readers must care enough about the main characters so that they *want* to step into those shoes.

Because children like to feel older, never younger, it helps, too, to make your main character as old as those in the upper age group who will be reading the stories. Publishers classify reading groups as six to nine, seven to eleven, eight to twelve, nine to thirteen, and young adult: ages ten and up.

To aid reader identification, most books for young people are written in single viewpoint, although multiple viewpoint can be used for young adult readers.

Gripping Beginnings

Young people from primary grades through the teen years are demanding readers. They will pick up a book, read the first few paragraphs—or even sentences—and if they aren't immediately captured they'll put down the book and reach for another. It's up to the juvenile mystery author to begin his story with intrigue, action, or suspense. The opening sentence should grab readers; the next few paragraphs should be fascinating enough to ensure that this book is going to be read.

While many mystery novels for adults start with a leisurely pace, taking time to offer a sense of place, set the scene, and introduce many of the characters before the events leading to the mystery begin to take shape, mystery novels for young readers immediately bring in the main character and toss him into the action.

For very young readers the opening sentences can be just slightly scary, with the realization that something is mysteriously out of order. Mystery stories for children in the primary grades could be called *puzzle mysteries*, and these puzzles fit into the reader's frame of reference. Perhaps something is missing. It might have been mysteriously switched for something else. It could be that something out of the ordinary has suddenly appeared. Maybe there's a shadow in the hall or a sound that can't be explained.

Humor is frequently used in books for beginning readers because it's a nice balance to tension; it creates the valleys between the peaks of suspense.

But readers in the eight to twelve and young adult categories want a full-fledged mystery, and they want to be shocked into tension, suspense, and fear right from the start. This means that after the opening scene that thrusts them into the mystery, flashbacks containing background information will often have to be woven into the story.

Flashbacks should contain only the most necessary information. It's often surprising how much background material really isn't important and can be left out. That which *is* important can be woven in through dialogue or through the main character's thoughts.

Original Ideas

With the exception of some mass-market series with single plotlines, today's successful juvenile mysteries deal with unusual, original situations, many of them relying on current problems that touch young lives.

The teenaged main character in Norma Fox Mazer's *Taking Terri Mueller* (Avon) is shocked and horrified when she begins to realize that she is a kidnapped child—kidnapped when she was only five by her father who had lost custody after a bitter divorce. Even though Terri's father has always said that her mother had died when she was five, Terri is sure that he had lied, and she sets about trying to find her mother.

Lois Duncan's main character, April, in *Don't Look Behind You* (Delacorte) is a teenaged girl whose father is a government witness with his life in danger; and the entire family must "disappear" with new identities. April is told she can't say good-bye to her friends and that she will not even be able to get in touch with them after the flight; but, brokenhearted at the thought of never seeing her boyfriend again, she breaks the rules, and a hit man from the crime syndicate is soon on the family's trail.

Betty Ren Wright deals with a haunted dollhouse in *The Dollhouse Murders* (Holiday House), as her main character, Amy, discovers that the dollhouse dolls are trying to give her the clues she needs to solve a murder that took place on the property many years ago.

Susan Beth Pfeffer writes of a family in which the younger brother mysteriously disappears without a clue in *The Year Without Michael* (Bantam). And in my mystery novel *The Other Side of Dark* (Delacort/Dell), a teenaged girl wakes from a four-year comatose state to discover not only that she is seventeen, instead of thirteen, but that she is also the only eyewitness who can identify the person who murdered her mother.

Demanding Plots

Plot and character development are so tightly interwoven that they grow together as the idea takes shape. The direction the story follows depends upon the main character's actions and reactions because the story belongs to the main character.

The successful juvenile mystery novel has two interrelated story lines: The main character has a personal problem that must be solved, and the main character has a mystery to solve.

Each of the mystery novels above contains this dual story line.

In *Taking Terri Mueller* the mystery is complex. Terri must discover her true identity and, without her father's knowledge, try to find her mother. Terri's emotions play a large part in this story: the torment she feels when she is sure her father has lied to her and is responsible for this strange, ever-moving life in which she can't put down roots or make real friends; the love-hate anguish at knowing her father has kept her from her mother all these years; and the fear that if she does contact her mother, her father will be put into prison. Terri has to handle her own feelings and come to a sensible course of action as well as solve the mystery.

April's identity and lifestyle are suddenly snatched away in *Don't Look Behind You*. Against her will even her name has been changed. Everything about her life seems to vary at the whim of the government agent in charge of her family; and she has to deal with the anger she feels toward the government, her father, her mother, and—eventually—even herself.

Amy, in *The Dollhouse Murders*, must deal with her own feelings of rejection by her mother; her jealousy of the attention her younger sister, Louann, is receiving; and her resentment of having to watch over this retarded sister.

As *The Year Without Michael* develops, Jody is devastated. She watches her family life crumble and those she loves split farther and farther apart. Desperately, she tries to bring them together as she aches with loneliness for the little brother she may never see again.

Stacy struggles to make up the four lost years of her life in *The Other Side of Dark*, at the same time mourning the death of her mother and trying to come to terms with the problems her eyewitness status is causing her family.

Anger, hatred, resentment, loss, fury, the desperate need to be loved—main characters in mysteries for young people have to learn to handle their personal problems as well as solve mysteries.

Suspense!

The mystery plot for today's impatient young readers is fast paced and filled with action. Writers should pull out all the stops and use any and every technique for establishing suspense. These are a few of the ways in which this can be done:

1. Use the description of the setting to help create and maintain suspense.

2. Your main character makes a mistake, which is obvious to readers, and takes a wrong course of action.

3. Time is rapidly running out. Will the main character make it?

4. The main character needs some information, and the person who has it is tantalizingly slow to come forward with it. The delay tantalizes readers, too.

5. Suspicion can be thrown on someone the main character has trusted. Maybe it's just the reader who becomes suspicious, and the main character is innocently unaware. When will the main character wake up and discover the danger she's in?

6. Unexpected surprises can make a sudden shift in the story's direction. Was it a wrong turn or a right one? Read and find out.

7. Readers are made aware that something dangerous or frightening will happen to the main character, but they don't know when it will take place.

8. Peculiar characters may fit only certain stories, but when they do appear they add suspense.

9. Chapters should end with dangling questions, creating such suspenseful curiosity that young readers can't put the book down and *must* go on to the next chapter.

Show, Don't Tell

Young readers have grown up with the highly visual drama presented in movies and television, and they think visually. A ninth-grade girl recently wrote to me, "I got really excited when suddenly Marti turned around and saw Emmet. I jumped because in my mind I was picturing the story; and if it were a movie, the volume of the music would have suddenly gotten louder and everyone would have jumped."

Writing can be every bit as visual as its media counterparts when it appeals to the imagination. Sensory perception and strong action verbs help writing become vivid and visual, and the frequent use of dialogue pulls readers into the story. If a story in a mystery novel moves from scene to scene, then narration will be minimal.

Be Sure of the Facts

It all comes down to respect for your readers. If you care about them, you'll double-check every fact. Be familiar with the background in your story. Write only about places in which you've lived or have traveled for the purpose of doing research.

If your story involves any type of police procedural, talk to someone at your local police headquarters. Make sure you've got it right. If you're including job information—anything from working in a fast-food place, an attorney's office, or an under-the-city sewer—do your research well, because there are kids out there who'll know if you're right or wrong, and they write letters. Do they ever! If you're right, they'll praise you, and if you're wrong, they'll let you know. If you lose their trust you've lost them as readers.

Of course, it's a foregone conclusion that as a good mystery writer you'll never withhold a clue or hold back information that's necessary to solve the crime.

Your mysteries can follow the path of detection or the back alleys of psychological suspense. They can reach afield to combine with science fiction, the Western, the historical, the romance, and the humor novel. They can open horizons and provide new directions. And because each year new crops of kids discover mystery novels and make them their reading favorites, juvenile mysteries will continue to rank high on publishers' lists.

THE JOYS AND CHALLENGES
OF THE SHORT STORY

■ *Edward D. Hoch*

The Joys

All right, why do I write short stories? Why does anyone, for that matter, in today's market? I've had well-known authors tell me if they thought of an idea good enough for a short story they'd expand it into a novel. I've had well-known literary agents tell me if they're taking an editor to lunch they want to be selling him a novel, not a short story.

There's no hiding the fact that the immediate financial gain from a novel is usually more than ten times greater than that from a short story. Unless you're selling to markets such as *Playboy*, short story payments generally range from three to ten cents a word, with some semiprofessional publications still offering the 1920s pulp rate of a penny a word. Occasionally an original anthology built around a highly marketable theme might offer a thousand or two thousand dollars, but that's about the limit.

However, there is money to be made from short stories over the long haul. I have dozens that have proven more profitable for me than the handful of novels I published thirty years ago. While a book publisher can tie up most rights, taking a cut from reprint and book club editions and sometimes even from foreign sales and film rights, magazine publishers generally purchase only first North American serial rights, occasionally with an option on first anthology rights as well. In most cases a writer is free to sell onetime nonexclusive rights to a story anywhere in the world—to a weekly newspaper in England, a radio station in Switzerland, or a mystery magazine in Japan. In this country there are frequent anthologies, compilations of short stories on audiotape, and even appearances in textbooks. (One of my early stories has been re-printed more than fifty times in textbooks for high school and junior high students.) If you're lucky, a single television sale can bring more than the advance on a novel.

But only a fool would write short stories solely for money. There has to be something more to it than that. In my case I am blessed (or cursed) with the ability to think up plots faster and more easily than I can fully develop them and set them down on paper. The novels I've attempted have dragged on for months in the writing, while all the time other ideas were crowding their way into my mind. I wanted to be done with the novel and on to the next story. The stories I write now, generally 6,000 to 7,000 words long, can be finished and polished in two weeks or less. That's just about right for me, and I'm usually starting the next story before the latest is in the mail.

Graham Greene once observed that an author is the same person when he starts and finishes a short story, whereas a novel that takes a year or more to write can find him a different person, with different views on some of the fundamental concepts of the book. A short story provides a writer with the exhilaration of completing a job, and in my case I can experience this exhilaration some twenty times a year! On a more practical note, if your short story doesn't happen to sell to the first or second editor who sees it, there's not the frustration of having wasted months or even a year of your life. Already you can be working on the next story while seeking other markets for the reject. And short story editors usually decide on submissions within a few weeks, not the several months often required for manuscripts of novels.

Short stories alone rarely make a writer famous, unless his name is Poe, but they can bring in a good income over the years, provide a nice change of pace for novelists, and offer the beginning writer a perfect opportunity to hone his skills before tackling a longer work.

Getting Started With Characters and Setting

The first thing for writers in our field to decide is whether they want to try a mystery or a suspense story. Either way, they need an opening that will grab the reader. If that opening can also introduce a character and establish a setting, so much the better. An opening line that did all three was Graham Greene's lead-in to his novel *Brighton Rock*: "Hale knew, before he had been in Brighton three hours, that they meant to murder him."

I tried something similar with the opening of my story "Murder of a Gypsy King," which begins: "On the long, lonely highway into Bucharest that sunny August afternoon, Jennifer Beatty suddenly changed her mind." In each of these examples, the reader is introduced to an important character and given the setting for the story. There is also a question implicit in each opening: Why do "they" want to murder Hale, and why did Jennifer Beatty change her mind? These questions are designed to hook the reader, to keep him or her going to find the answers.

If your story is set in the past, or in an unfamiliar city, some research will be necessary. I have built mysteries around Jumbo, the circus elephant, and the Wright brothers' first flight, among other things. Both required considerable research for just a few sentences of fact and description. For a story about America's centennial on July 4, 1876, I consulted microfilm copies of newspapers for that date.

My stories about British cipher expert Jeffery Rand and Romanian gypsy Michael Vlado are often set in European cities. The Rand stories sometimes venture even farther, and I was pleased when a reader complimented me on my authentic Hong Kong background in one of them. I'd never visited Hong Kong, but reading a couple of recent books gave me all the background I needed. I find two sources invaluable for research on unfamiliar cities: One is a street map of the city, and another is a guidebook containing photographs, particularly street scenes. Mentioning streets or airports or hotels, even if only in passing, can add greatly to a story's sense of realism. Guidebooks can also supply temperatures and rainfall frequency for different seasons. The entire world isn't like home. To have a sunny day during some city's rainy season or to forget that seasons are reversed in the Southern Hemisphere can be a fatal error.

Many mystery writers spend a great deal of time researching police procedure. I have never found this to be necessary in short stories with their limited space, mainly because such procedures can vary from city to city. My Captain Leopold stories, semiprocedurals, are set in an unnamed city where I feel the police can follow their own rules within certain limits.

In the close confines of a short story, character, plot, and setting are in a constant battle for space. If the plot and setting are to be developed, it's almost always characterization that suffers. With a series detective it's possible to overcome this problem over the space of several stories, giving the reader bits of character development as the series progresses.

But what about a nonseries mystery or a suspense story? Some characters in short mysteries seem to exist in a vacuum. Their pasts are never mentioned, and readers know nothing about them except for their actions within the time frame of the story. With the right sort of character, this can add a certain mystique to a plot, but to get the reader fully involved, it's much better to offer bits and pieces of the past—childhood, love affairs, military service, earlier cases. Occasionally there's a good reason for not revealing a character's past, at least not till the end of the story. One of my own nonseries stories deals with a wandering stranger who arrives in a small town and solves a murder. At the end the reader learns that the stranger himself is an escaped killer.

Plots and Clues

With a series character, the plot often flows from the character himself. A private eye investigates certain types of cases, often ones the official police don't know or care about. No private detective would be hired solely to investigate a murder or a bank robbery unless the authorities had failed in their task. Private detectives more often encounter murder while searching for a missing person or doing some sort of security work. In period pieces the private eye can still be seen gathering evidence for a divorce case, though the easing of divorce laws has made such investigations fairly uncommon today.

Of course the so-called amateur detective can be found investigating almost anything, and no one worries about all the bodies that seem to crowd into his life. In the eighteen years he's lived in the New England town of Northmont, my sleuth Dr. Sam Hawthorne has encountered more than sixty impossible crimes and locked-room murders—an improbable number by any standard.

Writers often find the germ of an idea in the pages of the daily newspaper, although I prefer to build plots around some odd fact or unusual setting. Occasionally I might even get the beginnings of a plot idea from a motion picture or novel, usually by thinking of ways I might have improved upon the author's original idea.

If your story is to be straight crime or suspense, possibly with a twist at the end, there need be no concern with clues. Even if the story is a mystery, there's no commandment that says an author must play fair with readers at all times. Conan Doyle's Sherlock Holmes often withheld information from the reader. Chesterton's Father Brown was better, but it was not until the advent of writers such as Agatha Christie and Ellery Queen that fair play became a necessity in true detective fiction.

I think many of today's writers view the planting and hiding of good clues as hard work that can easily be dispensed with. Admittedly, today's short story cannot contain the sort of involved explanations that Ellery Queen indulged in during the 1930s, but it can still find space for one or two good clues.

The easiest (laziest) sort of clue is the false statement by a suspect, or a statement that reveals knowledge the suspect shouldn't have had. For example, a man learns that his wife has been murdered and he immediately asks, "Do you know who shot her?" without having been told the cause of death. Other clues can involve some physical trait, such as the killer's being color-blind or right- or left-handed.

The dying message was a clue used extensively by Ellery Queen, especially in his later short stories, but the writer should try to make the circumstances of its use believable. There has to be a good reason the dying person would scrawl some obscure message rather than simply write the name of the killer. I once did a story about stolen icons in which the second victim was found dead of a bullet wound in his room, having lived long enough to print the word *ICON*. The man had committed the first murder himself. Wounded by a police bullet, he lived long enough to return to his room and start to write his confession. He died before he could finish the words *I CONFESS*.

A process of elimination sometimes reveals the killer's identity. Out of five suspects, perhaps only three had the physical strength to commit the crime. Only two of those had the knowledge that would give them a motive. And only one of them had access to the weapon that was used. Other clues might involve physical forces, such as gravity. In one of Isaac Asimov's science fiction detective stories, the killer has badly misjudged the distance he can throw an object, falling far short of his mark. The detective rightly concludes that the killer was more familiar with a world where the force of gravity was much less, and he arrests the only suspect just returned from a lengthy stay on the moon.

Perhaps the best clues are ones that make good use of the detective's special abilities, because of either special training or inherent knowledge. In one of her best Kinsey Millhone short stories, Sue Grafton's private eye spots a clue involving a woman's diaphragm—the sort of clue a female sleuth would spot more readily than a male.

Solutions and Conclusions

I think it was John Dickson Carr who once stated that the perfect locked-room mystery would have a solution that could be given in one sentence. That's true of any mystery, but if you want to play fair with the reader you'll need more space than that to point out the clues and explain the reasoning behind them. My stories generally run from twenty to twenty-five pages in manuscript, and I feel I can use two of these pages for the solution if necessary. Sometimes even that seems long, though. Certainly Carr's one-sentence windup is the goal to strive for.

It's not always necessary to surprise the reader with every story. Sometimes the plot may call for a more conventional ending. (Fred Dannay, one-half of Ellery Queen, once told me it's all right to let the reader solve the mystery occasionally.) With just about every story I write there comes a time when I sit back and think about the ending I'm heading for. I ask myself if it's an ending that would really satisfy me as a reader. If it isn't, I change it. With new writers, especially, an ending should be one that sticks in the readers' minds, one they remember the next time they encounter your name on the contents page.

The first story I ever read by Edgar Allan Poe was "The Pit and the Pendulum" in one of my school textbooks. I read those last four sentences:

> An outstretched arm caught my own as I fell, fainting, into the abyss. It was that of General Lasalle. The French army had entered Toledo. The Inquisition was in the hands of its enemies.

I read them, and I remembered their impact. I sought out every story of Poe's that I could find. It was an ending that completely satisfied the reader, as I'm sure it satisfied Poe. We can't all be Poe, but if we satisfy ourselves there's a good chance we'll satisfy the reader as well.

Selling Your Story

These days, with so few markets for short mystery fiction, there's no sure rule for success. Happily, both of the nationally distributed mystery magazines, *Ellery Queen Mystery Magazine* and *Alfred Hitchcock's Mystery Magazine*, are especially hospitable to stories by new writers. Beyond that, an increasing number of original anthologies is being published—as many as twenty a year—

though often they are not open to the beginning writer. There are also a few semiprofessional mystery magazines published without national distribution. Their rates are often low, but someone just breaking into the field should consider them.

If a story doesn't sell to the first few editors who see it, there's a tendency to change and revise it, especially if an editor has offered concrete objections to certain plot points. My own feeling is that if you believe in a story you should stick with it, revising it only if a contract is offered. My Edgar-winner story "The Oblong Room" was rejected a few times before finding a home in *The Saint Magazine*. Only one of my ten stories that have appeared on American television sold to the first editor who saw it. The other nine had all been rejected at least once.

As I indicated earlier, literary agents aren't too interested in handling short stories these days, even for established clients. As a short story writer you're pretty much on your own. Still, it's a good feeling when those letters of acceptance arrive in the mail. It's not even that bad when a rejection comes in, because there's always the possibility of selling to a new market and reaching a whole new audience.

Recommended Reference Books

Adey, Robert. *Locked Room Murders and Other Impossible Crimes: A Comprehensive Bibliography*. Rev. and expanded. Minneapolis: Crossover Press, 1991.

Breen, Jon L. *What About Murder? A Guide to Books About Mystery and Detective Fiction*. Metuchen, N.J.: Scarecrow Press, 1981.

———. *What About Murder? (1981–1991): A Guide to Books About Mystery and Detective Fiction*. Metuchen, N.J.: Scarecrow Press, 1993.

Contento, William G. and Martin H. Greenberg. *Index to Crime and Mystery Anthologies*. Boston: G.K. Hall, 1991.

Cook, Michael L. *Mystery, Detective, and Espionage Magazines*. Westport, Conn.: Greenwood Press, 1983.

Cook, Michael L., and Stephen T. Miller. *Mystery, Detective, and Espionage Fiction: A Checklist of Fiction in U.S. Pulp Magazines, 1915–1974.* (2 vols.) New York: Garland Publishing, 1988.

Cook, Michael L., comp. *Monthly Murders: A Checklist and Chronological Listing of Fiction in the Digest-Size Mystery Magazines in the United States and England.* Westport, Conn.: Greenwood Press, 1982.

Lachman, Marvin. *The American Regional Mystery.* Minneapolis: Crossover Press, 2000.

Recommended Story Collections

Chesterton, G.K. *The Innocence of Father Brown.* New York: John Lane Company, 1911. Still the outstanding single-author collection of detective short stories.

Pronzini, Bill, Martin H. Greenberg, and Charles G. Waugh, eds. *The Mystery Hall of Fame: An Anthology of Classic Mystery and Suspense Stories Selected by the Mystery Writers of America.* New York: Morrow, 1984.

Queen, Ellery, ed. *101 Years' Entertainment: The Great Detective Stories, 1841–1941.* Boston: Little, Brown and Company, 1941.

THE MEDICAL THRILLER

■ *Tess Gerritsen*

I've lost count of how many people I have watched die. You probably think this is merely a figurative statement by a mystery author, but it is, in fact, the truth—a truth shared by every other physician who has practiced clinical medicine. During our training, we doctors dash off to countless code blues, pump on so many chests, and thread endotracheal tubes down so many throats that the dead begin to blend together in our memories. Over the years, we see so many patients die that the scene loses its power to shock us. Medical crises that the public would consider high drama are just part of a day's work for a doctor, and we do not realize how fascinating our jobs must seem to everyone else.

That, in large part, is why it took me so long to write my first medical thriller.

For eight years, while working part-time as a physician, I wrote romantic suspense novels. I chose topics that I considered exciting: international espionage, crimes of passion, and women on the run. It didn't occur to me that readers might hunger to know about the world of hospitals and doctors—the very world I just happened to work in every day.

Then the premise for a medical thriller practically dropped into my lap. I'd heard a horrifying rumor from an ex-cop who'd been traveling in Russia. He claimed that children were being kidnapped in Moscow, to be sacrificed as organ donors. Immediately the plot of *Harvest* sprang to life in my head, as did the characters: one a crippled but resourceful Russian child who would survive by his wits alone, the other a woman physician on the cusp of achieving her lifelong dream as a transplant surgeon.

When I pitched this idea to my agent, she said: "It's a great premise for a medical thriller. But only a doctor would have the credibility to write it."

"I never told you this," I confessed. "I am a doctor. A board-certified internist."

Her impassioned response: "Then why on earth *aren't* you writing medical thrillers?"

Her reaction, as well as the subsequent success of *Harvest*, demonstrated to me just how much the public loves medical suspense. Every day, life-and-death dramas play out in hospitals, where we experience the best and the worst times of our lives: the birth of a child, the death of a loved one. Here is where we witness both joy and tragedy, and because of this, we regard hospitals with apprehension and even fear. Yes, hospitals are where we go to be healed, but they're also places where we're stabbed with needles and probed with tubes and where all sorts of painful things are done to our bodies. They're places where we could very well die. What better setting for a suspense novel?

But the hospital setting alone is not enough to make a novel a medical thriller. While many fine suspense novels take place in hospitals, they lack the essential element that makes this particular subgenre so unique. The definition I myself use for the term *medical thriller* is this: It is a suspense novel set in the world of medicine, with characters who are medically trained. It is *also* a novel in which the central conflict or evil involves medical science or medical ethics. These different elements combined—the hospital setting, the physician or nurse protagonist, and a premise based on situations unique to medicine—are what make these novels so compelling.

Where does one find a good medical thriller premise? If you've worked in the medical field, you can probably list a number of them right off the top of your head, from the perils of managed care to corruption in the pharmaceutical industry. The popular media—from wire stories to the *The National Enquirer*—is another fertile source of thriller premises, although I tend to shy away from topics that are widely publicized because I know that every other thriller writer will be racing to use them. When Dolly the sheep was created, we could all guess that cloning would be the next hot thriller topic. Sure enough, two best-selling cloning novels, Ken Follett's *The Third Twin* and John Darnton's *The Experiment*, were soon published.

I've found that even better sources for a medical thriller premise are scientific journals. I'm fascinated by cutting-edge medical research, so I look for plot ideas in magazines such as *Science*, *Nature*, *Discover*, and *Scientific American*. Their articles often focus on rather esoteric subjects, but they show us the direction in which future medical developments are headed. For example, an article in *Science* about the manipulation of fruit fly genes, resulting in flies with multiple eyes, inspired my novel *Life Support*. The plot of my NASA medical thriller, *Gravity*, was based on a research article about the bizarre growth of cell cultures in zero gravity. Whenever I learn about some new scientific discovery, I ask the question: "What are its possible consequences to humanity? How could this advance turn into disaster?" Then I search for the scientific evidence to back up my scenario. While imagination fuels my stories, I limit myself to what is scientifically achievable. Above all, these thrillers must be medically possible and grounded in *real* science—not pseudoscience.

Beyond the basics of plot and character, we get down to the actual writing, and here is where many of these thrillers fall apart. The usual reason is that the medical details are unconvincing or just plain wrong. Again and again, as a reader, I've found myself stopping cold in the middle of a book because of a glaring medical error. The plot and characters may be superb, the action pulse pounding, but that one error will destroy the author's authority for me. It will break the spell he has worked hard to weave.

The most frequent mistakes are due to the author's lack of familiarity with the medical training process. Writers have confused "premed students" with "medical students," used "cardiologist" and "cardiac surgeon" interchangeably, and mistakenly referred to the "chief of medicine" as the "chief medical resident." Any doctor or nurse who spots these errors will either groan or burst out laughing—not the reaction you want your readers to have! So here, in a nutshell, is what you need to know about medical training.

It starts off with four years of college, in which the undergraduate premed takes the prerequisite science courses to apply to medical school. The premed has *not* taken any medical courses. He does not know how to diagnose illnesses or perform surgery. He is an undergraduate like any other college student and may in fact be a nonscience major. (I myself was an anthropology major.) He then applies to medical school, takes the Medical College Admission Test (MCAT), and keeps his fingers crossed that he's accepted. Getting into medical school is the most competitive stage in the entire process. Once a student is accepted to medical school, he is almost assured his M.D., so fictional scenarios involving cutthroat competition to graduate from medical school are unrealistic.

Medical school is four years long. The first two years tend to be lab and classroom work, so don't have your fictional first-year medical student performing surgery. He wouldn't know how to hold a scalpel! At the end of these four years, the student is awarded his M.D., but he's still not qualified to practice medicine. He must go on to a residency training program, the first year of which is called the internship. (Note: An "intern" is an M.D. in his first year of training; an "internist" is a fully qualified physician who has completed an internal medicine residency.) Depending on the specialty the doctor chooses, the residency program will usually last between three and five years. Internal medicine is a three-year residency; general surgery requires five years. At the end of this residency, he is eligible for specialty certification and may open a practice. Or, he may choose to pursue additional years of subspecialty training, at the end of which he'll be roughly seventy years old and ready for retirement.

Okay, so I'm exaggerating. A newly minted neurosurgeon is most likely about thirty-two years old. My point is, medical training is long and arduous, and at the end of it, the physician may have accumulated hundreds of thousands of dollars in educational debts. During those years, he worked eighty- or even hundred-hour weeks, witnessed countless tragedies, and made mistakes that may have killed people. Because of the selection process he has endured, he is almost certainly intelligent, skillful, and determined—in other words, he is superb material on which to base either a hero or a villain.

Now your job, as a novelist, is to make your doctor character come alive on the page through action and dialogue. Here is where medical thriller writers can again lose credibility, by not understanding the basics of "doctor-speak." Readers of these books are hungry for the inside details. My agent once told me, "We all want to know what doctors know. We want to know your secret code, to be brought into a world we can't otherwise visit." This means you the author must get the language right so your doctors sound like real doctors.

The most popular source of accurate doctor-speak is the TV show *ER*. Here the characters don't stop to define every term; what the audience hears is rapid-fire dialogue punctuated by unfamiliar words. ("Stat!" "V-fib!" "IV push!") Does the audience need to know what these words mean? Not really. Simply by the context in which a word is used, and how other characters react, we understand that an announcement of "V-fib!" is very, very bad news indeed.

Watch a few episodes of *ER*, and you'll hear how doctors speak to one another. They don't say "He had a heart attack"; they say, "He had an MI." And so should the doctors in your novel. Technically accurate dialogue is the best way to demonstrate your authority as a medical thriller writer. You don't need to write pages and pages of it; in fact, just a few key scenes with spot-on accurate dialogue will probably convince your readers you know far more about medicine than you really do.

A doctor's medical training spans seven years or more, and it's impossible for the nonphysician novelist to match that experience with just a few weeks of research. To write a convincing medical thriller, you will need to turn to expert sources for guidance on dialogue and medical procedures. If you've got an M.D. in your family, lucky you! If not, you'll have to cultivate friendships with physicians. Retired physicians are especially good sources of information because they have a lifetime of anecdotes they can share. Nurses, too, make good expert sources since they work on the same hospital wards, understand doctor-speak, and can usually spot errors in your manuscript. Most medical personnel will be happy to address specific issues, but don't hand them pages of questions or treat the visit as a fishing expedition. Do your homework ahead of time so that you know at least a little about the subject you're researching. And don't show up at your own doctor's appointment with a surprise manuscript in hand for his "expert" proofreading. I can guarantee, your physician will *not* be pleased to get it.

Although I'm an M.D., I'm well aware of huge gaps in my own medical knowledge, and I keep a large library of textbooks that I frequently refer to. Every medical thriller writer should own, at the very least, a comprehensive medical dictionary, a recent *Physicians' Desk Reference (PDR)*, and a recent *Manual of Medical Therapeutics* (otherwise known as "the Washington Manual," published by Little, Brown). In addition, I often consult my copies of *Harrison's Principles of Internal Medicine*, Schwartz's *Principles of Surgery*, and textbooks on anatomy, gynecology, infectious diseases, and pharmacology. These are rather expensive books, so if you live near a hospital or medical school, I recommend you contact the medical librarian for access to the institution's collection. The librarian probably won't let you check out the books but will allow you to use them on premises.

I've also found the Internet to be a terrific source for obscure bits of information and for recent journal articles. One excellent medical Web site is hosted by the National Library of Medicine at www.ncbi.nlm.nih.gov/PubMed. Here I can search for a list of every recent article published about, say, mad cow disease. Then I take this list to my local medical library, where I can read the articles themselves.

Beyond technical accuracy and doc-talk, there is one more characteristic about medical thrillers that makes them unique: They allow us to see the world through a nurse's or a doctor's eyes, to experience the sounds and smells and emotions this person confronts on the job. It's these sensory details that grab a reader's attention. The feel of the needle tip "popping" into a vein. The smell of burnt flesh as it's cauterized. The screech a bone saw makes as it cuts through the sternum. These are things only medical personnel have experienced, and to learn these details, you will have to turn to your expert sources.

What they will not tell you, however, are the things they're ashamed of: all the mistakes they've made, or the days they've broken down sobbing in the ICU, or how they wished a certain patient would hurry up and die. Yet it's these very secrets, these dark and shameful emotions, that can make your fictional hero come alive. Here is where your skill as a novelist comes in, when you create a character whose flaws transform him from a stock M.D. figure into a real—and imperfect—human being.

And that, in the end, is what our novels should be about: not icons in white coats rushing about saving lives, not brilliant heroes who never make mistakes, but believably imperfect and complex people who—yes—just happen to be doctors.

LEGAL THRILLERS

■ *Linda Fairstein*

Perhaps you have made a decision to write a legal thriller because you have been a participant in a dramatic courtroom battle— as a defense attorney whose skill exonerated an innocent client, as the beneficiary of family heirlooms in a hard-fought will contest, or as a juror who second-guessed the tactics of the litigators throughout a protracted trial. Maybe your fascination with this category of crime novels is that you have practiced law on the civil side but have fantasized about delivering the stirring summation in a high-profile murder trial. Or maybe you simply enjoy the prospect of entering this world because you like lawyers.

That last possibility brings me directly to the subject of the willing suspension of disbelief, something that most of us count on in our readers when we set about to plot our stories.

Once you have selected this subgenre as your setting, I think there are critical issues to face before you start pounding out the pages. Whether you are writing a courtroom drama or using a legal eagle as an amateur sleuth, remember that you have chosen to portray a profession—like medicine—that requires an advanced degree and is governed by a lot of rules and procedures. Even if your characters are going to break those rules, you have to know what they are in order to heighten the tension of any ethical dilemma or criminal verdict.

For thirty years, I have been a prosecutor in the great office of the district attorney in New York. When I set out to write a series about an assistant district attorney with a similar job, I felt that what I could bring to the books was the authenticity of what my work has been—investigating homicides and sexual assault cases with my colleagues in the NYPD.

Because of my professional experience, when I pick up a legal thriller, I prefer to read books written by experienced lawyers or by authors who have studied the practice seriously. They know the language and attitude of the courtroom, they move their characters about it with ease, they sit them at the proper counsel table, they craft their arguments to the judge with appropriate rhetoric, and they know when to make objections. Many other readers who have no reason to be familiar with legal procedures won't care about getting these details right, so you first need to figure out who your target audience might be.

I'm going to assume that some of you who are reading this chapter are doing so because you have that Juris Doctor degree. You still have a lot of choices to make about the direction you will take in writing fiction. Let's examine the many options some of the masters of this specialty have given us.

From my earliest days as a prosecutor, I was haunted by the model that Erle Stanley Gardner had laid before the American public, first in his stories and then in their adaptation to the television screen. While Perry Mason was the most popular and widely known defense attorney in fiction, I found myself sympathizing with Hamilton Burger. How many times could the poor guy get it wrong and actually not figure out his mistake until the murder case was literally ready to be put in the hands of the jurors? In my first few trials, I used to get the jitters during the defense summations, fearful that someone in the benches behind me (which were never as densely populated as Gardner's) would stand up and proclaim his guilt, preventing the miscarriage of justice because of Mason's skill as a cross-examiner.

In the many years that I thought about creating the Alexandra Cooper series, I dreamed of righting that vision of the bumbling prosecutor, the one simply anxious to nail a culprit rather than do justice. My books were designed to be procedurals, rather than courtroom dramas, and to show the actual manner in which cases are investigated in our jurisdiction, since we have an unusually close partnership with the homicide detectives from the moment a murder is discovered through the trial of the case.

You can tell that I use my own novels to set the world back in a better place . . . from my own personal perspective. And I think whatever personal reasons bring you to the story you want to tell help to drive the writing. Scott Turow's *Presumed Innocent* remains, to my view, one of the most brilliant examples of this genre. There is, of course, the genius of the plotting. But there is also the unmistakable skill of Turow, the lawyer, who guides his carefully drawn characters—most of whom are also lawyers—through stunning scenes in a criminal trial that were clearly enhanced by his own experience at the bar.

I hope you haven't forgotten that the murder victim in that book was, unfortunately, a sex crimes prosecutor. Her debut was one of the first times the mystery genre featured an assistant district attorney in that rather unique specialty. Since that has been my field of concentration since our office established the country's pioneering unit in the 1970s, another of my personal goals in creating Alex Cooper was to let people in on the work that has riveted me and kept me in the job for so long.

Give some thought to whether your protagonist will be a professional or an amateur. It is hard for me to imagine anyone working in law enforcement today who is not familiar with the ways in which DNA technology has revolutionized the criminal justice system. Just five years ago, serologists at the police lab needed substantial amounts of blood—a stain the size of a quarter—to link a suspect to crime scene evidence. Today, the skin cells that have sloughed off onto my computer mouse as I write this chapter would be able to create a genetic profile sufficient to identify me every bit as conclusively as a vial of my blood or saliva. If you have a law degree and practiced in the trusts and estates department of a large firm for ten years, be sure and make yourself familiar with the most up-to-date forensic developments before you sit your characters in the well of a criminal courtroom.

In my three decades as a prosecutor, no one in my very large and eclectic jurisdiction has died after eating poisoned mushrooms. Even though some homicides have remained unsolved for a very long time, I have never worked on a murder with Manhattan North homicide detectives during which a spunky nun, a retired veterinarian, or a hungover private investigator has cracked the case before New York's Finest was able to do so. I can suspend my disbelief and devour amateur sleuth stories as often as the next guy, but it's harder to swallow a protagonist in the legal profession who does not know the law and legal procedures.

Are you doing a stand-alone, or do you think you have the genesis of a series? The former gives you more latitude to take risks with the characters you are creating, because you don't have to worry about how the choices they make in this book will affect their return appearances. An unethical attorney who does something outrageous may get away with it once or twice, but sooner or later, he's likely to be disbarred. If you believe that you are giving birth to a cast of continuing characters, how they behave will be determined—at least in part—by their backstory, and by how your readers will greet them when they reappear in the sequel.

One of the real advantages about entering this subgenre is the enormous range it offers in the methods of telling stories. While the wonderfully fast-paced novels of John Grisham and David Baldacci are often categorized as legal thrillers, Grisham's *A Time to Kill*, with the same essential elements as his later best-sellers (a crime, the professional involvement of lawyers, the use of the courtroom), is frequently described as a quiet, reflective book, given the more dignified label of literary fiction.

Richard North Patterson is one of the most eloquent, elegant writers working today. His stories are intellectually challenging, exploring issues of morality in American social and political life. They involve murders and crises of legal conscience and consequence, and they feature lawyers who are skilled and smart. Patterson has won many awards—including our own Edgar—and while

the law is at the center of his fictional world, I would not character-
ize his books as thrillers. His work makes me think, instead, of
Pulitzer prize–winning Harper Lee, the lawyer whose only novel,
To Kill a Mockingbird, was a stunning courtroom drama, but
also a profound and moving examination of conscience and racism
in the American South.

Once you breathe life into your legal protagonist, you have to
decide with whom she or he practices law. When Alex Cooper
gets ready to leave public service and hang out a shingle, she'll be
planning to do job interviews at firms peopled with any lawyers
created by Lisa Scottoline. Now this is not simply because Scottoline is another Edgar-winning author, but because her Portias are
all so damn smart *and* have a riotously fine time together. Judy
Carrier, the accused's mouthpiece in *The Vendetta Defense*, has
the great good fortune to work at Rosato and Associates, where I
would dearly love to practice myself. She demonstrates once again
that the combination of intelligence, guts, humor, and knowledge
of the law is unbeatable—both in fiction and in the courtroom.

This works on both sides of the pond. I am always engaged by
the novels of Frances Fyfield, who shows us the practice, legal
and literary, from abroad. Her fiction, steeped in crime, is also rich
in psychological nuance and texture. Before you even think of
moving your characters around internationally—something that
Grisham does masterfully—remember that unlike many professions, the rules vary under different systems of law. The way in
which Fyfield's Crown Prosecutors are assigned their cases and
how they prepare them for trial is wildly different from the American method. There are barristers and solicitors, and you need to
know the distinctions between their roles before you get to dressing
your lawyers up in wigs and robes.

What if you are determined to do a legal thriller but have never
practiced law? There are a variety of ways to do research. Even
though cameras are not welcome at trials in every state in the country, the public *is*. Violent crime figures may be down, but there
isn't a prosecutor's office anywhere that doesn't have a couple of
murder cases pending. Befriend the assistant district attorney. For
the painless price of an acknowledgment, most of us are only too

happy to explain the system and describe behind-the-scene events that are often the most scintillating parts of the case, but never make it into the trial because of evidentiary rules.

There are also invaluable human resources available through the members of MWA. If you're writing about the law, I'll presume you've read a lot of crime novels that feature lawyer-protagonists. How I wish I could go back and pick the brains of someone like Robert Traver, who wrote the stunning courtroom drama *Anatomy of a Murder*. Too late for that, for me. But you should identify the style of book you like and read everything you can by those authors. Whether it's legal procedurals, crime-ridden thrillers, dazzling courtroom scenes, or moral dilemmas that you long to write about, study the classics, and immerse yourself in the books you most admire.

Like the practice of law, the opportunity to write about the legal system offers an endless array of subjects for conflict; a colorful palette of character traits to draw from in creating heroes, heroines, and villains; and a constantly evolving justice process that allows us to explore, in fiction, what is still fluid and changing before our highest courts. Don't kill all the lawyers, as Shakespeare's Dick the Butcher urged, because some tough prosecutor, such as Alex Cooper, will be looking to send you up the river. But do join those of us who have stood before a jury and tried to keep our characters within—or just beyond—the reach of the long arm of the law.

HISTORICAL MYSTERIES:
THE PAST IS A
FOREIGN COUNTRY

▪ *Laurie R. King*

"The past is a foreign country: they do things differently there."
Far be it from me to argue with L.P. Hartley, but I'm not
so sure I agree. The first part of the statement, granted: 1920s England
is a foreign country even to a London native, or 1940s Los Angeles
to most Angelinos. But doing things differently? From a writer's
point of view, one of the most valuable things about the past is
precisely that human beings don't change all that much, that the
similarities we share with our ancestors vastly outweigh the
differences.

Faded Times: Why?

There are any number of reasons, of course, why we choose to
write, or to read, stories set in faded times. Historical fiction has
long been saddled with the "escapism" charge, doubly so when the
fiction is also classified as a mystery. And it is true, one of the
pleasures in reading a good historical is that it's like a trip to a
foreign country without the inoculations. A historical novel that
makes full use of its setting can be as invigorating as a jaunt to

Tijuana or Amsterdam, and if it's decently researched you might even learn something—keeping in full view the caveat that we writers lie for a living.

In my own case, the historical period I ended up in was more or less chosen for me, when I wished to write about a young woman who comes face-to-face with Mr. Sherlock Holmes. Unless I wanted to have him so decrepit he had to be trundled about the Sussex Downs in a Bath chair, the year 1915 was about as late as I could begin, some months following the last (by internal date) of the Conan Doyle stories. This plunged me into the very midst of the Great War. I would like to think that I'd have gotten there eventually, even if Ms. Russell's particular needs had not taken me there, because I have come to find the years following August 1914 one of the most fascinating, enchanting, moving, terrifying periods in history. Women's rights, the agony of modern warfare, the devastation of a nation's innocence, heroism and tragedy and heart-stopping stupidities and all the building blocks of today's political turmoil. I feel like a cook surveying her magnificently stocked pantry: Any random choice can make a feast.

So that's one of the reasons, an abundance of colorful and emotionally satisfying material, the landscape of a foreign country out of which will grow a story.

Then there's the simple fact that it is the past, that even if the tale I am reading is set in medieval China and none of my ancestors has set foot out of Ireland in two thousand years, it is my past as well, with the potential of teaching me something about where I have come from.

Furthermore, the past resonates. When I set a story in 1919 Palestine, my character's innocence of what the century will bring allows me to utilize foreshadowing on a grand scale. When she muses of the millennia of man's inhumanity to man that has played itself out on the rocky hills over Jerusalem, then goes on to wonder if perhaps the torment might be coming to an end, the modern reader looking over her shoulder sets that faint hope against the actual events of the intervening years and is given a sense of omniscience and sorrow for the character's optimism. (That, at any rate, was the intention.) A story set, say, in London during the early months of 1666 would throb with hidden suspense, for the reader would know what the characters do not: that despite the gaiety of theatres and bawdy taverns and the creeping threat of plague in the slums, the Great Fire is flickering catastrophically just over the horizon, waiting to obliterate a city.

One of the most valuable, and subtle, strengths of the historical is found in the space between the resonations of the past and its odd familiarities. Do "they" do things differently? Yes, of course they do. No, of course they don't. In foreign travel, some of the most intense experiences are those that are peculiarly unforeign, things that are tilted just enough off-center to make us look more closely, at them and at ourselves—such as the utterly familiar glass bottle of Vaseline I bought in India to soothe my infant's rash, which, when opened, reeked of raw gasoline (petroleum jelly, no?). Or the jolt felt at spotting a pair of Birkenstocks among the water buffalo–hide sandals at the entrance to an Asian temple. Or giggling figures craning over a shared mirror to correct makeup and hairstyles, only these figures are not Californian teenagers, they're middle-aged Papuan males preparing for a ritual dance.

The slight electrical shock imparted by incongruity, the familiar among the strange or the foreign in the known, is one of the purposes of fiction. When we read the Brother Cadfael stories of Ellis Peters, we are not seeing some ex-Crusader-turned-monk whose motives and belief system are nine centuries out of date; we are seeing a man, a human being: ourselves. And when we chuckle at the tribulations of Amelia Peabody, it is not because Elizabeth Peters has captured a foreign land and society so well; it is because the familiar human frailties and idiosyncrasies come into greater focus when in that unfamiliar setting, and show us known faces looking out from the odd costumes.

Last, but by no means least, one of the great pleasures of historical fiction is the scope it offers for richness of language. If I am writing a story about a homicide inspector in the San Francisco Police Department, a tale that opens this morning, my language will reflect that setting and the themes I am working on. My verbs and nouns will be precise, my sentence structure straightforward, my modifiers as minimal as I can make them in order to keep the story moving right along. If, however, I am writing a book that begins in 1915, recalling those distant events through the filtering eyes of the protagonist some seven decades later, then my language will be very different—the vocabulary rich, verging on the ornate, the sentences more formal, the descriptions more complete, the delight in language palpable.

How Not to Do It

With all the reasons speaking in favor of the historical mystery, there are pitfalls to be avoided.

First and foremost, beware the idea that sticking a story in the past simplifies matters. Yes, Brother Cadfael need not concern himself with Miranda rights and the laws of search and seizure, but in truth, from a fiction writer's point of view, those legal parameters are easily incorporated into a story. Yes, I have the advantage of allowing my amateurs to aid (or even take over from) Scotland Yard in 1920s England, but I still have to know the organizational structures of the various police bodies, I have to know early forensic techniques and when they came into use, I have to know the ground and the politics and . . .

On the other hand, the hazards of research are manifold. Research can become an addiction, and the temptation is powerful to make use of every laboriously gleaned fact, every appealing tidbit and prized iota of knowledge. When I was writing the book about 1919 Palestine, for example, I came across mention of how the army would lay out rabbit wire onto the desert floor to keep staff cars from getting bogged down in the sand. Oh, frabjous fact! I had to have it. So there I am writing away, ushering my quartet of pseudo-Bedouins toward Beersheva and across the sandy wastes where battle has raged fourteen months before, and I gleefully drag in my rabbit wire. Great tangling sheets of the stuff, strewn across the sand, rough edged, half-buried, catching at the boots of our intrepid heroine and tripping the pack mules, giving opportunity for a lengthy and oh-so-clever peroration about battle techniques and the self-importance of staff officers and the resentment of the common soldier forced to stumble along through the deep sand to one side of the wire and . . . And I entirely forgot why my characters were headed to Beersheva in the first place. The rabbit wire got ripped up, trimmed to a brief line or so, and we continued our trudge through the cold desert air.

Beware the siren call of research facts; beware the temptation to use each and every one of those hard-gained three-by-five cards. Far better to have your character pause midconversation to gesture with the buttonhook in her hand than to subject the reader to a step-by-step description of its application to the boot. If you want to see how it's done, read Steven Saylor's Gordianus series set in ancient Rome: Meticulously researched, his books manage to read as if he simply lived there. And don't we all?

Beware as well the hazards of anachronism. This warning may appear obvious, certainly to anyone who has caught a writer using an object or phrase from a story's future, but it works the other way as well. A number of times I have come across contemporary mention of an object or, more often, a phrase that I hadn't realized was yet in existence. One school of thought says, Use it, for the good of the reader. (Andrew Taylor, who nudged my memory when it came to this chapter's opening quotation, is one proponent of this way of thinking: If it's provable, it's usable.) However, I personally am chary of interrupting what John Gardner called the fictional dream; I would rather do without a phrase than have my reader's attention snagged by a thing, unless it can be smoothly incorporated into the plot.

Research Techniques

And that brings us neatly to the question of research itself. Myself, I am a book researcher, in part by training—primary source material is all that really counts in Old Testament theology—and also because I live out in the country, and my modem is therefore as torpid as a lizard in winter. Mainly, however, I prefer to handle the actual volume of Great War memoirs that some reader first held in 1919, or to read the execrable best-sellers of 1923 that no one has checked out since 1957, or even (where's my white cane?) to spin through the microfilmed *London Times* to study the adverts, head-lines, and photographs of balls and hunts.

If I did not live within striking distance of a good research library, I might be forced to troll the Internet for those bits of information (and, alas, misinformation) others have found of use. In this case, I would probably begin with the Web site (http://world.std.com/~swrs) compiled by the excellent and erudite Sarah Smith, with its sections "research historical fiction" and "Virtual Victoria" as well as valuable links to specific sites at home and abroad. Similarly, most major museums have Web sites, and although by unwritten law there is never the precise information you desire, they offer you a place to begin.

Certainly if I went to an area about whose past I was writing, I would search out the newspaper records office and, above all, any of the myriad of tiny museums that continue to spring up across the globe. Costume museums showing Roman sandals and whale-bone stays, antique auto collections, the archaeological display in one corner of a town's art museum, a bizarre collection of freak animals in formaldehyde next to stuffed hamsters dressed up and arranged as a classroom of schoolchildren—it's all grist for the writer's mill. It is also extraordinary how eager people are to share their expertise, once they hear you are a writer doing research. If you are willing to spend copious hours learning all about starting handles and steering linkages, you might even find yourself be-hind the wheel of a Stanley Steamer.

My own system of historical research tends to be twofold. The early stages are very general, even desultory, skimming memoirs and histories, on the lookout for interesting ideas and links, getting a clear sense of the time, place, and concerns of the people, all the while listening for that "ting" of inspiration. I need a character to provide my protagonists with certain information? There was mention of salt trading in that 1910 Baedeker's guide to Palestine—voilà! Mr. Bashir, a salt trader, enters my story. Later, once the story is more or less set in my mind—and indeed, after the book is written and I can see the glaring gaps in my knowledge—I will return to certain areas for closer, more focused attention. The build-ing techniques in country houses, the sorts of motorcars common in

England at the close of the war, when crepe rubber soles came into use, the actual wording of the death notifications sent to the families of executed soldiers—all those specific facts that I didn't know I might need when I began the book, yet that didn't have sufficient importance to force me to pause in my writing to clarify them, I will go back and hunt down once I have come to the end of the first draft. Here, too, is when assistance comes into play, when I have a list of specific questions: I do so hate wasting an informant's time.

A mirror fascinates because it reflects, but also because it distorts, giving back a face reversed and in a rare state of watchful repose. Crime fiction fascinates because it, too, introduces a rare distortion, a murder, that drops into a community like a rock in a pond, shattering the calm surface into a turmoil of dark and light, evil and good, rapacious and noble, and flashing glimpses of ourselves with every tossing ripple. Historical fiction transports us to a lost time, as if someone handed us cracked and sepia-tinted photographs of streetcars and gas lamps and we saw our own faces looking out at us.

The past is indeed a foreign country. We do things the same there.

From the Cradle to the Pen: The Evolution of a True Crime Writer

■ *Ann Rule*

A s far back as I can remember, I wanted to be a cop. My grand-father and then my uncle were sheriffs in a small Michigan county, and I spent my childhood vacations literally in *jail*. It was a mom-and-pop jail where the living quarters, the office, and the jail itself were all under one roof. I constantly asked my grandfather *why* anyone would want to grow up to be a criminal. Of course, it wasn't that simple to explain. But I know now that my curiosity about criminal behavior was really a struggle to understand the psychopathology of the criminal mind. Today, I'm just curious—I know the right terms to use.

I *did* become a cop, a policewoman in Seattle, but after only eighteen months, I had to resign. I was so nearsighted that I couldn't pass the eye test, and in those days you couldn't wear contact lenses. It was the biggest disappointment of my life, but a few years later, I found that I could be involved in crime solving after all. Most writers are nearsighted, but it doesn't stop us from writing, and I found another career in writing about crime.

Way back in 1969, after five years of rejection slips, I was so thrilled to receive an assignment from *True Detective* to cover a murder case that I didn't stop to evaluate the emotional impact that came with the genre. As I spoke with a Seattle homicide detective about the unsolved murder of an eighteen-year-old bride and looked at the crime scene photographs, I suddenly realized, "I'm going to be making a living because of other people's tragedies." Even though I was supporting four small children on my own and really needed this job as the Northwest territory "stringer" for five true crime magazines, I wondered if I could do it. And if I could deal with facing stark and brutal reality constantly, would I eventually grow hardened?

To face my dilemma, I arranged for one hour with a psychiatrist and asked him the question that haunted me. He smiled and said, "Ann, don't you realize that half the people in the world make a living from the other half's problems—firefighters, police officers, doctors, morticians, insurance salespeople, and so on? What matters is how *you* feel about those you write about."

The answer was easy for me. I really did care about the crime victims and their families. Fourteen hundred homicide cases later, I haven't become immune to the pain of what I've seen and heard. Instead, I think I am much *more* aware of victims' rights and feelings. Surprisingly, I have come to believe that the mass of humanity is not evil. For every conscienceless killer I research, I find several dozen "heroes"—detectives, prosecutors, witnesses who testify even when they're frightened. The good guys always seem to win in the end.

I love my career and I am grateful to have it, but every genre has its own peculiar demands and drawbacks. True crime has more than most. Successful true crime writers have to be self-starters. Many times a week, fledgling authors ask me how they can be crime writers. I tell them as gently as possible that the very nature of the genre requires writers who will find a way themselves. We must not only be writers—but detectives. In researching a crime, we must figure out how to elicit information that seems impossible to get. We have to ask people about pain and horror they would rather forget. We must ask detectives and prosecutors to share their investigations and their feelings with us. And it isn't easy. I still get butterflies in my stomach.

I've just finished my twentieth book, but each time I start working on a new book, I am still convinced that I will *never* get enough information, that nobody is going to talk to me, and that I'll end up with a pathetically thin book. And each time I end up with more details and inside information than I can squeeze behind two covers. So as you begin, you just have to have faith that it will all come together.

The most important decision you will make is to choose a subject—not a hero but an antihero. I always look for cases in which the accused are the last people in the world you would expect to be arrested for murder. They seem to have everything: good looks, brilliance, charm, charisma, talent, wealth, fame, love, success, respect—basically the traits that any of us would be happy to have. But "my people" are never content; they always want more, and they don't care what burns down or who gets killed for them to get their ways. They have no empathy at all for others, and they don't feel guilt or regret. If you pick a fascinating, antisocial subject, the book almost writes itself.

I always go to the places where the crimes happened. I want to take my readers along with me as I revisit a case. I want them to know what the houses look like, where locals go to eat, what flowers and trees grow there, and what the air feels like so they can feel as though they have been there too. I've been in Kansas in a blizzard, Florida in a hurricane, Atlanta during a beautiful autumn, and San Antonio during a ten-minute ten-inch rainfall—an hour after which the sun was much too hot for a Seattle dweller. I have stood with a convicted killer (then paroled) in a basement where two murders occurred. I have slogged into brushy fields where signs said "BEWARE: Attack Dogs on Duty" and have seen the insides of more jails than I can count, to interview felons. Even though I know I'll be coming out again, I dread the sound of that "clank" as the locks close behind me.

But this is all *after* trial. The cardinal rule in true crime is that we must wait until a case has been adjudicated before we write. Certainly, I follow cases that look promising, save newspaper clips, and jot notes in a folder. I also note the trial dates. But I never want to "spook" the prosecutor or the detectives, so I contact them and assure them that while I'll be in the courtroom, I will not write my book before trial, nor will I approach potential witnesses. Those of us who write true crime books have an advantage over reporters for television and newspapers; they have daily deadlines while we can afford to wait for the verdict.

Even though I'm gambling on a conviction (because if the defendant is acquitted, I can't write a book), I always begin research with the trial of the accused. Sitting in a courtroom for a week, a month, or even three months can be wearying, and the benches are *hard*. But there you will see the "characters" in this "play." You will hear the testimony and be able to describe the witnesses and the defendant and to capture the ambiance of the courtroom. You can decide for yourself who is telling the truth. Yes, some days are boring, but most days are compelling. I take my own notes continuously. They are my best source.

Another excellent reason to attend the trial is that you get to know the witnesses, families, and officials you will need to interview after the trial is over. They can see that you care enough about the outcome of this trial to be there every day. Even if you only discuss the weather or the Christmas lights outside the courthouse, you will get to know each other, and you can exchange addresses and phone numbers.

If I miss trial sessions because of other writing commitments, I purchase the transcripts for those sessions from the court reporters. These cost from $.50 to about $3.50 a page. If you are really lucky, the prosecutor's office will provide copies of transcripts free of charge. In most jurisdictions, you can get copies of motions filed by both the prosecution and the defense from the clerk's office for the price of copying.

I try to have at least three sources for everything I write. I have been sued a few times over the years—usually by convicted killers who insisted I had "ruined their reputations." No one has ever collected because I do keep careful files of my sources. Examples of sources are my own trial notes, transcripts, newspaper articles, videos, tapes of interviews, telephone records, letters, court documents, even tapes from my answering machine.

Sometimes, detectives will give you copies of their follow-up reports, but only after the trial is over. These are very helpful.

In order to speak the language of detectives, a competent crime writer must take advantage of every chance to understand her or his highly specialized field. Very early in my true crime career, I realized I didn't know enough about forensic science. Although I have a four-year degree in creative writing, I went back to college and got a two-year degree in police science. At the time, *True Detective* et al. wouldn't let me write under my own name; I had to be "Andy Stack" because my editor said readers wouldn't believe that a woman knew anything about solving crimes. After I graduated with an A.A. degree, that same editor said, "Ann, you know more than all our male writers—you can use your own name." But by then I knew the benefits of being anonymous, and I stayed with Andy Stack, at least in the fact-detective magazines.

Going to college at night, I took crime scene investigation, crime scene photography, arrest, search and seizure, criminal law, and police management, and I learned a number of things that most girls don't need to know. But *I* did. I learned how to dust for fingerprints, how to collect evidence and keep it inviolate from contamination, what medical examiners look for in an autopsy, what livor mortis and rigor mortis really are, and even what kind of "splotch" blood makes when it is dropped from varying heights.

Local law enforcement agencies let me sit in on their training courses. I rode with the state police, the county sheriff, the city police department, paramedics. I also spent three hundred hours riding with the Seattle Fire Department's arson investigators and viewed a whole new kind of detective work.

If I had to, I know how to work a homicide scene and how to spot an arson fire. I'm sure my neighbors must have wondered why I came home smelling like smoke! I even had a card signed by the fire chief that said I could enter any burning building I wanted. (It's really not that much fun inside a burning building.)

After I have chosen my subject for an upcoming book, attended the trial, interviewed dozens of people, and piled all my research around me, I have to decide where to plunge in. I want to begin at a gripping point in the case, at a scene that will convince a book browser that the first page is just a sample of an enthralling story to come. After I give a glimpse at the beginning without revealing too much, I go back in time—two or three generations, if I can find that much information on both the killer and the victim—and write in a linear fashion until I come to the point where I started. Thereafter, the skeins of the story weave together.

True crime books should be suspenseful. It's easier to create complete suspense in fiction, but it's still possible to hold back the denouement of a real case for a few hundred pages. It's always a temptation for new writers to give the whole thing away in the first chapter, leaning very heavily verbatim on police files. If you do that, your book will sound stilted *and* it will go downhill rather than building tension.

After three decades, I'm still finding new ways to dig deeper into the backstories that lead inexorably toward violent death. True crime writing is constant trial and error, always swallowing your anxiety and approaching subjects who may not want to talk to you, and often landing in a strange city with no idea where the courthouse is and *if* officials will let you into the trial.

Every writer has a slightly different way of looking at criminal cases and presenting them to the reader. But I have found that some rules and techniques don't change for me. Today, I am offered more than five hundred cases a year by families, detectives, or others with an interest. I can do a book only about every nine months, so I must choose that book with great care.

I'm going to list Rule's Eleven Rules for True Crime Success.

1. If you can, start now to attend classes in police science at a college near you. A few courses in psychology will help too. Read books already written on true crime cases. Become as expert as you possibly can on all the elements of crime solving.

2. Examine your own motivations. Can you be professional and compassionate at the same time? I always weigh whether I should reveal everything I've learned. Some incidents will hurt innocent people far more than they would add to my book. I leave those out. You will hold people's emotions in your hand as you write about the crime.

3. Choose a case no more than ten years old. The newer, the better. Be sure the characters are interesting (see my criteria above) and the case itself is convoluted enough that it isn't a "slam dunk" for detectives. You don't want to pad your book because you run out of story. Avoid cases with too much publicity, for example, JonBenet Ramsey, O.J. Simpson, and Chandra Levy/Gary Condit. You'll be competing with dozens of other writers, and every periodical has already told the story.

4. Don't pick an unsolved case. There has to be an ending to please the reader.

5. Prepare a proposal on the case you have selected, even though the trial lies ahead. With an outline and three sample chapters (to prove you can write) you may well interest an agent and have a book contract—based on the outcome of trial. (I had a contract to write the book that turned out to be *The Stranger Beside Me* six months before I knew my friend Ted Bundy was the prime suspect, and it took another five years before I could write it.)

6. Gather every newspaper article, scrap of paper, video, or other resource material you can find, and start a file on "your" case. Write or call the jurisdiction where the trial will be held, and ask what credentials you will need to sit in the media section. You can usually find some editor of some periodical to give you the precious little card that says "Press."

7. Attend the trial, with your fingers crossed that there will be a conviction. Unless the defendant is a juvenile, these trials are open to everyone. If you couldn't arrange a press pass, get there early to get a seat! You will end up with stacks of yellow legal tablets. It's always a gamble to spend weeks at a trial, but I've never guessed wrong yet on conviction.

8. You may use the real names of public officials, the deceased, and convicted felons. I usually change the names of children and of people who have no direct involvement in the case. When you interview subjects, ask them if they have a preference.

9. Titles are the most difficult writing in the whole book! Start thinking now of a title that will give a clue to your story and will intrigue agents, editors, and, we hope, readers. Make it short.

10. Finding photographs isn't easy. Family will often let you make copies of precious pictures. If you want to use newspaper photographs, you must pay the photographer or the paper in order to use them. Payment usually starts at about $200 a photo. If you're handy with a camera, take some of your own photographs of neighborhoods, houses, witnesses (outside the courtroom), police, prosecutors, and judges. Don't approach the latter officials until trial is over, of course. Often the police or prosecutors will give you some pictures connected to the crime. I *never* use gruesome or grisly pictures of the victim. In my newest book, *Every Breath You Take*, I have one photo of the victim, who is lying far from the camera, but I asked her family's permission first.

11. Last, I urge you to protect yourself. When I began writing true crime, I suspected that I would undoubtedly annoy some dangerous felons, many of whom would eventually get out of prison. I would not let fear blunt my life. Either I would pick another genre or go ahead, be careful, and not dwell on the danger. My choice was to go ahead and take the chance, but I took a few more than normal precautions. I don't have a listed phone number, except for my office. I don't have my address listed in the phone book. I wouldn't think of having a vanity license plate that said "CRM-ATHOR" or anything like it. I use a box number for all my mail. My home and office have burglar alarms, and I have three large dogs. (Got them because I love them, but they're very protective.)

I would love to put myself out of business, but, sadly, there will always be murders. The most any of us can hope for is to warn readers of ruses and devices used by killers. At the same time, we can give them tips so that they *don't* become victims. The best reader letters I get are the ones that begin, "I would be dead now, but I remembered something I read in one of your books. . . ." That makes me smile all day.

Good luck on *your* career as a true crime writer!

E-Media—Crime Fiction E-Volves

■ *G. Miki Hayden*

You, the author, create your mystery novel by sitting at your newest, hyperpowered electronic wonder and typing in some wickedly devious, double-twisting, red-herringed-up-the-kazoo plot, with characters ever so decent and some so evil that the reader will gnash her teeth in a furious desire to see justice done. The end.

What is it that you now have at your very fingertips, what do you see on the screen? A novel that—with a little work—can be sent almost directly to any printing press in the nation. You have, more or less, typeset your own book, which makes its transformation into some other font, point size, or software-manipulated format not *easy* but at least imaginably possible.

E-media (electronic media) which includes handheld readers, print on demand (POD), Web publishing, and more, opens up new ways for you to showcase the novel you've just completed. We have only seen the beginning of the technological breakthroughs in the publishing industry. And new forms will quickly emerge.

One such technology is ability to print books as needed. Machines will soon be in every bookstore to print on demand, in perfect book form, one of thousands of titles programmed to be delivered within minutes of an order. (WH Smith has Zoom Systems e-Stores in most of its airport shops already, offering a mere twenty-five instant titles; and a PerfectBook device, now being mass-produced, will cost other retail spots a very reasonable thirty thousand dollars to install.) Although POD publishing is still in the trial stage, this technology appeals to many writers because their books will not go out of print.

As for the e-book itself, the New York publishing giants are pouring millions into making digital versions of textbooks and novels. Further, many of the publishing houses aim to have their best-sellers so electronically convertible that a single title will be producible in any media, at any time.

The small presses jumped into electronic media years ago, and every new mystery publisher that has recently emerged—and many have—prints trade paper books one at a time, via POD technology. Numbers of other "presses" are preparing files to be read on personal computers, as well as on portable e-book readers (still considered by some publishing experts to be "too pricey" to become a standard for books on disk).

All of this technology implies one thing to those who write mysteries: a world of new markets. And that's what should interest us most about the e-discussion, the encouraging revelation that more producers of books might be willing to examine (and even publish) our manuscripts.

More mystery markets exist now because the computer is a democratizing device. New authors—and even somewhat worn and tattered ones—no longer have to give up after a series of rejections from the "mainstream," or New York, publishing houses. A few short years ago, if New York wouldn't have your novel, no one else would. But today, the expansion of technology has made the entrepreneurial publisher the logical next step for submissions.

The lines between POD and e-book-only publishers have blurred. Many of the imprints that began solely as electronic enterprises now publish in all media, including POD. Despite our new love of the e-book, many authors and readers still like to hold the old-fashioned paper-and-ink book in their hands, and the possibility of getting an actual book at the same time that the electronic version comes out (in a "jewel case," complete with cover or via the Web or e-mail) elicits high interest.

The e-book sale is ancillary to the print agreement. And that option is not just for Robert Parker (the beloved Spenser-series author) who signed with RosettaBooks years after publishing a book with Random House. How about Diana Kirk whose *A Caduceus Is for Killing* published by Hard Shell Word Factory won the first EPPIE (an e-book award) for best thriller? Kirk, a featured author in Writer's Digest Publishing Successes, has had her books issued in electronic, audio, and print formats, all at once.

The e-book gives the mystery author added revenue potential. In the case of those who win an award, such as the EPPIE, sponsored by the Electronically Published Internet Connection (EPIC), the author gains not only a publication credit, but a certain amount of prestige.

Even if you haven't had a book published in the traditional format, you might want to consider the e-book market. Publication in print is possible if the e-book sells well, and sometimes a good review of the e-book—yes, e-books *do* get reviewed, in many venues—will prime the pump for a print sale. In addition, the e-book-only publisher might, in the future, bring out a version in POD format.

While the reading audience for e-books might still be small, e-books provide a number of special advantages for certain audiences, thus making the group larger than you may think. Consider, for example, the person who travels extensively and carries several books on disk for long-distance journeys, or the person with poor eyesight who wants to notch up the point size when she reads. Consider the person with arthritis who has a hard time holding a heavy hardcover. Or the husband who gets enough illumination on the backlit screen so he doesn't have to keep on the light, which bothers his wife. Or the twenty-something who is accustomed to reading on a monitor and simply likes doing it that way. People definitely buy e-books.

One marvelous advantage of submitting to the e-book market is that you will save a lot in postage. The great majority of the e-book publishers accept e-mailed submissions, usually in standard manuscript format, as a word processing attachment to an e-mail. You'll also save by not printing out the manuscript, taking it to the post office, and standing in line.

Those who decide to try to get an e-book published will, obviously, want to find all the houses that issue mysteries. To find these markets, first visit author pages and get the names of a few of their publishers. Then you can search for, or link to, those Web sites. If the author's e-mail is given, you can also personally connect with a writer who has published at that imprint. A politely worded inquiry might get you information about what it's like to work with that publisher. One thing about e-book and small press publishers: Authors seem to enjoy publishing with them. E-publishers generally are open to input from the authors.

Sometimes, however, the e-book publishers are swamped, especially those that have been around a while and that have gained a name and good reputation. You might never receive an answer to a submission, or a response can take just as many months as it takes the mainstream press. Due to that fact, you ought to consider making several simultaneous submissions. Don't fret—the upside is bigger than the minuscule possibility that you'll be caught and thought poorly of. After all, writers with agents have their novels simultaneously submitted to several publishers all the time. Go ahead—if two acceptances arrive at your door, take the better offer, of course.

Some of the new e-book publishers are inexperienced in the business and might not deal with you intelligently. A writer I know mentioned having a deal with one publisher. She was going to receive the contract the next week. But when she finally heard, the editor requested substantial changes to the book, which the author was not willing to undertake. Had the editor been in the business a bit longer, she would have realized that assuring publication prematurely was bad form.

Because some of the older, established e-book publishers have books scheduled well into the future, you might want to find the newest and most untried e-publishers for your submission. Sometimes the best moment to hit a press is early on, when the editors need material and will spend more time reading your novel.

What you will do first, in submitting, is to follow the guidelines on the publisher's Web site. The imprint will usually invite authors either to query or to submit a partial. Often, the format of a query is specified, requiring something like a 250-word description of the mystery plus a bio. Always include some type of cover letter that begins with a hook ("When Rona Bennet finds a dead body on her seaside property, she knows that she will be a suspect. A year before, she was tried and acquitted after a similar killing."). Include the name of the novel, the length, a couple of sentences describing the story, and a sentence or two about your own writing background.

If an editor is interested in your query, she will then invite you to submit either fifty pages of the manuscript or the entire thing. If you're invited to submit only part of the manuscript, be sure you have a summary of the entire novel available to send along with it. A summary typically runs three to seven pages and provides details of all the major action in the mystery. And, as with traditional publishers, you must reveal the identity of the killer.

If the e-publisher is interested in more, you will then send the entire mystery. Remember to include the summary this time, too, as well as the first chapters you had sent before. (You'll also do this when you send your novel to a print publisher that invites submission of the complete manuscript.) Always write a brief cover e-mail with the attachment. Make sure to include the publisher's invitation to submit the full novel at the end of your reply. Now all you have to do is wait.

This is not the time to withdraw your mystery from consideration elsewhere. Sit tight. Even when a full manuscript is requested, you might not get a response for months—or ever—from a busy press. Some have a policy of only responding when they are interested, a sad, rude facet of the new face of publishing. For that reason, don't dwell on the submission, but continue to track down new markets and query them.

When you do receive an offer, read the contract carefully. Some unscrupulous companies will take advantage of new writers. Luckily many e-publishers' contracts are on their Web sites. If you receive a contract, check out the contracts of other e-publishers. If something in the contract seems unusual, such as that the e-publisher demands to own the copyright, you may want a lawyer who understands publishing and intellectual property laws to look at your contract. Sometimes you can convince the publisher to change clauses in the contract. However, first decide how hard you will push and where you will draw your line in the sand. Request a change, but never haggle unless you are genuinely willing to withdraw the book from consideration if your need is not met. Remember what your goals are as an author and decide based on that.

The crucial considerations in contracts for the e-mystery are the length of time the contract covers (and the means by which the deal may be terminated) and royalties. Contracts generally go into effect for one year with an option to renew at the end of the period, but some publishers have gotten away from that typical clause. A few might have a contract with no time limit but an option for either party to terminate with an e-mail. Another might have an initial two-year period in which no termination is permitted except by mutual agreement. Others require ninety days' notice to terminate. The ability to terminate a contract is an important point because deals in publishing, as in the rest of the world, can sometimes go sour. If the contract stipulates that termination must be by mutual agreement, try to arrange a one-party withdrawal.

Royalties, normally paid within thirty days of the end of the quarter, run up to 50 percent—although some publishers offer more if the author provides the cover art. Other houses may schedule royalties. For example, an author may receive 25 percent on the first 1,000 copies sold, 30 percent on the next 5,000 copies, 40 percent on the next 3,000 copies, and 50 percent on sales of 9,000 copies and above. Keep in mind, however, that e-books have not sold well so far. Sales in the thousands are possible, but such sales are more likely for big-name authors or authors who work hard to market their books. Even the sale of 100 copies is not too shabby.

Random House offers royalties of 50 percent on its e-book line. But, said Richard Sarnoff, the company's president of new media and corporate development, "Part of the investment we're making is our willingness to act diseconomically in acknowledging the future economics. We want to have the authors as our partners."

What should you expect in terms of editing? That will depend on the philosophy and editorial standards of the publisher. Some will provide a light edit; others will edit heavily. Some imprints will not touch your work at all. Advantages to all three approaches exist, depending on the skill of the author and the skill of the editor. Despite rumors to the contrary, a "professional" edit can introduce errors—but, then again, an edit can prevent howlingly funny mistakes.

The use and quality of cover art can also depend on the e-publisher. If you're a designer, or you know one, you might offer to do the cover. On the other hand, covers to e-books are generally capably produced. Check other titles on the e-publisher's list to see if its covers are something you'd be proud to have on your book.

Authors have also been self-publishing in e-book formats since the concept came along. In a recent netletter column, author Joyce Jace admitted to having done just that. Invited to participate in a workshop for Mystic-Ink, she brought her self-produced diskette and gave it to one of the publishers attending the conference. A few weeks later, the phone rang with the offer of a traditional publishing contract. The deal was not for the book she had passed around but for a different book—one that was to come out both in hardcover and in e-book form. Self-publishing gave Jace a way to break into print.

POD books are now the way to go for those who want to self-publish inexpensively in print, however. A number of online services offer a means to put out a book, with the site doing the heavy lifting—pulling your file into the proper format, obtaining the ISBN (a number needed to sell in bookstores), designing the cover, and interacting with the POD printer. The cost of these services varies from ninety-nine dollars on up. Sometimes, for a much higher charge, the book is also given an editorial once-over.

With a great deal of effort at marketing, an author can sell his or her POD book in the same way as any other mystery novel in print. Or nearly. One catch with some of the PODs delivered via the online services is that they are nonreturnable. Bookstores are accustomed to being able to return copies of a title that don't sell. Consequently, many of the retailers have banned POD, feeling that they can't afford to take on a product they can't send back. Add to that stumbling block the fact that all PODs are trade paperbacks and higher priced to the consumer, and the difficulty increases for the author who wants to sell books. This isn't to say it can't be done, just that doing so is very difficult.

When it comes to marketing, focus on promoting e-books online. After all, this is your natural audience. One great way to get your name out there is to join listservs and chat groups of mystery readers/writers and e-book and general authors. Posting will begin to promote your name in the world of the mystery and the Internet writer, a big plus. Many writers have had their success greatly enhanced by developing a presence on the Internet. For an e-book author, appearing on the Web is a must.

Having a Web site of your own in order to promote your book has pros and cons. Some mystery writers say they do well with home pages—they get a lot of traffic and enhance sales. Others claim that the time spent keeping the site fresh and the cost for Web site hosting aren't worth the bother. If you're a natural techie or know someone who will create a nice page—cheap—go for it. You don't have that much to lose.

Getting people to visit your page might not be easy. Consider creating a monthly or quarterly netletter advertising yourself but containing additional beneficial content for readers. You might review or interview other authors, provide market news, or get people to contribute articles. Build your subscription list by posting the availability of your electronic newsletter on the lists to which you now belong. Never add anyone without a request. Some people don't like unsolicited e-mail for fear of acquiring a computer virus.

With book promotion of any type, remember one (double) rule: Be polite and, whatever you do, be sure your target readers receive a benefit, some information they didn't have before. Suppose you're a deep-sea fisherman and that's the background of your book. Join lists of people who love to fish. Then post your own fishing information. Your signature line is the ad for your book. Explore the niche audience to whom your mystery will appeal. Maintain a presence on some of the "traditional" mystery reader lists—such as DorothyL—and post general items, not just information about your book.

Should you spend money to advertise? You aren't going to make much cash on the book, so think about your finances. Consider trading ads with other authors who have Web sites, or write online or print articles in exchange for ads—or just for your tag line.

Winning an award provides great publicity for your book. In addition to the EPPIE, which is geared entirely to e-book offerings, books in e-media are eligible to win a range of traditional honors. First to accept e-book submissions was England's Booker Prize. E-books can also be submitted, under existing categories, for the National Book Award, which carries a ten-thousand-dollar prize. And Mystery Writers of America allows e-books (print copies required) to be considered for various categories of the coveted Edgar Award. POD books may, naturally, be submitted across the board, since they are no different from any other book, and a self-published POD title was recently nominated for a Shamus, given by The Private Eye Writers of America.

Now you have an idea of the range of opportunities e-publishing can offer, take time to explore them to see if they're right for you.

Resources

Author Network: www.author-network.com/index.html

The Authorized Directory of eBook Publishers: www.thewisd omkeeper.com/director.html

eBook Connections: www.ebookconnections.com

Electronic Publishers Coalition: www.epccentral.org

Electronically Published Internet Connection (EPIC): www.ep icauthors.org

THE BEST OF THE GENRE AND A REFERENCE LIST OF BOOKS ON WRITING AND TECHNICAL INFORMATION

Angela Zeman
Barry Zeman

W hen the first MWA *Mystery Writer's Handbook* was published in 1956, the editor, Herbert Brean, included a section on the best mysteries ever written. It was his learned contention that "it goes without saying that anyone interested in writing mysteries should be reasonably well read in the mystery field." He defined "well read" as "knowledge both of the cornerstones of the past and a generous sampling of more recent output." We have reprinted here the historical cornerstones for your use but also felt it would be important to take Brean's advice by giving you an up-to-date picture of the best of more contemporary writings in the genre.

The "historical cornerstones" were first chosen and published by Howard Haycraft, an eminent historian and critic of the detective story, in his 1941 publication, *Murder for Pleasure*, the first definitive history of the genre. In 1951, Fred Dannay (half of the famous writing team known as Ellery Queen), a preeminent mystery author, editor, and historian, joined Haycraft in updating the cornerstones. The Haycraft Queen (HQ) List, as the joint compilation became known, is a master list of the definitive and historical library of detective-crime-mystery fiction up until 1952.

The more recent selections came from contributors to this volume. We asked them to suggest the most important and influential works (or authors) of recent vintage that in their opinion would be of benefit to new or aspiring writers. Generally, the suggestions encompass works published in the last five years, but some listings date back as far as the last thirty years. The books or writers listed are those our distinguished contributors considered "the best." Their choices are varied, perceptive, and instructive. Some contributors also asked colleagues for their opinions. We hope you will find this addition to the handbook helpful.

The Haycraft Queen Definitive Library of Detective-Crime-Mystery Fiction

Two Centuries of Cornerstones (New and Revised List)
[*Asterisks denote titles added to the list by "Ellery Queen"]

1748 Voltaire, *Zadig*. The great-great-grandfather of the detective story.

1794 William Godwin, *Things as They Are: or, The Adventures of Caleb Williams*. The great-grandfather of the detective story.

1828–9 François Eugène Vidocq, *Memoires de Vidocq*. The grandfather of the detective story.

1845 Edgar Allan Poe, *Tales*. The father of the modern detective story.

1852–3 Charles Dickens, *Bleak House*; 1870, *The Mystery of Edwin Drood*.

1856 "Waters" [William Russell], *Recollections of a Detective Police-Officer*. The first English detective yellow-back.

1860 Wilkie Collins, *The Woman in White*. An important "transitional" book.

1862 Victor Hugo, *Les Misérables* (first edition in English, also 1862).

1866 Feodor Dostoevski, *Crime and Punishment* (first edition in English, 1886).

1866 Emile Gaboriau, *L'Affaire Lerouge*; 1867, *Le Dossier No. 113*; 1868, *Le Crime D'Orcival*; 1869, *Monsieur Lecoq*. The father of the detective novel.

1866 Seeley Regester [Metta V. Victor], *The Dead Letter*. An example of the pioneer American detective novel—published twelve years before Anna Katharine Green's *The Leavenworth Case*. Detective: Mr. Burton.

1868 Wilkie Collins, *The Moonstone*. The father of the English detective novel.

1872 [Harlan Page Halsey], *Old Sleuth, The Detective*, 1885. The first dime novel detective.

1874 Allan Pinkerton, *The Expressman and the Detective*.

1878 Anna Katharine Green, *The Leavenworth Case*. Generally conceded to be the mother of the American detective novel.

1882 Robert Louis Stevenson, *New Arabian Nights*; 1886, *Strange Case of Dr. Jekyll and Mr. Hyde*.

1887 Fergus W. Hume, *The Mystery of a Hansom Cab*.

1887 A. Conan Doyle, *A Study in Scarlet*; 1890, *The Sign of Four*; 1892, *The Adventures of Sherlock Holmes*; 1894, *The Memoirs of Sherlock Holmes*; 1902, *The Hound of the Baskervilles*; 1905, *The Return of Sherlock Holmes*; 1915, *The Valley of Fear*; 1917, *His Last Bow*; 1927, *The Case-Book of Sherlock Holmes*.

1892 Israel Zangwill, *The Big Bow Mystery*.

1894 Mark Twain, *The Tragedy of Pudd'nhead Wilson*.

1894 Arthur Morrison, *Martin Hewitt, Investigator*.

1895 M.P. Shiel, *Prince Zaleski*.

1897 Bram Stoker, *Dracula*.

1899 E.W. Hornung, *The Amateur Cracksman*.

1903 [Erskine Childers], *The Riddle of the Sands*.

1905 Baroness Orczy, *The Scarlet Pimpernel*; 1909, *The Old Man in the Corner*.

1906 Godfrey R. Benson, *Tracks in the Snow*.

1906 Robert Barr, *The Triumphs of Eugène Valmont*.

1907 Jacques Futrelle, *The Thinking Machine*.

1907 Maurice Leblanc, *Arsène Lupin, Gentleman-Cambrioleur*; 1910, *"813"* The Leblanc-Lupin masterpiece; 1922, *Les Huits Coups De L'Horloge*.

1907 Gaston Leroux, *Le Mystère de la Chambre Jaune*; 1908–9, *Le Parfum de la Dame en Noir*.

1907 R. Austin Freeman, *The Red Thumb Mark*. The First Dr. Thorndyke book. 1909, *John Thorndyke's Cases*; 1911, *The Eye of Osiris*; 1912, *The Singing Bone*. The first "inverted" detective stories.

1907 Joseph Conrad, *The Secret Agent*. Said to be a favorite with both Eric Ambler and Graham Greene.

1908 Mary Roberts Rinehart, *The Circular Staircase*. The founding of the Had-I-But-Known school.

1908 O. Henry, *The Gentle Grafter.*

1908 G.K. Chesteron, *The Man Who Was Thursday*; 1916, *The Innocence of Father Brown.*

1909 Cleveland Moffett, *Through the Wall.* A neglected high spot.

1909 Carolyn Wells, *The Clue.* The first Fleming Stone book.

1910 A.E.W. Mason, *At the Villa Rose.* The first Hanaud book. 1924, *The House of the Arrow.*

1910 William MacHarg and Edwin Balmer, *The Achievements of Luther Trant.*

1912 Arthur B. Reeve, *The Silent Bullet.* The first Craig Kennedy book.

1913 Mrs. Belloc Lowndes. *The Lodger.*

1913 Sax Rohmer, *The Mystery of Dr. Fu-Manchu.*

1913 E.C. Bentley, *Trent's Last Case* (first U.S. title: *The Woman in Black*).

1914 Ernest Bramah, *Max Carrados.* The first blind detective.

1914 Louis Joseph Vance, *The Lone Wolf.*

1915 John Buchan, *The Thirty-Nine Steps.*

1916 Thomas Burke, *Limehouse Nights.*

1918 Melville Davisson Post, *Uncle Abner.*

1919 J.S. Fletcher, *The Middle Temple Murder.*

1920 Agatha Christie, *The Mysterious Affair at Styles.* The first Hercule Poirot book. 1926, *The Murder of Roger Ackroyd.*

1920 Freeman Wills Croft, *The Cask*; 1924, *Inspector French's Greatest Case.*

1920 H.C. Bailey, *Call Mr. Fortune*; 1932, *The Red Castle.*

1920 "Sapper" [Cyril McNeile], *Bull-Dog Drummond.*

1920 Arthur Train, *Tutt and Mr. Tutt.*

1920 E. Phillips Oppenheim, *The Great Impersonation.*

1921 Eden Phillpotts, *The Grey Room.*

1922 A.A. Milne, *The Red House Mystery.*

1923 G.D.H. Cole, *The Brooklyn Murders.*

1923 Dorothy L. Sayers, *Whose Body?* The first Lord Peter Wimsey book. 1934, *The Nine Tailors*; 1930, with Robert Eustace, *The Documents in the Case.*

1924 Philip MacDonald, *The Rasp.* The first Colonel Anthony Gethryn book. 1938, *Warrant For X* (English title: *The Nursemaid Who Disappeared*).

1925 Edgar Wallace, *The Mind of Mr. J.G. Reeder.*

1925 John Rhode, *The Paddington Mystery.* The first Dr. Priestley book. 1928, *The Murders in Praed Stree*t.

1925 Earl Derr Biggers, *The House Without a Key*. The first Charlie Chan book.

1925 Theodore Dreiser, *An American Tragedy*.

1925 Liam O'Flaherty, *The Informer*.

1925 Ronald A. Knox, *The Viaduct Murder*.

1926 S.S. Van Dine, *The Benson Murder Case*. The first Philo Vance book. 1927, *The "Canary" Murder Case*.

1926 C.S. Forester, *Payment Deferred*.

1927 Frances Noyes Hart, *The Bellamy Trial*.

1928 W. Somerset Maugham, *Ashenden*.

1928 Leslie Charteris, *Meet the Tiger* (U.S. title: *Meet—The Tiger!*, 1929).

1929 Anthony Berkeley, *The Poisoned Chocolates Case*; 1937, *Trial and Error*; 1932 [Francis Iles], *Before the Fact*.

1929 Ellery Queen, *The Roman Hat Mystery*. The first Ellery Queen book. 1942, *Calamity Town*; 1932 [Barnaby Ross], *The Tragedy of X*. The first Drury Lane book. 1932, *The Tragedy of Y*.

1929 Rufus King, *Murder by the Clock*.

1929 W.R. Burnett, *Little Caesar*.

1929 T.S. Stribling, *Clues of the Caribbees*. The only Professor Poggioli book.

1929 Harvey J. O'Higgins, *Detective Duff Unravels It*. The first psychoanalyst detective.

1929 Mignon G. Eberhart, *The Patient in Room 18*.

1930 Frederick Irving Anderson, *Book of Murder*.

1930 Dashiell Hammett, *The Maltese Falcon*. *The Glass Key*; 1944, *The Adventures of Sam Spade*.

1930 David Frome, *The Hammersmith Murders*. The first Mr. Pinkerton book.

1931 Stuart Palmer, *The Penguin Pool Murder*. The first Hildegarde Withers book.

1931 Francis Beeding, *Death Walks in Eastrepps*.

1931 Glen Trevor (James Hilton) *Murder at School* (U.S. title: *Was It Murder?*, 1933).

1931 Damon Runyon, *Guys and Dolls*.

1931 Phoebe Atwood Taylor, *The Cape Cod Mystery*. The first Asey Mayo book.

1932 R.A.J. Walling, *The Fatal Five Minutes*.

1932 Clemence Dane and Helen Simpson, *Re-Enter Sir John*.

1933 Erle Stanley Gardner, *The

Case of The Velvet Claws. The first Perry Mason book. 1933, *The Case of the Sulky Girl.*

1934 Margery Allingham, *Death of a Ghost.*

1934 James M. Cain, *The Postman Always Rings Twice.*

1934 Rex Stout, *Fer-De-Lance.* The first Nero Wolfe book. 1935, *The League of Frightened Men.*

1935 Richard Hull, *The Murder of My Aunt.*

1935 John P. Marquand, *No Hero.* The first Mr. Moto book.

1938 John Dickson Carr [Carter Dickson], *The Crooked Hinge*; 1938, *The Judas Window*; 1945, *The Curse of the Bronze Lamp* (English title: *Lord of the Sorcerers,* 1946).

• On his original list, Mr. Haycraft chose *The Arabian Nights Murder* by Carr and *The Plague Court Murders* by Dickson; but on page 493 of his *The Art of the Mystery Story* Mr. Haycraft wrote: "After careful, and possibly maturer, re-reading I beg to change my vote" to *The Crooked Hinge* and *The Judas Window.*

1938 Nicholas Blake, *The Beast Must Die.*

1938 Michael Innes, *Lament for a Maker.*

1938 Clayton Rawson, *Death from a Top Hat.* The first Great Merlini Book.

1938 Graham Greene, *Brighton Rock.*

1938 Daphne du Maurier, *Rebecca.*

1938 Mabel Seeley, *The Listening House.*

1939 Ngaio Marsh, *Overture to Death.*

1939 Eric Ambler, *A Coffin for Dimitrios* (English title: *The Mask of Dimitrios*).

1939 Raymond Chandler, *The Big Sleep.* The first Philip Marlowe Book. 1940, *Farewell, My Lovely.*

1939 Georges Simenon, *The Patience of Maigret.*

1939 Elliot Paul, *The Mysterious Mickey Finn.* The first Homer Evans book.

1940 Raymond Postgate, *Verdict of Twelve.*

1940 Frances and Richard Lockridge, *The Norths Meet Murder.*

1940 Dorothy B. Hughes, *The So Blue Marble* (or *In a Lonely Place,* 1947).

1940 Cornell Woolrich [William Irish], *The Bride Wore Black*; 1942, *Phantom Lady.*

1940 Manning Coles, *Drink to Yesterday*; 1941, *A Toast to Tomorrow* (English title: *Pray Silence,* 1940). The first two Tommy Hambledon books.

1941 H.F. Heard, *A Taste For Honey.

1941 Craig Rice, Trial By Fury (or Home Sweet Homicide, 1944).

1942 H.H. Holmes [Anthony Boucher], *Rocket To The Morgue.

1942 James Gould Cozzens, *The Just and the Unjust.

1943 Vera Caspary, *Laura. A modern "psychothriller."

1944 Hilda Lawrence, Blood Upon the Snow.

1946 Helen Eustis, The Horizontal Man.

1946 Charlotte Armstrong, *The Unsuspected.

1946 Lillian de la Torre, *Dr. Sam Johnson, Detector.

1946 Edmund Crispin, The Moving Toyshop (or Love Lies Bleeding, 1948).

1947 Edgar Lustgarten, One More Unfortunate (English title: A Case to Answer).

1947 Roy Vickers, *The Department of Dead Ends.

1948 Josephine Tey, The Franchise Affair.

1948 William Faulkner, *Intruder in the Dust.

1948 Robert M. Coates, Wisteria Cottage.

1948 Stanley Ellin, Dreadful Summit.

1949 John [Ross] Macdonald, The Moving Target.

1950 Eleazar Lipsky, The People Against O'Hara. Rated by Dorothy B. Hughes as the best detective novel of the year.

1950 Evelyn Piper, The Motive. Anthony Boucher considers this book a "major milestone" in the history of the whydunit, as opposed to the whodunit and the howdunit.

1950 Thomas Walsh, Nightmare in Manhattan.

1950 Helen McCloy, Through a Glass, Darkly.

1950 Bart Spicer, Blues for the Prince.

1950 Charlotte Armstrong, Mischief. Possibly to replace The Unsuspected, 1946.

1950 Raymond Chandler, The Simple Art of Murder. To replace an earlier choice or to be added.

1951 Dorothy Salisbury Davis, A Gentle Murderer.

1952 Lord Dunsany, The Little Tales of Smethers.

A Selected List of Detective Story Anthologies
(Arranged alphabetically by compilers;
U.S. dates, titles, publishers given)

General

Macgowan, Kenneth, *Sleuths: Twenty-Three Great Detectives of Fiction and Their Best Stories* (New York, Harcourt, Brace, 1931).

Queen, Ellery, *Challenge to the Reader: An Anthology* (New York, Stokes, 1938).

Sayers, Dorothy, *The Omnibus of Crime* (New York, Payson & Clarke, 1929).

———.*The Second Omnibus of Crime* (New York, Coward-McCann, 1932).

———.*The Third Omnibus of Crime* (New York, Coward-McCann, 1935).

———.*Tales of Detection* (London, Dent [Everyman's Library], 1936).

Starrett, Vincent, *Fourteen Great Detective Stories* (New York, Modern Library, 1929).

Thwing, Eugene, *The World's Best 100 Detective Stories* (New York, Funk & Wagnalls, 1929).

Wright, Lee, *The Pocket Book of Great Detectives* (New York, Pocket Books, 1941).

Wright, Willard Huntington, *The Great Detective Stories* (New York, Scribner's, 1927).

Wrong, E.M., *Crime and Detection* (New York, Oxford University Press [World's Classics], 1926).

Juvenile

Haycraft, Howard, *The Boys' Book of Great Detective Stories* (New York, Harper, 1938).

———.*The Boys' Second Book of Great Detective Stories* (New York, Harper, 1940).

Specialties

Allingham, Margery, and others, *Six Against Scotland Yard* (New York, Doubleday, Doran, 1936).

Detection Club of London, *The Floating Admiral* (New York, Doubleday, Doran, 1932).

———.*Ask a Policeman* (New York, Morrow, 1933).

Rhode, John [for the Detection Club], *Line-Up* (New York, Dodd, Mead, 1940).

Permission to reproduce this list has been kindly granted by the Scott Meredith Literary Agency L.P. for the Ellery Queen Estate.

Best of Genre as Selected By . . .

This handbook's contributors recommended a wide array of mystery novels as "best of genre," "most influential novels or writers," or "must-reads." Interestingly, few books but several writers were mentioned more than once as follows:

Classics
Josephine Tey, *Brat Farrar*.
All of the Sherlock Holmes Stories.

Contemporary
Sue Grafton, *"A" Is for Alibi*.
Dennis Lehane, *Darkness, Take My Hand*.
Walter Mosley, *Devil in a Blue Dress*.
Don Winslow, *California Fire and Life*.

In addition to the above, authors mentioned frequently were Michael Connelly, Reginald Hill, Laurie R. King, Elmore Leonard, Ruth Rendell, and Ross Thomas.

Most Influential Books in Recent Years and Best of the Genre: An Editor's View

Ruth Cavin, mystery editor at St. Martin's, admits (understandably) that she "cannot find the time to read broadly enough to judge this topic wisely." However, she certainly makes an astute observation: "I think the subgenres are so varied as to be uncomparable (as opposed to incomparable)." Choosing a number of authors rather than specific books, she often goes back significantly farther than five years. She explained: "The early Robert B. Parkers were damn good mysteries with a sleuth unlike the tough detectives in books that preceded him. Ross Thomas mixed sophistication, literary craftmanship, and action/adventure in his incomparable books. Reginald Hill, for superb characterization; Carl Hiaasen for sharp irony; and Tony Hillerman for being what he is."

Cavin asked some of her editor colleagues which books they felt were the most influential in recent years. Interestingly, they named two noir books: Thomas Harris's *The Silence of the Lambs* and Michael Connelly's *The Poet*. Walter Mosley's *Devil in a Blue Dress* came in third but brings with it a debate whether it can be firmly tagged as noir. Cavin herself thinks differently about noir being the most influential subgenre. "The most significant developing trend in mystery novels, . . . still in transit . . . , is the way the good mystery novel is growing closer and closer to a good novel that happens to contain a crime. It is a work whose past is composed of people of depth and complexity, and whose current story is rooted firmly in reality." Her author choices in this category are Laurie R. King and Charles Todd.

On the "best books" question, two of Ruth Cavin's editor colleagues agreed on Walter Mosley's *Devil in a Blue Dress* and Dennis Lehane's *Darkness, Take My Hand*. Also mentioned by one editor were Margaret Maron's Edgar-winning book, *Bootlegger's Daughter*; *The Man Who Liked Slow Tomatoes* by K.C. Constantine; *Black and Blue* by Ian Rankin; *A Grave Talent* by Laurie R. King; *Down by the River Where the Dead Men Go* by George Pelecanos; Iain Pears's *An Instance of the Fingerpost*; and *California Fire and Life* by Don Winslow—which John Lutz names as his nomination for the best book in the last five years. He calls Winslow a "unique voice" with a "superminimalist style that might inspire imitation."

Best of Genre: Writers' Choices

Jan Burke

To add to the Haycraft Queen cornerstone list of classics, Burke (and Margaret Maron) named *Brat Farrar* by Josephine Tey. Not that Howard Haycraft and Ellery Queen ignored Tey. They selected *The Franchise Affair*.

Burke's other top choices for must-read books from the last thirty years include Joe Wambaugh's *The Onion Field*, Dick Francis's *Whip Hand* (which won the Edgar in 1981), and books from two writers whom other contributors listed as favorites: *"A" Is for Alibi* by our editor, Sue Grafton; and *The Black Echo*, Michael

Connelly's blockbuster debut. Just under Burke's top four are Dick Lochte's *Sleeping Dog*; one of Elizabeth Peters's Amelia Peabody mysteries, *The Crocodile on the Sandbank*; and the late Ross Thomas's 1985 Edgar-winning novel, *Briarpatch*.

Loren D. Estleman

Loren D. Estleman, in his thoughtful essay, presents an extensive and instructive list of mystery and other novels classified by points of view. Echoing the theme of this chapter, that good writers should read widely, Estleman takes us a step further by recommending a number of excellent books outside the genre stating, "Most of the true artists in this [mystery] form read widely, in part because restricting oneself to one's own specialty is about as nutritious a practice as a shark devouring its own intestines."

Linda Fairstein

Linda Fairstein states that Scott Turow's *Presumed Innocent* is "one of the most brilliant examples of this [legal] genre." She also selects *Postmortem* by Patricia Cornwell, *The Spy Who Came in From the Cold* by John Le Carré, and *L.A. Requiem* by Robert Crais. Beyond these she added the classic *Anatomy of a Murder* by Robert Traver. Fairstein says that she reads Le Carré's book every other year "for the best plotting, character, and spare prose style."

Jeremiah Healy

Jeremiah Healy picks three novels of the last decade from which writers can "read and learn":

> Jeffrey Deaver, *A Maiden's Grave*. "An absolutely mesmerizing example of a stand-alone thriller."
>
> Janet Evanovich, *One for the Money*. "Terrific example of introducing a new series character."
>
> Richard Russo, *Nobody's Fool*. "Not a mystery . . . [but] read this one to learn writing style from a master."

Tony Hillerman

For new writers, Tony Hillerman highly recommends Ed McBain for "a look at the techniques of a master." He also suggests anything by Fred Harris, former U.S. senator, "who takes you back into Depression dust-bowl days"; Steve Brewer; James Doss, an ex–Los Alamos lab scientist; and Giles Blunt's *Forty Words for Sorrow*, "a new [to me] Canadian writer just being published by Putnam in the U.S., for a superb example of multiple viewpoints, plots, and the world outside the window." He also recommends the short story collection *The Best American Mystery Stories of the Century*, published by Houghton Mifflin, which he and Otto Penzler edited.

Edward D. Hoch

The absolute master mystery short story writer of today, Edward D. Hoch recommends a number of short story collections, including one on the HQ List: Chesterton's *The Innocence of Father Brown*. Hoch calls this "the outstanding single-author collection of detective short stories." Other recommended must-reads are Ellery Queen's *101 Years' Entertainment* and *The Mystery Hall of Fame: An Anthology of Classic Mystery and Suspense Stories Selected by the Mystery Writers of America* edited by Bill Pronzini, Martin H. Greenberg, and Charles C. Waugh (1984). See Hoch's essay for a full list of great story collections and references.

Laurie R. King

Must-read mysteries chosen by Laurie R. King are: Reginald Hill's *Pictures of Perfection* (1994) and two of Peter Dickinson's books: *A Summer in the Twenties* (1981) and *The Last Houseparty* (1982). She also notes that "pretty much everything by Hill and all the nonhistorical novels by Dickinson are worthwhile."

Dick Lochte

Dick Lochte says that there are a number of recent books that could serve as inspiration to a novice writer, but he raves about one in particular: Kenneth Abel's *Cold Steel Rain*, published in 2000 by Putnam. Lochte devotes a full page to the attributes of this book, including how Abel spins a yarn, holds suspense, and handles the mystery elements, raising all "up a notch." He sums up by opining, "For the mystery fan, *Rain* is an enjoyable piece of work. For the new writer, it's an indispensable object lesson."

John Lutz

Don Winslow's *California Fire and Life* is "the best book in the last five years," according to John Lutz. However, to expand the Haycraft Queen List, he nominates the first Sue Grafton, *"A" Is for Alibi*, and Sara Paretsky's debut, *Indemnity Only*, as "they did exemplify a new direction and were seminal." Lutz also feels the more recent books by Marcia Muller are important must reads.

Ann Rule

Nonfiction, Recent:
Jerry Bledsoe, *Bitter Blood*.
Mikal Gilmore, *Shot in the Heart*.
Darcy O'Brien, *Two of a Kind*.

Nonfiction, Classic:
Thomas Thompson, *Blood and Money*.
Truman Capote, *In Cold Blood*.

Fiction:
Edna Buchanan, *Garden of Evil*.
John D. MacDonald, *The Executioners* (also published as *Cape Fear*).
James Patterson, *Along Came a Spider*.
Ruth Rendell, *Murder Being Once Done*.
Rule also recommends "almost anything by Elmore Leonard."

Sandra Scoppettone

Dennis Lehane and Annette Meyers.

Carolyn Wheat

Michael Connelly, *The Concrete Blonde*.

Angela Zeman

In Barbara D'Amato's *Good Cop, Bad Cop*, "Barbara links an original plot with superb everything else. This book is a jewel with every facet perfect."

Books on Writing Chosen by More Than One Contributor

Lawrence Block, *Telling Lies for Fun and Profit*

Jan Burke, Ruth Cavin, Warren Murphy, and Angela Zeman all chose this book. A number of others, including Jan Burke and Warren Murphy, include Block's other books on the craft of writing, including *Spider, Spin Me a Web* and *Writing the Novel*.

John Gardner, *The Art of Fiction: Notes on Craft for Young Writers*

This title is recommended by Laurie R. King and Angela Zeman.

John Gardner, *On Becoming a Novelist*

Laurie R. King and Warren Murphy both highly recommend this volume.

Stephen King, *On Writing*

Ruth Cavin and Warren Murphy chose Stephen King's book about writing.

William Strunk Jr. and E.B. White, *The Elements of Style*

This simple and eminently useful book has been in print for so long, over forty years, that it is considered a standard text. It was chosen by Loren D. Estleman, Sue Grafton, and Barry Zeman.

A Good Dictionary

Many, including Jan Burke, Tony Hillerman, and Julie Smith, said a good dictionary is essential, but Loren D. Estleman advises to stick to the *Webster's New International Dictionary*, second edition. "Burn all later editions, particularly the execrable Eleventh."

Bartlett's Familiar Quotations
Tony Hillerman and Julie Smith use this often.

Roget's Thesaurus
Julie Smith and Marilyn Wallace both keep this close at hand. Margaret Maron rates it her number one aid and gives a more specific explanation of why it's important: "The one reference book I should hate to be without is *Roget's Thesaurus*. I am referring, of course, to the indexed version wherein similar ideas are grouped together, not the dictionary version which is no more useful than the thesaurus found on your word-processor program. A thesaurus is not a synonym finder. It is a tool for helping you to express the exact nuance of an idea when the first word you used isn't quite right." Loren D. Estleman adds another opinion, "Go with the original, avoid *Roget's II* at all costs."

Books on Writing Chosen by Individual Contributors

Jan Burke
All the Lawrence Block books on writing.
Oakley Hall, *The Art and Craft of Novel Writing.*
Anne Lamott, *Bird by Bird.*
Kirk Polking, *The Beginning Writer's Answer Book.*
Edward D. Johnson, *The Handbook of Good English.*
Patricia T. O'Conner, *Woe Is I: The Grammarphobe's Guide to Better English in Plain English.*
A good dictionary.

Ruth Cavin
Lawrence Block, *Telling Lies for Fun and Profit.*
Stephen King, *On Writing.*

George C. Chesbro
Georges Polti, *The Thirty-Six Dramatic Situations.* Mongo's creator explains, "Most of the text is useless, but I find

Polti's arguable breakdown of dramatic situations into categories very useful for noodling plots."

Loren D. Estleman

Stephen Glazier, *Word Menu*.
William Strunk Jr. and E.B. White, *The Elements of Style*.
Roget's Thesaurus, the original.
Webster's New International Dictionary, second edition.

Sue Grafton

William Strunk Jr. and E.B. White, *The Elements of Style*.
Christopher Vogler, *The Writer's Journey*.

Jeremiah Healy

John F. Baker, *Literary Agents: A Writer's Introduction*. (See also Baker's essay.)
Michael Seidman, *Fiction: The Art and Craft of Writing and Getting Published*. "Like having a three-hundred-page drink with one of the deans of New York publishing."

Tony Hillerman

Bartlett's Familiar Quotations.

Laurie R. King

John Gardner, *The Art of Fiction: Notes on Craft for Young Writers*, *On Becoming a Novelist*, and *On Moral Fiction*.
Encyclopedia Britannica, eleventh edition (1910). "A valuable tool for anyone writing about the early part of the century."

Margaret Maron

Roget's Thesaurus.

Warren Murphy

Any of the writing books by Lawrence Block, Stephen King, or Dean Koontz.
Leonard Bishop, *Dare to Be a Great Writer*. "Bishop is a great

writer and his book is brimful of suggestions on how to get that way."
John Gardner, *On Becoming a Novelist.*

Joan Lowery Nixon

Francis L. and Roberta B. Fugate, *Secrets of the World's Best-Selling Writer: The Storytelling Techniques of Erle Stanley Gardner.*

The Haunting, Nixon's own book. This is a young adult mystery that emphasizes characterization and suspense, yet highlights the reader's involvement in solving clues.

Julie Smith

Roget's Thesaurus.
Bartlett's Familiar Quotations.
A good dictionary.

Marilyn Wallace

The Oxford Dictionary of Quotations.
Roget's Thesaurus.
The Chicago Manual of Style.

Carolyn Wheat

Renni Browne and Dave King, *Self-Editing for Fiction Writers.*
Robert Ray, *The Weekend Novelist Writes a Mystery.*

Angela Zeman

Lawrence Block, *Telling Lies for Fun and Profit.*
John Gardner, *The Art of Fiction: Notes on Craft for Young Writers.*
Robert McKee, *Story.*
Gary Provost, *100 Ways to Improve Your Writing.*

Barry Zeman

William Strunk Jr. and E.B. White, *The Elements of Style.*

Technical Information

Our contributors have kindly agreed to share with you key reference books they use frequently, a wide-ranging array of technical works that will be of invaluable use to any mystery writer.

Bear in mind that investigative techniques and law enforcement procedure and organizations change and advance over time. Be sure the work you consult is the latest, unless of course you're doing a period piece and need reference books of that specific era. Older editions of *The Mystery Writer's Handbook* can also be helpful resources as they date from the 1950s through 1989.

The Internet is a rich source of data and information, and it's especially helpful in researching historical topics. See G. Miki Hayden's essay on e-media for a good list of Internet publishing resources and author networking sites. A few of the better reference sites include the Internet Public Library at www.ipl.org and www.findlaw.com to research a specific state, federal, or foreign law. Various city and state government sites reveal everything from vacation locations to local government agencies and law enforcement details. An easy-to-use and easy-to-understand Web site for anything regarding the U.S. government is www.first.gov. A great place for encyclopedic/historical information is www.Britannica.com. Web sites of specific countries and various library sites are also valuable. Of course there are also plenty of chat rooms and e-groups, including Murder Must Advertise, DorothyL, and E-MWA for active members of Mystery Writers of America.

For research tips, see Stuart M. Kaminsky's essay. It includes wonderfully helpful (and fun) sources.

Technical Reference Books Chosen by More Than One Contributor

Barry Fisher, *Techniques of Crime Scene Investigation*
This one's a favorite of both Jan Burke and Tony Hillerman.

David Fisher and Reginald Bragonier Jr., *What's What*
Dick Lochte and Marilyn Wallace included this title in their preferred technical references.

Vernon J. Geberth, *Practical Homicide Investigation*
This volume is by far the single most respected reference work on investigation. Its readers include Jan Burke, P.M. Carlson, Aaron Elkins, and Ann Rule.

The Howdunit Series
This well-known series published by Writer's Digest Books offers eight books on different topics germane to crime and mystery writers. Nancy Pickard and Sandra Scoppettone specifically mentioned this series.

Technical Reference Books Chosen by Individual Contributors

Jan Burke
Barry Fisher, *Techniques of Crime Scene Investigation.*
Vernon J. Geberth, *Practical Homicide Investigation.*
Marcella Sorg and William Haglund, *Forensic Taphonomy: The Postmortem Fate of Human Remains.*
Charles R. Swanson, Neil C. Chamelin, and Leonard Territo, *Criminal Investigation.*

P.M. Carlson
Vernon J. Geberth, *Practical Homicide Investigation.*

Aaron Elkins
Vernon J. Geberth, *Practical Homicide Investigation.*
G.T. Kurian, *World Encyclopedia of Police Forces and Penal Systems.*

Loren D. Estleman
Yale Kamisar, Wayne R. LaFave, and Jerold H. Israel, *Modern Criminal Procedure: Cases, Comments and Questions,* fifth edition.
F. Philip Rice, *Outdoor Life Gun Data Book.*
Robert A. Rinker, *Understanding Firearm Ballistics.*

Carl Sifakis, *The Encyclopedia of American Crime.*
Sir Sidney Smith, *Mostly Murder.*

Linda Fairstein

Linda Fairstein's essay contains excellent resources for use when writing the legal thriller.

Tess Gerritsen

For a good list of medical references and where to find them, see Tess Gerritsen's excellent essay.

Sue Grafton

Charles O'Hara, *Fundamentals of Criminal Investigation.*

Tony Hillerman

Barry Fisher, *Techniques of Crime Scene Investigation.*
Bartlett's Familiar Quotations. "When you want to make a character seem erudite, a pseudo- intellectual, etc."

Edward D. Hoch

See Hoch's essay for a stellar list of recommended story collections and reference books about the short story.

Stuart M. Kaminsky

Martin Roth, *The Writer's Complete Crime Reference Book.* "The one book a person who writes about crime should have within arm's reach."

Laurie R. King

Encyclopedia Britannica, eleventh edition (1910). "A valuable tool for anyone writing about the early part of the century."

Dick Lochte

David Fisher and Reginald Bragonier Jr., *What's What.* Dick Lochte says this is a totally unique reference work that should be on every writer's desk. It's a "picture dictionary that identifies objects and their parts."

Margaret Maron

Roget's Thesaurus.

Sara Paretsky

Sara Paretsky says the following books provide a good idea of who's writing and what's out there:

Willetta Heising, *Detecting Women* and *Detecting Men.*
Maureen Reddy, *Sisters in Crime.*

For historical background she uses the following:

Bruce Cassiday, *Roots of Detection: The Art of Deduction Before Sherlock Holmes.*
Audrey Peterson, *Victorian Masters of Mystery: From Wilkie Collins to Conan Doyle.*

Nancy Pickard

Any of the crime-related volumes of the Howdunit series from Writer's Digest Books.

Ann Rule

Michael Baden, M.D., *Dead Reckoning: The New Science of Catching Killers.*
————. *Unnatural Death: Confessions of a Medical Examiner.*
Sheree Bykofsky and Jennifer Basye Sander, *The Complete Idiots Guide to Getting Published.*
Vernon J. Geberth, *Practical Homicide Investigation.*
Twentieth Century Day by Day, published by Dorling Kindersley.

Sandra Scoppettone

Writer's Digest's *Howdunit* series of eight books on various crime-related subjects.

Julie Smith
> Any book of baby names.

Marilyn Wallace
> E.W. Count, *Cop Talk*.
> David Fisher and Reginald Bragonier, Jr., *What's What*.
> Tony Lesce, *Police Products Handbook*.
> Anne Svenssen, Otto Wendel, and Barry Fisher, *Techniques of Crime Scene Investigation*.
> *The World Almanac*.
> Golden Nature Guides: Trees; Flowers, Mammals of North America, etc.

Wallace's best piece of advice: "I buy tons of reference books in secondhand stores on every subject so I can use the right specific words to name things."

Angela Zeman
> Robert Ressler and Tom Shachtman, *Whoever Fights Monsters* and *I Have Lived in the Monster*.

About the Contributors

John F. Baker

John F. Baker is vice-president and editorial director of *Publishers Weekly*, where he has worked for over twenty-five years. He is the magazine's regular columnist for its "Hot Deals," about new book signings, and the twice-weekly "Rights Alert" e-mail column, and he frequently lectures on questions of interest to authors and publishers. He is married to an agent, Barbara Braun.

Lawrence Block

Lawrence Block's novels range from the urban noir of Matthew Scudder (*Hope to Die*) to the urbane effervescence of Bernie Rhodenbarr (*The Burglar in the Rye*), while other characters include the globe-trotting insomniac Evan Tanner (*Tanner on Ice*) and the introspective assassin Keller (*Hit List*). He has published articles and short fiction in *American Heritage*, *Redbook*, *Playboy*, *GQ*, and *The New York Times*, and has published several collections of short fiction in book form, the most recent being *The Collected Mystery Stories*. Block is a Grand Master of Mystery Writers of America. He is a past president of The Private Eye Writers of America and the Mystery Writers of America.

Jan Burke

Jan Burke is the author of eight novels, including *Bones*, which won the Edgar for best novel, and *Flight*. She is also an award-winning short story writer. She has taught mystery writing through the UCLA Extension Writers' Program and has served as the president of the Southern California Chapter of Mystery Writers of America. You can learn more about her at www.janburke.com.

Robert Campbell

The late Robert Campbell was the author of the Edgar Award–winning *Junkyard Dog*, the first book in the Jimmy Flannery

Mystery Series. He wrote the La-La Land series that features Whistler, an aging Hollywood private eye. His last book in that series was *Sweet La-La Land*. He also wrote for the screen and television.

P.M. Carlson

P.M. Carlson writes mysteries featuring the bright, lively, and sometimes outrageous Maggie Ryan, who is statistician, mom, and sleuth. Carlson's other series features Marty Hopkins, a deputy sheriff. *Murder Unrenovated* was a finalist for both Anthony and Macavity Awards. Her latest book, *Renowned Be Thy Grave: The Murderous Miss Mooney*, is a collection of mystery short stories featuring Bridget Mooney, a nineteenth-century actress.

Ruth Cavin

Ruth Cavin is a senior editor–associate publisher for Thomas Dunne Books for St. Martin's Press. Mystery novels and related works are the backbone of her list, but she does publish nonfiction and other kinds of fiction as well. Cavin has worked in public relations, produced advertising copy, been the author of published books (none of them mysteries), and in the distant past written some plays that were never produced. She's had to take seriously her own advice to new authors: "Don't give up your day job." But editing is a day job she loves.

George C. Chesbro

George C. Chesbro is the critically acclaimed, internationally renowned author of twenty-three novels, hundreds of short stories, articles, and poems. He is the creator of the Mongo mystery series. Mongo, a private detective who has a Ph.D. in criminology and is a former professor with a black belt in karate who just happens to be a dwarf, is unique in the mystery literature. Chesbro has acquired a cult following in this country, and his Mongo mysteries, along with *Bone*, approach best-seller status in France. A popular lecturer at writing seminars, he is a frequent guest at arts conferences and festivals, here and abroad. He served three years as executive vice-president of Mystery Writers of America. His latest book is *PRISM: A Memoir as Fiction*.

Michael Connelly

Michael Connelly, a former crime reporter, is the author of the best-selling series of Harry Bosch crime novels, including the recent, *Angels Flight*, and of the best-sellers *Blood Work* and *The Poet*. He lives in Los Angeles. Connelly's first novel, *The Black Echo*, won the Edgar Award for best first novel.

Aaron Elkins

Aaron Elkins has won an Edgar, an Agatha (with his wife, Charlotte), and a Nero Wolfe Award. His two continuing series feature anthropologist-detective Gideon Oliver and art curator–sleuth Chris Norgren. In addition, he and Charlotte coauthor a mystery series about a struggling female golfer, Lee Ofsted. Aaron Elkins's Gideon Oliver adventures have been translated into a major ABC-TV series, and his books have been selections of the Book-of-the-Month Club, The Literary Guild, and the Reader's Digest Condensed Mystery Series. His work has been published in eleven languages. He and Charlotte live on an island near Seattle, their marriage having survived (more or less intact) their continuing collaboration on novels and short stories.

Loren D. Estleman

Loren D. Estleman has published nearly fifty novels in the fields of mystery, historical Western, and mainstream. His Amos Walker detective series has earned four Notable Book of the Year mentions from the *The New York Times Book Review*, and he has been the recipient of sixteen national writing awards. He has been nominated for the Edgar Allan Poe Award, England's Silver Dagger Award, the National Book Award, and the Pulitzer prize. His latest novel, *Sinister Heights*, was published in 2002. Estleman is the current president of the Western Writers of America. He lives in Michigan with his wife, author Deborah Morgan.

Linda Fairstein

Linda Fairstein is the author of the Alexandra Cooper series of crime novels. Her first novel, *Final Jeopardy*, was an ABC-TV movie of the week in 2001. That book was followed by *Likely to Die, Cold Hit*, and *The Deadhouse*. Her nonfiction book, *Sexual Violence*, was a *New York Times* Notable Book of the Year. Fairstein is a graduate of Vassar College and the University of Virginia School of Law, and has been a prosecutor in the office of the New York County District Attorney for thirty years. For most of that time she has been the bureau chief of the Sex Crimes Prosecution Unit.

Russell Galen

Russell Galen is the president of Scovil Chichak Galen Literary Agency, Inc.

Tess Gerritsen

Tess Gerritsen is a physician as well as a *New York Times* best-selling author of five medical thrillers: *Harvest, Life Support, Bloodstream, Gravity*, and *The Surgeon*. She lives in Maine.

Bill Granger

Bill Granger has written twenty-four books. He won the Edgar Award from the Mystery Writers of America for *Public Murders* and is the author of the November Man Series, including *League of Terror* and *The Man Who Heard Too Much*. "Drover" is his latest series character. He has been a journalist for the *Chicago Sun-Times*, United Press International, and the *Chicago Tribune*.

He lives in Chicago and for many years authored a regular column for *The Chicago Tribune Magazine*.

■

G. Miki Hayden

G. Miki Hayden, the author of *Pacific Empire, By Reason of Insanity*, and *Writing the Mystery*, teaches at Writers Online Workshops and is a prepublication editor as well as an MWA board member.

■

Jeremiah Healy

Jeremiah Healy, a graduate of Rutgers College and Harvard Law School, was a professor at the New England School of Law for eighteen years. He is the creator of John Francis Cuddy, a Boston-based private investigator. Healy's first book, *Blunt Darts*, was selected by *The New York Times* as one of the seven best mysteries of 1984. His second work, *The Staked Goat*, received the Shamus Award for the best private eye novel of 1986. He has been a Shamus nominee for thirteen books and short stories. Healy's later novels include *So Like Sleep, Swan Dive, Yesterday's News, Right to Die, Shallow Graves, Foursome, Act of God, Rescue, Invasion of Privacy*, and *The Only Good Lawyer*. A legal thriller, *The Stalking of Sheilah Quinn*, and a collection of his short stories, *The Concise Cuddy*, were published in 1998. His current Cuddy novel, *Spiral*, was published in 1999. He is the president of the International Association of Crime Writers.

■

Tony Hillerman

Tony Hillerman was born in 1925 in the Oklahoma farm community of Sacred Heart. He attended boarding school for American Indian girls for the first eight grades, served in an infantry rifle company in WWII, attained rank of private first class twice, and won the Silver Star, Bronze Star with cluster, and Purple Heart. With journalism degrees from The University of Oklahoma and The University of New Mexico, Hillerman has worked as a police reporter, editor, and professor of journalism. He is the author of twenty-three books, including fourteen mysteries now printed in nineteen languages, and he won the Edgar Allan Poe Award and was named an MWA Grand Master. He is the former president of the MWA. He's been married to Marie for fifty-three years and has six children. He lives in Albuquerque, New Mexico.

Edward D. Hoch

Edward D. Hoch, past president of the Mystery Writers of America, is the author of more than 850 published short stories and 18 novels and story collections. He has had a story in every issue of *Ellery Queen Mystery Magazine* since May 1973, and from 1976 to 1995 edited *The Year's Best Mystery and Suspense Stories,* a yearly anthology. He is an MWA Grand Master and the field's foremost practitioner of the short story form. Hoch and his wife, Patricia, live in Rochester, New York.

Stuart M. Kaminsky

Stuart M. Kaminsky is a six-time nominee for the Edgar Allan Poe Award, which he won in 1989 for his novel *A Cold Red Sunrise.* He has served as president of MWA and as Edgar Awards chair. Winner of the Prix Du Roman d'Aventure for best mystery novel published in France, Kaminsky is the author of more than fifty published mystery novels, including those in the Toby Peters, Porfiry Rostnikov, Lew Fonesca, Abe Lieberman, and Jim Rockford series. His screenwriting credits include *Once Upon a Time in America, Enemy Territory,* and *Hidden Fears.* His television credits include *A Woman in the Wind* for the A&E Short Story series and *Immune to Murder* for the Nero Wolfe series on A&E. In addition to writing, Kaminsky is the editor in chief of Mystery Vault, Inc., which is devoted to publishing new books and new editions of out-of-print titles.

Faye Kellerman and Jonathan Kellerman

Faye Kellerman's most recent novel is *The Forgotten.* She has written a number of other novels, including and acclaimed historical mystery, *The Quality of Mercy*. Her series characters are Peter Decker and Rina Lazarus. Edgar-winning Jonathan Kellerman's novels include *When the Bough Breaks, Blood Test, Over the Edge, The Butcher's Theater, Silent Partner*, and *Time Bomb*. His latest novel is *Flesh and Blood*. Like his detective hero, Kellerman was trained as a clinical psychologist specializing in children. He is the author of two volumes of psychology and one book for children. The Kellermans live in Los Angeles with their three children.

Laurie R. King

Laurie R. King is a third-generation northern Californian with a B.A. in comparative religion from the University of California, Santa Cruz, a master's in Old Testament theology from the Graduate Theological Union in Berkeley, and an honorary doctorate from the Church Divinity School of the Pacific. She has combined the heady interest in things theological with a longtime, hands-on passion for renovating old houses and the equally challenging job of raising children. She occasionally regards writing as a nice holiday.

Dick Lochte

Dick Lochte's current books include a short story collection, *Lucky Dog, and Other Tales of Murder*, and *L.A. Justice*, a legal thriller written in collaboration with attorney Christopher Darden. Winner of the Nero Wolfe Award for his novel *Sleeping Dog*, Lochte has written for both feature films and television. His column of mystery reviews appears biweekly in the *Los Angeles Times*, and his articles and essays have appeared in numerous other publications, including *The Oxford Companion to Crime and Mystery Writing*. A native of New Orleans, Louisiana, he now resides with his wife and son in southern California.

John Lutz

John Lutz is the author of more than 30 novels and approximately 250 short stories and articles. He has served as president of both

Mystery Writers of America and The Private Eye Writers of America. Lutz won the Mystery Writers of America Edgar Award in 1986 and The Private Eye Writers of America Shamus Award in 1982 and 1988. In 1989 he won the Trophee 813 Award for best mystery short story collection translated into the French language. In 1995 he was the recipient of The Private Eye Writers of America Life Achievement Award. He is the author of two private eye series: the Carver series, set in Florida, and the Nudger series, set in his hometown of St. Louis, Missouri. Also the author of many nonseries suspense novels, his *SWF Seeks Same* was made into the hit movie *Single White Female*, starring Bridget Fonda and Jennifer Jason Leigh. His novel *The Ex* was made into an HBO film of the same title, for which he coauthored the screenplay. His short story collection *The Nudger Dilemmas* and a suspense novel *The Night Caller* were published in 2001.

Margaret Maron

Margaret Maron lives on her family farm a few miles southeast of Raleigh. She's the author of seventeen mystery novels and a collection of her short stories that were published here and abroad. Her works have won most of the major national awards in the field, including the Edgar for best novel, and are on the reading lists of various courses in contemporary Southern literature. She is a past president of Sisters in Crime and of the American Crime Writers League, and a former national director of MWA. Visit her Web site at www.MargaretMaron.com.

Warren Murphy

Warren Murphy was born in Jersey City, New Jersey. He worked as a reporter and editor, and after service during the Korean War, he drifted into politics. Murphy, who created the long-run Destroyer and Trace series, is also a screenwriter. He has been an adjunct professor at Moravian College, Bethlehem, Pennsylvania, and has also run workshops and lectured at many other schools and universities. His books and stories have won a dozen national awards, including two Edgars and two Shamuses from the Private Eye Writers of America. Encyclopedia Mysteriosa called him "a mentor and teacher to a whole generation of crime and thriller writers." Visit his Web site at www.warrenmurphy.com.

Joan Lowery Nixon

Joan Lowery Nixon has authored over 130 books, the most recent of which is the young adult mystery *Playing for Keeps*. She has won four Edgars from Mystery Writers of America, two Western Writers of America Spur Awards, and many children's choice awards throughout the United States. A former president of Mystery Writers of America, she is listed in *Contemporary Authors of Children's Literature; Something About the Author*, volume 78; *Something About the Author Autobiography* series, volume 9; and *Who's Who in America*.

Sara Paretsky

The recipient of numerous awards, including the 1996 Mark Twain Award for distinguished contributions to Midwestern literature and a Visiting Scholarship at Oxford University in 1997, Sara Paretsky helped found Sisters in Crime in 1986. A graduate of The University of Kansas, Paretsky holds a Ph.D. in history and an M.B.A. in finance from The University of Chicago. She has founded two scholarships at The University of Kansas and mentors students in Chicago's inner city schools. She lives in Chicago with her husband, physics professor S.C. Wright.

Nancy Pickard

Nancy Pickard is the author of three award-winning mystery series featuring amateur sleuths: Jenny Cain, director of a charitable foundation; Marie Lightfoot, a true crime writer; and Eugenia Potter (created by Virginia Rich), whose adventures launched the popular genre of culinary mysteries. Pickard, who is also an award-winning short story writer, lives in the Kansas City area.

Ann Rule

Ann Rule graduated from the University of Washington with a degree in creative writing, and she has an associate degree in police science from Highline Community College. She's been trying to get published since the late fifties, and she sold her first article in about 1962 to *The Seattle Times*. She wrote for *True Detective* magazine and her "sister" magazines—*Cosmopolitan*, *Ladies' Home Journal*, *Good Housekeeping*, *Redbook*, et al.,—for fifteen years, selling fourteen hundred true crime articles. Her first book was *The Stranger Beside Me* (about Ted Bundy), published in 1980. She has published nineteen books since then, including *Small Sacrifices*, *If You Really Loved Me*, *Dead by Sunset*, *Bitter Harvest*, and *. . . And Never Let Her Go*. Her newest book, published in December 2001, is *Every Breath You Take*. She also writes a series called Ann Rule's Crime Files. She has been on *The New York Times* best-seller list seventeen times, and has two Anthony Awards, a Peabody Award, and three Edgar nominations (no wins!). Rule is a former Seattle police officer and lectures to law enforcement officers both local and FBI. Currently she has contracts with Free Press/Simon and Schuster and Pocket Books for five more books.

Sandra Scoppettone

Writing as Jack Early, Sandra Scoppettone was given a Myster Writers of America Edgar nomination in the 1984 best first mystery category for *A Creative Kind of Killer* and was nominated by The Private Eye Writers of America for a Shamus, which she won. The following year, as Scoppettone, she was nominated for an Edgar in the YA division. Starting with *Everything You Have Is Mine*, she created the Lauren Laurano series. There are five books in the series. All the Jack Early books have been reprinted under Scoppettone's name, and most of her books have been published in many languages.

Julie Smith

Julie Smith has written about both San Francisco and New Orleans. In more than a dozen novels, she chronicles the adventures of amateur sleuths, Rebecca Schwartz and Paul Mcdonald, PI Talba Wallis, and New Orleans cop Skip Langdon. The first in the Skip Langdon series, *New Orleans Mourning*, won the Edgar for best hardcover novel in 1991. Julie Smith is a former reporter for the New Orleans *Times-Picayune* and the *San Franciso Chronicle*.

Marilyn Wallace

Marilyn Wallace has served Mystery Writers of America as president of the Northern California Chapter, as a national board member, and as general award chair of the Edgar Allan Poe Awards. Her three-book series featuring Oakland, California, homicide detectives Jay Goldstein and Carlos Cruz includes *A Case of Loyalties*, a Macavity Award winner, and *Primary Target* and *A Single Stone*, both Anthony Award nominees. The focus shifts to psychological suspense in *So Shall You Reap*, *The Seduction*, *Lost Angel*, and *Current Danger*. Editor of the five-volume award-winning *Sisters in Crime* short story anthologies, which highlight the work of American women mystery writers, and coeditor with Robert J. Randisi of *Deadly Allies*, she has led numerous writing workshops across the country.

Carolyn Wheat

Carolyn Wheat, multiple award-winning author of the Cass Jameson legal mysteries, is also the editor of two mystery story anthologies, *Murder on Route 66* and *Women Before the Bench*. Her own stories are available in the collection *Tales Out of School*.

Phyllis A. Whitney

Phyllis A. Whitney has long been a best-seller in the mystery-suspense field. She received the Grand Master Award from Mystery Writers of America in 1988. She also received an Agatha Award from Malice Domestic in 1990. Both were given for lifetime achievement. For many years she taught writing at New York University, and her books on writing include *Guide to Fiction Writing* and *Writing Juvenile Stories and Novels*.

Angela Zeman

Angela Zeman is author of the Mrs. Risk "witch" story series published in *Alfred Hitchcock's Mystery Magazine* and other venues. Her Mrs. Risk novel, *The Witch and the Borscht Pearl*, was published in November 2001. A Mrs. Risk story was also chosen for the recent MWA anthology *The Night Awakens*, edited by Mary Higgins Clark, which has been published in a number of countries and languages and is also available in audiobook. One suspense-thriller story, "Hello?," included in the 1999 trade paper anthology *Mom, Apple Pie, and Murder*, edited by Nancy Pickard, was reviewed by *Publishers Weekly* as "magical." Both anthologies are still in print. A new story will appear in the upcoming MWA anthology, *Hot and Sultry Nights*, edited by Jeffrey Deaver. Over the years Zeman has served MWA in various capacities, most notably on the board of directors and twice as chairperson of the annual MWA writers symposium.

Barry Zeman

A noted mystery historian and antiquarian, nonfiction writer Barry Zeman is an expert in the field of mystery and detective fiction and contributes articles to journals, magazines, and books. He has lectured and participated on panels at national and international meetings. Currently MWA's Executive Vice President and New York regional chapter president and recently national publications chair, he has been for many years their archivist and librarian and served over ten years as a board member and five years as treasurer. He twice cochaired the annual symposium and has chaired and served on a number of Edgar Award committees.

Index

"A" Is for Alibi, 279, 280, 283
Abel, Kenneth, 282
Abrahamsen, David, 88
Absurdity, 149-150, 152
Accuracy, 210, 211, 239
Action, 212, 219, 223
Advance, 195
Agents, 3, 187, 190-196, 200, 265
Alfred Hitchcock's Mystery Magazine, 176, 230
Along Came a Spider, 283
Amateur sleuth, 79-90, 243
American Regional Mystery, The, 232
Anatomy of a Murder, 245, 281
Antihero, 255
Appointment in Samarra, 120
Art of Fiction: Notes on Craft for Young Writers, 284, 286, 287
Asimov, Isaac, 229
Atmosphere, 2, 48, 54, 210, 212
Attribution, 134, 185
Authenticity, 11-12, 34, 35, 136, 241

Background, 48-55, 54, 210, 219, 223
Baker, John F., 190-196, 293
Baldacci, David, 243
Barnard, Robert, 134
Barnes, Linda, 7
Barr, Nevada, 126
Beginning, 3, 184, 206-208, 218-219
Believability, 71, 90, 129, 185, 210, 229
Best American Mystery Stories of the Century, The, 282
Big Sleep, The, 119
Bishop, Paul, 34
Bitter Blood, 283
Black and Blue, 280
Black Echo, The, 280
Black Ice, The, 62-64
Black Orchids, 128
Bledsoe, Jerry, 283
Blessing Way, The, 101
Blind Descent, 121, 126
Block, Lawrence, 8, 166-172, 284, 285, 286, 287, 293
Blood and Money, 24, 283
Blunt, Giles, 282
Bone, 96
Books, best mystery, 271-284

Books, on writing, 284-288
Books, reference, 231-232, 238, 284-292
Bootlegger's Daughter, 280
Brat Farrar, 66-67, 279, 280
Brewer, Steve, 282
Briarpatch, 281
Brighton Rock, 226
Buchanan, Edna, 283
Bum Steer, 82
Bundy, Ted, 88
Buried Dreams: Inside the Mind of a Serial Killer, 88
Burke, Jan, 180-189, 280, 285, 288, 289, 293
Burns, Rex, 135
Busman's Honeymoon, 66
Butcher's Theater, The, 38
Butler, Gwendoline, 207

Caduceus Is for Killing, A, 264
Cain, James, 89
California Fire and Life, 279, 280, 283
California Roll, 128
Campbell, Robert, 10, 105-111, 293-294
Cape Fear, 283
Capote, Truman, 283
Carlson, P. M., 160-165, 289, 294
Case of Loyalties, A, 17
Category mystery, 197, 198-200
Catskill, 214
Caunitz, William J., 34, 119
Cavin, Ruth, 205-215, 285, 294
Chandler, Raymond, 8, 9, 20-21, 49, 53, 61, 76, 119
Chapters, 98, 99, 100, 101, 123, 128, 143, 183, 222
Characters, 2, 3, 11, 16, 48, 94, 103, 105, 106, 107, 129, 178, 184, 185, 198, 212, 218, 226-227, 235, 241, 281
   development of, 17, 57-64, 65-71, 108, 132, 209-210, 220-221
   main, 141, 142, 219, 220, 221, 222
   secondary, 38
   series, 72-78, 281
Chesbro, George C., 91-97, 285, 294-295
Chesterton, G.K., 228, 232, 282
Christie, Agatha, 66, 68, 76, 119, 160, 163, 165, 228
City Primeval, 120

Clark, Mary Higgins, 14
Cleeves, Ann, 125
Climax, 3, 146
Close third-person, 69
Clues, 2, 3, 123, 160-165, 174, 175, 176, 177, 223, 227-229
Coffin's Game, 207
Cold Red Sunrise, A, 137
Cold Steel Rain, 282
Columbella, 140
Conclusion, 105, 229-230
Concrete Blond, The, 283
Conflict, 15, 59-60, 72, 74, 75, 144, 234, 245
Connelly, Michael, 57-64, 126, 128, 279, 280, 281, 283, 295
Consistency, 184
Constantine, K.C., 280
Continuity, 75
Contracts, 195, 196, 200, 266-267
Cook, Robin, 33
Cop Talk, 292
Cornwell, Patricia, 281
Cozy mystery, 1, 122
Crais, Robert, 8, 164, 281
Creative Kind of Killer, A, 89
Crime, 1, 2, 59, 87, 89, 103, 164, 211, 244, 280
Crime novel, 14, 34, 53, 61, 73, 74, 124, 183, 202, 209, 240, 245, 252, 258
Crime scene, 122, 162, 257
Crime writing, 72-73, 140, 228, 253-261, 289, 290
Criminal Investigation, 289
Criminal justice system, 3, 242
Crocodile on the Sandbank, 281
Cross, Amanda, 74
Crumley, James, 119
Culprit, 10-11, 86 *See also* Villain
Curiosity, 141, 146, 211

D'Amato, Barbara, 284
Dance Hall of the Dead, 103
Danger, 142, 145, 146, 222
Dannay, Fred, 230, 271
Dark Wind, The, 103
Darkness, Take My Hand, 279, 280
Darnton, John, 235
Daughter of Time, The, 119
Davis, Dorothy Salisbury, 77
"Day of the Picnic, The," 176
Dead Crazy, 82

Dead Reckoning: The New Science of Catching Killers, 291
Death, 9, 72, 148, 258
Deaver, Jeffrey, 281
Demon in My View, A, 119
Denouement, 108, 258
Description, 2, 54-55, 62, 128, 143, 184, 249
Details, 49, 58-59, 64, 70, 154, 212, 239
Detecting Men, 291
Detecting Women, 291
Detective, 160, 161, 162, 164, 242, 254
Detective stories, 96, 123, 129, 228, 278
Devil in a Blue Dress, 279, 280
Dialect, 38, 136-137
Dialogue, 2, 3, 57, 105, 128, 129-138, 177, 184, 185, 223, 237, 238
Diamond in the Buff, 51-52
Dickinson, Peter, 72, 72-73, 282
Disaster, impending, 144
Disbelief, 80-82, 240, 243
Dold, Gaylord, 213
Dollhouse Murders, The, 220, 221
Donato and Daughter, 87, 89
Don't Look Behind You, 220, 221
Doss, James, 282
Double Indemnity, 89
Down by the River Where the Dead Men Go, 280
Doyle, Conan, 72, 228, 247
Dr. Jekyll and Mr. Hyde, 120
Drafts, 93, 94, 166, 180, 181, 182
Duncan, Lois, 220, 221
Dunlap, Susan, 15, 51-52

E-books, 1, 262-270
Eccentricity, 142
Editing/editors, 3, 128, 186, 190, 191, 195, 198, 201, 205-215, 231, 265-266, 268
Electronic media, 1, 262-270
Elkins, Aaron, 33, 129-138, 289, 295
Ellery Queen Mystery Magazine, 176, 230
Emotion, 14, 18, 142, 146-147, 178, 221, 258
Empty bracket, 149, 150-152, 153
Encyclopedia of American Crime, The, 290
Ending, 16, 147, 173-179, 227
Errors, 186-187
Estleman, Loren D., 8, 112-120, 281, 286, 289, 295-296
Evanovich, Janet, 281
Every Breath You Take, 260

Except the Dying, 208
Executioners, The, 283
Experiment, The, 235
Expertise, 3, 33-40, 42, 43, 188, 238

Facts, 223
Fairstein, Linda, 240-245, 281, 290, 296
False clues, 163, 165
Fatal Addiction, 88
Fatal Vision, 88
Feedback, 187-188
First chapter, 98, 99, 128, 183
First draft, 93, 94, 166, 180, 181, 182
First-person narrative, 9-10, 69, 74, 96, 97,
    112-114, 117, 118, 119, 142, 186
Five Red Herrings, The, 163
Flashback, 219
Flow of a story, 62, 63
Fly on the Wall, 102
Follet, Ken, 235
Ford, Miriam Allen, 88
Forensic science, 3, 243, 257
*Forensic Taphonomy: The Postmortem Fate
    of Human Remains*, 289
Foreshadowing, 174, 175, 176, 178, 247
Forty Words for Sorrow, 282
Frame, 163
Franchise Affair, The, 280
Francis, Dick, 14, 21, 121, 280
Friedman, Mickey, 15, 49-50
Friends of Eddie Coyle, The, 119
Fright, 219, 222
Fundamentals of Crime Investigation, 290
Fyfield, Frances, 244

Galen, Russell, 197-204, 296
Galton Case, The, 127
Garden of Evil, 283
Gardner, Erle Stanley, 241
Gardner, John, 121, 250, 284, 286-287
Gash, Jonathan, 65
Gaudy Night, 76
Gender, 7, 34, 74, 77, 145
Generous Death, 81-82
Gerritsen, Tess, 233-239, 290, 296
Gilmore, Mikal, 283
Glass Key, The, 119
Goals, opposing, 144
Good Cop, Bad Cop, 284
Gores, Joe, 34, 51
Grafton, Sue, 7, 164, 229, 279, 280, 283,
    286, 290

Grammar, 186-187
Granger, Bill, 148-159, 296-297
Grave Talent, A, 280
Gravity, 235
Greeley, Andrew, 33
Greenberg, Martin H., 282
Greene, Graham, 225, 226
Grisham, John, 243, 244
Guide to Literary Agents, 193
Guilt, 2, 7, 146
Gun in Cheek, 127

"H" Is for Homicide, 126
Hall, Parnell, 11
Hamilton, Steve, 207
Hammett, Dashiell, 8, 9, 53, 116, 119, 121
Hansen, Joseph, 8, 49
Harris, Fred, 282
Harris, Thomas, 38, 86, 119, 280
Harvest, 234
Haunting, The, 287
Haycraft Queen List, 271, 272-277, 280,
    283
Hayden, G. Miki, 262-270, 288, 297
Hayes, John R., 214
Healy, Jeremiah, 6-12, 281, 286, 297
Hero, 7, 9, 10-11, 64, 75, 237, 255
Hiaasen, Carl, 279
Higgins, George V., 119
"High Stakes," 178
Highsmith, Patricia, 89
Hill, Reginald, 279, 282
Hillerman, Tony, 14, 53, 98-104, 134, 213,
    279, 281, 286, 288, 290, 297-298
Historical mysteries, 1, 223, 246-252, 288,
    290
Hoch, Edward D., 224-232, 282, 290, 298
Hound of the Baskervilles, The, 114
Howdunit series, 289, 291
Humor, 127, 198, 219, 223
Hunter, The, 119, 171
Hurricane Season, 49-50, 54

I Have Lived in the Monster, 292
Ideas, 3, 13-19, 160, 219-220
Identification, reader, 84, 218
Impending disaster, 144
Impression, 54, 175, 176
In Cold Blood, 283
In the Heat of the Summer, 33
Incongruity, 248
Indemnity Only, 283

Index to Crime and Mystery Anthologies, 231

Innocence of Father Brown, The, 232, 282

Innocent Bystanders, 86-87

Instance of the Fingerpost, An, 280

Internet, 23, 42, 43, 238, 251, 269, 288

Intrigue, 219

Irony, 156

Jargon, 35, 38, 128, 130

Jennings, Maureen, 208

Journals, 38-39

Jungle of Steel and Stone, 97

Juvenile mystery writing, 140, 141, 217-224

Kaminsky, Stuart M., 41-47, 137, 288, 290, 298

Katzenback, John, 33

Kellerman, Faye and Jonathan, 33-40, 298-299

Kersh, Gerald, 119

Killing Zone, The, 135

King and Joker, 73, 75

King, Laurie R., 246-252, 279, 280, 282, 286, 290, 299

King of the Corner, 117

King, Stephen, 48, 118, 140, 284, 285, 286

Kirk, Diana, 264

L.A. Requiem, 281

Language, 37, 38, 84, 248, 249

Lanier, Virginia, 65

Last Coyote, The, 60

Last Good Kiss,The, 119

Last Houseparty, The, 282

Latham, Emma, 74

Law and Order, 120

Law Student, A, 208

Le Carré, John, 74, 281

Lee, Harper, 244

Legal thrillers, 1, 34, 240-245, 281, 290

Lehane, Dennis, 279, 280, 283

Leonard, Elmore, 11, 119, 124, 279, 283

Libraries, 23, 39, 45, 141, 251

Life-or-death problem, 141, 144

Life Support, 235

Listening Woman, 99

Literary Market Place (LMP), 191, 199

Little Saigon, 122, 125

Location, 48-55

Lochte, Dick, 20-25, 281, 282, 288, 290, 299

Locked Room Murders and Other Impossible Crimes, 231

Logic, 184

Los Angeles, 8, 53, 64, 164

Lutz, John, 10, 173-179, 283, 299-300

Lyons, Arthur, 8

MacDonald, Jeffrey, 88

MacDonald, John D., 21, 283

Macdonald, Ross, 53, 126

Magazines, 46, 90, 92, 203-204, 225, 230, 231, 235, 254

Maiden's Grave, A, 281

Main character, 141, 142, 219, 220, 221, 222

Mainstream mystery, 197-198

Maling, Arthur, 75-76

Maltese Falcon, The, 116

Man Who Liked Slow Tomatoes, The, 280

Manuscript preparation, 186-188, 204, 208-209

Marketing, 195, 197-204, 268-269

Maron, Margaret, 65-71, 280, 286, 291, 300

Marriage is Murder, 82

Matera, Lia, 34

Mazer, Norma Fox, 220, 221

McBain, Ed, 281

McCoy, Horace, 119

McGinniss, Joe, 88

Medical thrillers, 1, 33, 233-239

Metaphor, 54, 64, 125, 126-127, 128, 161

Meyers, Annette, 283

Miami Blues, 87

Millar, Margaret, 89

Misery, 48

Misstatement, 156

Modern Criminal Procedure: Cases, Comments and Questions, 289

Modifiers, 249

Monthly Murders: A Checklist and Chronological Listing of Fiction, 232

Mood, 48, 50, 51, 64, 125, 131, 132

Mosley, Walter, 279, 280

Mostly Murder, 290

Motivation, 89, 90, 105, 211

Motive, 89, 103, 131, 160, 161

Mrs. McGinty's Dead, 160

Muller, Marcia, 8, 283

Murder, 2, 3, 15, 86-87, 160, 161, 162, 202, 211, 241, 242, 243, 253, 260

Murder Being Once Done, 283

Murder for Pleasure, 271

Murder in the Queen's Armes, 132
Murder Must Advertise, 75
"Murder of a Gypsy King," 226
Murder of Roger Ackroyd, The, 119
Murderers, The, 88
Murderers Sane and Mad, 88
Murdering Mind, The, 88
Murphy, Warren, 26-32, 286, 300-301
Mystery, Detective, and Espionage Fiction, 231-232
Mystery, Detective, and Espionage Magazines, 231
Mystery Hall of Fame: An Anthology . . . , 232, 282
Mystery novel, 16-17, 68, 91, 96, 129, 145, 202, 209
Mystery Writer's Handbook, The, 288
Mystery Writers of America, 1, 4, 140, 199, 204, 245, 270, 288
Mystery writing, 6-11, 226, 227, 289

Narcissist, 87, 89
Narration, 158, 223
Narrative voice, 69-70 *See also* First person narrative; Third person
Networking, 191, 194, 288
New Orleans Mourning, 50-51, 52-53
Night and the City, 119
Nixon, Joan Lowery, 217-223, 287, 301
No Body, 82
No Pockets in a Shroud, 119
Nobody's Fool, 281
Noir, 280
Noodling, 91, 92, 93, 95
North of Nowhere, 207
Novel & Short Story Writer's Market, 204

"Oblong Room, The," 231
O'Brian, Tim, 88
O'Brien, Darcy, 283
O'Conner, Patricia, 186, 285
O'Hara, John, 119
Oklahoma Punk, The, 115
Omniscient narrator, 69, 70, 96, 114-115, 118, 119, 186, 247
On Writing, 284, 285
One Foot in the Grave, 73, 74
One for the Money, 281
101 Years' Entertainment: The Great Detective Stories . . . , 232, 282
Onion Field, The, 280

Openings, 99, 128, 183-184, 206-208, 214, 218-219, 226
Opinion, 48, 53, 54
Other Side of Dark, The, 220, 221
Outdoor Life Gun Data Book, 289
Outlining, 3, 93, 94, 98-104, 105-111, 171-172

Pacing, 2, 9, 57, 139-147, 179, 184, 185
Paperbacks, 199, 201, 269
Paragraph, opening, 206-208
Paretsky, Sara, 7, 72-78, 164, 283, 291, 301
Parker, Dorothy, 180
Parker, Robert B., 11, 264, 279
Parker, T. Jefferson, 122, 125
Parody, 126
Partners, 26-32
Passion, crime of, 87, 89
Past, 62-63, 226, 246-258
Patterson, James, 283
Patterson, Richard North, 243
Pears, Iain, 280
Pelecanos, George, 280
Penzler, Otto, 282
Personal style, 61, 121-128
Peters, Elizabeth, 65, 248, 281
Peters, Ellis, 248
Petievich, Gerald, 34, 37
Pfeffer, Susan Beth, 220, 221
Pickard, Nancy, 11, 79-90, 289, 291, 301-302
Pictures of Perfection, 282
"Pit and the Pendulum, The," 230
Plausibility, 175, 176, 178
Plot, 2, 3, 7, 10, 16, 17, 48, 52-53, 57, 62, 65, 66, 68, 91-97, 109, 129, 143, 160-165, 169, 198, 202, 210, 211, 220-221, 227-229, 235, 242, 281, 282
Poe, Edgar Allan, 16, 113, 226, 230
Poet, The, 280
Point of view, 3, 96, 112-120, 185-186
Poison Apples, 214
Police procedures, 2, 3, 84, 122, 152, 223, 227
Police Products Handbook, 292
Possibility, 175, 178
Postman Always Rings Twice, The, 89
Postmortem, 281
Practical Homicide Investigation, 289, 291
Present tense, 97, 124
Presumed Innocent, 36, 242, 281
Prey to Murder, A, 125

Primary Target, 14
Print on Demand books (POD), 262-263, 268-269
Private eye, 1, 2, 7-11, 39, 74, 77-78, 122, 164, 165, 227-232
Problems, 7, 73-74, 141, 144, 166-172
Process of elimination, 229
Production notes, 94
Professional killer, 87
Promotion, 195, 269-270
Pronzini, Bill, 11, 127, 232, 282
Prose, 57, 149, 152-155, 198, 211, 281
Protagonist, 34, 59-61, 62, 64, 72, 77, 90, 100, 101, 103, 116, 131, 180, 183, 184, 185, 186, 234, 242, 244
Psychological suspense, 2, 96, 144, 223, 244
Psychopath, 87, 88, 89
Publicity, 196, 270
Publisher, 191, 196, 198, 200, 262-270
Puzzle mystery, 2, 165, 219

Queen, Ellery, 27, 228, 229, 230, 232, 271, 280, 282
Query letter, 192, 194, 200, 202, 266
Quest plot, 164-165

Randisi, Robert, 11
Rankin, Ian, 280
Razzamatazz, 89
Reader identification, 84, 218
Reading aloud, 137-138, 185
"Real Shape of the Coast, The," 176
Realism, 142, 210, 227
Recurring hero, 75
Red Carnelian, The, 140
Red Dragon, 86
Red Harvest, 53
Red herrings, 2, 160-165, 177
Red Highway, 115
Red is for Murder, 140
"Red Wind," 49
Reference books, 231-232, 238, 271-292
Rendell, Ruth, 119, 131, 279, 283
Research, 3, 23-24, 33-40, 41-47, 57, 141, 223, 226-227, 244-245, 249-252, 256, 288
Resolution, 72
Revision, 166, 180-189, 212
Rewriting, 29, 35, 93, 123
Rights, 224-225
Roots of Detection: The Art of Deduction Before Sherlock Holmes, 291

Royalties, 195, 201, 267-268
Rule, Ann, 253-261, 283, 289, 291, 302
Rules of mystery writing, 6-11
Russo, Richard, 281

Saint Magazine, The, 231
Saint Mystery Magazine, The, 178
Samedi's Knapsack, 213
Sanders, Lawrence, 127
Sapir, Richard Ben (Dick), 30-32
Say No to Murder, 82
Sayers, Dorothy L., 66, 68, 75, 76, 77, 163
Scene, 11, 107, 133
Schedule, work, 20-25
Schutz, Benjamin, 8
Science fiction, 223, 229
Scoppettone, Sandra, 86-90, 283, 289, 291, 302
Scottoline, Lisa, 244
Second Horseman Out of Eden, 94
Secondary character, 38
Secret, 144
Self-publishing, 268
Senses, 54-55, 223, 239
"Sentence, The," 14
Sentences, 248, 249
Sequel, 72, 243
Series, 72-78, 227, 243, 281
Serpentine, 24
Setting, 8, 48-55, 65, 103, 126, 129, 140, 198, 222, 226-227, 234, 246, 248
Sherlock Holmes, 72, 228, 247, 279
Short story, 2, 16-17, 68, 224-232, 282, 290
Shot in the Heart, 283
Shotgun, 118, 120
Silence of the Lambs, The, 38, 86, 120, 280
Silent Partner, 36-37
Simile, 126-127
Simon, Roger L., 128
Sisters in Crime, 291
Skeleton-in-Waiting, 73
Sleeping Dog, 22, 281
Smith, Julie, 48-55, 287, 292, 303
Sociopath, 87, 88, 89
Solutions, 229-230
Speech, 70, 130
Speech descriptor, 133-134
Speech, parts of, 124, 134, 146, 248
Spelling errors, 186-187
Spy Who Came in From the Cold, The, 281
Stark, Richard, 119, 171
Stevenson, Robert Louis, 119

Story flow, 62, 63
Stout, Rex, 128
Stranger Beside Me,The, 259
Strong Poison, 75, 76
Structure, 91-97, 184
Stumbling blocks, 3, 166-172. *See also*
  Writer's block
Style, 3, 57, 121-128, 211
Subjective depiction, 155, 156
Such Nice People, 86
Summer in the Twenties, A, 282
Suspects, 163, 164
Suspects, 119
Suspense, 2, 3, 16, 96, 97, 139-147, 211,
  219, 221-222, 258, 282
Suspense story, 33, 122, 223, 226, 227, 228,
  234
Suspicion, 222

Taking Terri Mueller, 220, 221
"Tale of Two Pretties, A," 16-17
Tanay, Emanuel, 88
Technical reference books, 288-292
Technique of the Mystery Story, The, 129
Techniques of Crime Scene Investigation,
  288, 289, 290, 292
Technology, 262-270
Telling Lies for Fun and Profit, 284, 285,
  287
Tempo, 130, 146
Tense, 97
Tension, 183, 219, 258
Tey, Josephine, 65, 66-68, 119, 279, 280
Theme, 3, 17, 103, 248
Thieves, 89
Third person narrative, 9, 10, 69, 96,
  114-115, 116-118, 119, 142, 185-186
Third Twin, The, 235
Thomas, Ross, 279, 281
Thompson, Thomas, 24, 283
Threat, 145, 146, 211
Thriller, 202
Time, 143-144, 222
Time to Kill, A, 243
Timothy Files, The, 127
Title, 16-17, 93, 260
To Live and Die in L.A., 37
Todd, Charles, 280
Tone, 2, 3, 130
Town of Masks, A, 77
Trapdoor, The, 165
Traver, Robert, 245, 281

Trials, 255-257
True crime, 1, 87
True Detective, 253, 257
Turow, Scott, 34, 36, 242, 281
Two of a Kind, 283

Uhnak, Dorothy, 34, 119
Underground Man, The, 126
Underplaying, 149, 152-155
Understanding Firearms Ballistics, 289
Understatement, 153, 156
Unexpected, the, 143
*Unnatural Death: Confessions of a Medical
  Examiner*, 291

Vachss, Andrew, 53-54
Valin, Jonathan, 8
Veil, 97
Veiled One, The, 131-132
Vendetta Defense, The, 244
Veracity, 135-136
Verbs, 124, 133-134, 146, 223
Verisimilitude, 38, 135-136
Victim, 148, 156, 160, 161
*Victorian Masters of Mystery: From Wilkie
  Collins to Conan Doyle*, 291
Viewpoint, 9, 96, 112-120, 123, 142, 143,
  185-186, 218, 282
Villain, 10-11, 64, 86-90, 165, 237
Violence, 2, 8-9, 84, 148-159
Vocabulary, 10, 130, 249
Voice, 11, 69-70, 96, 130, 185, 213-214
Void Moon, 126, 128

Wallace, Marilyn, 13-19, 287, 288, 292, 303
Wambaugh, Joseph, 34, 280
Waugh, Charles C., 282
Weapons, 9, 82, 84, 163, 165
Web sites, 23, 188, 238, 251, 266, 269, 288
Weekend Novelist Writes a Mystery, The,
  287
Westlake, Donald, 89, 171
Wetering, Janwillem van de, 208
*What About Murder? A Guide to Books
  About Mystery . . .* , 231
What's What, 288, 290, 292
Wheat, Carolyn, 15, 121-128, 283, 287, 303
Whip Hand, 280
Whiskey River, 114
Whitney, Phyllis A., 139-147, 303-304
Whodunit, 2, 86, 164
Whoever Fights Monsters, 292
Willeford, Charles, 87

Winslow, Don, 279, 280, 283
Woe Is I: the Grammarphobe's Guide to Better English, 186, 285
Woman Without a Past, 143
Work schedules, 20-25
World Encyclopedia of Police Forces and Penal Systems, 289
Wright, Betty Ren, 220, 221
Wright, Nancy Means, 214
Writer's block, 140-141, 167 *See also* Stumbling blocks
Writer's Complete Crime Reference Book, The, 47, 290

Writers conferences, 193-194, 196
Writer's Digest books, 193, 204, 289, 291
Writer's Digest magazine, 193, 204
Writers groups, 187, 194, 215
Writer's Market, 199, 204
Writing, 6-11, 18, 21-25, 93, 111
Writing, books about, 284-288
Writing partners, 26-32

Year Without Michael, The, 220, 221
Young readers, 140, 141, 217-223, 287

Zeman, Angela and Barry, 271-292, 304